Hot Springs
of Western Canada
— A complete guide —

Also includes some hot springs in
Washington and Alaska

2nd Edition

Glenn Woodsworth

Revisions include extensive updates on eight springs

- Meager Creek
- Skookumchuck (St. Agnes Well)
- Sloquet
- Halcyon
- Cave and Basin, at Banff
- Middle, at Banff
- Lakelse (Mount Layton)
- Aiyansh

---

and minor updates on nine springs

- Harrison
- Sol Duc, in Olympic National Park
- Ainsworth
- Nakusp
- Canyon
- Fairmont
- Radium, in Kootenay National Park
- Upper, at Banff
- Miette, in Jasper National Park

Gordon Soules Book Publishers Ltd.
West Vancouver, Canada
Seattle, U.S.

First edition published 1997
Second edition 1999

Canadian Cataloguing in Publication Data

Woodsworth, G. J.
   Hot springs of Western Canada – 2nd edition

   Includes bibliographical references and index.
   ISBN 0-919574-03-3

   1. Hot springs–Canada, Western–Guidebooks.   2. Canada, Western–Guidebooks.   3. Hot springs–Alaska–Guidebooks.   4. Hot springs–Washington (State)–Guidebooks.   I. Title
   GB1198.4.C3W66 1999   917.1204'3   C99-910517-5

Published in Canada by
Gordon Soules Book Publishers Ltd.
1359 Ambleside Lane
West Vancouver, BC V7T 2Y9
(604) 922-6588 or (604) 688-5466
Fax: (604) 688-5442
E-mail: books@gordonsoules.com
Website: http://www.gordonsoules.com

Published in the United States by
Gordon Soules Book Publishers Ltd.
PMB 620, 1916 Pike Place #12
Seattle, WA 98101–1097
(604) 922-6588 or (604) 688-5466
Fax: (604) 688-5442
E-mail: books@gordonsoules.com
Website: http://www.gordonsoules.com

Front cover photo: Lussier Hot Springs, in the East Kootenays. See page 155
Cover designed by Harry Bardal
Maps by Glenn Woodsworth
Typeset by Joy Woodsworth
Printed and bound in Canada by Transcontinental Printing

CONTENTS

List of Maps

Acknowledgments

This guide had its beginning when Jim McDonald and Gordon Soules, author and publisher, respectively, of the original *Hotsprings of Western Canada,* asked me to work on a revised edition. Jim soon bowed out of the project, but without his initial push I doubt that I would have finished this book.

Books don't spring ready-made onto the shelves, and I find it humbling to reflect on how much I owe to others.

Many people shared information and photos. Without their contributions, this book would have been far less complete and contained far fewer pictures. Thanks to: Bob Anderson, John Baldwin, Mary Lou Bevier, John Clarke, Lisel Currie, Carol Evenchick, Hu Gabrielse, Susie Gareau, Norm Graham, Steve Grasby, Jim Haggart, Doug Herchmer, Geordie Howe, Paul Kroeger, Jim Logan, Don Murphy, Charlie Roots, Margi Rusmore, Tim Sadlier-Brown, Mike Sato, Rick Sheppard, Rob Skelly, Jill and Barrie Taylor, Derek Thorkelson, Per Tjaden, my brother Bob, my daughter Karen, and all those at the commercial springs who cheerfully answered my questions.

Near the end of the project, photographers Karl Arsh and Eva Fabian made available a large selection of colour photographs. These were of such high quality that they required a rethink of the illustrations and led to the inclusion of the colour section.

Jack Souther encouraged me throughout this project, provided photos, and reviewed an early draft of the manuscript. In particular, his thoughtful comments on the Introduction led to a thorough overhaul of that section. Doug Herchmer, Ralph McGreevy, and staff and students of Johnston Heights Secondary School read drafts of the manuscript and made many useful comments.

Mary Akehurst and Steve Lunsford provided obscure publications and illustrations. Mary Conibear and Vic Marks of Hartley & Marks, Publishers, Mary Yates and Rebecca Myers of Gordon Soules Book Publishers, and Peter Renner helped in various bookish ways.

My son, David, one of my regular companions on hot springs trips, made a large and important contribution to this book. His critical reading of two drafts of the manuscript and meticulous editing of the maps caught many errors.

My editor, Nancy Flight, not only fixed stylistic and organizational problems but critically read the manuscript from the viewpoint of one who has never visited a hot spring. Her work was invaluable, thoroughly professional, and greatly appreciated.

Paul Adam joined me in many hot springs trips, supplied many photos, and critically read the manuscript. His help extends far beyond these tangible contributions, though, through his genial prodding and encouragement and by feeding me stray bits of information that crossed his path. Above all, continuing discussions with him over the years have helped shaped my own ideas about what a guidebook should be. He did at least let me buy him a cup of coffee.

My wife, Joy, an uncertain hiker but a great companion in and out of the pools, worked hard on all aspects of this book. In particular, she did the unenviable job of verifying what was in the manuscript against my hand-written notes. Thanks, Joy! Now, on to all those Italian hot springs.

Photo Credits

The author and publisher gratefully acknowledge the following sources for photographs.

FRONT COVER

Karl Arsh and Eva Fabian

COLOUR PHOTOS

Karl Arsh and Eva Fabian, 194, 195 top and bottom, 196 top and bottom, 198, 200 top and bottom, 201, 202 top, 207 bottom
Courtesy of Fairmont Hot Springs, 203
Hu Gabrielse, Geological Survey of Canada, 208 bottom
Steve Grasby, 207 top
Al Harvey, 206 bottom
Courtesy of Canadian Rockies Hot Springs, 204, 205
Charlie Roots, Geological Survey of Canada, 208 top
David Woodsworth, 197
Joy Woodsworth, 199, 202 bottom

MODERN BLACK AND WHITE PHOTOS

Karl Arsh and Eva Fabian, 17, 67, 109, 125, 135, 159, 246, 261, 267
Carol Evenchick, 255
Doug Herchmer, B.C. Forest Service, 226
Christian Reiner, 131
Mathias Rickli, courtesy of Susie Gareau, Geological Survey of Canada, inside back cover
Mike Sato, 37
Rick Sheppard, 111
Jack Souther, Geological Survey of Canada, 21, 41
David Woodsworth, 85, 87, 99
Joy Woodsworth, 170

HISTORICAL PHOTOS

Heritage Photo Co-op, Penticton (photo attributed to Wm. Nottman & Son), 60 top
Whyte Museum of the Canadian Rockies, Banff, Alberta (catalogue no. V263-NA71-557, photographer unknown), 171 (catalogue no. V263-NA71-3539, photographer unknown), 178

All other photos are by the author or are historical photos by unknown photographers from the author's collection.

Disclaimer

Using the hot springs and travelling to and from the hot springs and other destinations in this guidebook can be dangerous. Users of this guidebook assume responsibility for their own safety, including evaluating whether their health and physical condition allow them to use hot springs and evaluating whether their fitness level, their outdoor travel training and experience, their driving skills and experience, and the type and condition of their vehicle allow them to travel to and from the hot springs and other destinations in this guidebook.

Information in any guidebook is subject to change and error. As well, this guidebook does not list all possible hazards or describe conditions as they may be encountered on any particular day. Neither the author nor the publisher accepts responsibility for any outdated information, omissions, or errors in this guidebook, nor does either of them accept responsibility for mishaps, accidents, injuries, illnesses, damages to person or property, or death of any persons using any of the hot springs in this guidebook or travelling to or from any of the hot springs or other destinations in this guidebook.

The information in this guidebook on travelling on private land and using hot springs on private land is given for information purposes only and does not imply any legal right of access. Neither the author nor the publisher accepts responsibility for the possibility that users of this guidebook may trespass on private property.

Future Editions of this Book

Any guidebook is only as good as the information in it. Corrections and clarifications to material in this book are most welcome, as are descriptions of new springs and suggestions for future editions. Please send all information and suggestions to me, care of the publisher. Thank you.

Glenn Woodsworth
c/o Gordon Soules Book Publishers Ltd.
1354-B Marine Drive
West Vancouver, BC, Canada V7T 1B5
Fax: (604) 688-5442
E-mail: books@gordonsoules.com

Preface

Of the roughly 110 known hot and warm springs in Canada, most are in British Columbia, and the rest are in Alberta, Yukon Territory, and the westernmost Northwest Territories. These springs, which are often in spectacular surroundings, include steaming pools, reached after a long hike up a mountain valley, tide-washed streams where you can dangle your toes in the ocean while you stay deliciously warm, rustic wooden pools beside gravel roads, and fully developed commercial resorts. Finding a new hot spring and settling in for a long, relaxing soak is one of life's great pleasures. And revisiting a familiar hot spring is like a visit to an old friend: it's comfortable but never the same as the time before.

Hot springs make a great focus for a trip: hiking, boating, car-camping with the kids, or enjoying a weekend getaway for two at an elegant resort. It's hard to worry about work when you are up to your neck in hot, soothing water in a beautiful mountain setting. For the moment, life seems simpler.

The first comprehensive guide to hot springs in Canada, Jim McDonald's *Hotsprings of Western Canada: A Complete Guide,* was published in 1978. The fact that it was in print until recently shows the continuing popularity of hot springs as a recreational destination. In recent years, the popularity of hot springs has increased dramatically. But access to many of the springs and the facilities at the springs have changed over the last 20 years, particularly in southern British Columbia, and it is time for a new guide.

This book gives descriptions of all Canadian hot and warm springs that I know of, including some that have never been thoroughly described before. Cold springs are not included, since few people are interested in them for recreation. For good measure I've included seven springs in northern Washington and two springs in southeastern Alaska just outside British Columbia. Commercially operated springs in British Columbia, Alberta, and Yukon Territory are fully described; the rest of the descriptions are split between partly developed (but free) springs and undeveloped wilderness springs. You can drive to many of the springs; others require a short walk that can easily be longer if you can't get up the roads. A few springs require serious hiking, and some are accessible only by boat or plane. I've also mentioned springs that are rumoured to exist, on the assumption that (to rework an old phrase) where there's steam there's hot water. Whatever your interests, there are plenty of hot springs to discover and enjoy.

Introduction

About Hot Springs

Guidebook writers often face a conflict between the desire to keep special places secret and the wish to let others enjoy them too. As more people become aware of special spots, they are used much more and increased pressure is placed on sensitive ecosystems. In this guide I've tried to achieve a balance by encouraging visits to some springs while providing information about why hot springs are special and how to treat them responsibly. I believe that we, the public, must soon make some hard land-use decisions about many of the hot springs described in this book and that those decisions will best be made by an educated and informed public with full access to all relevant data. The following brief description of the natural history of hot springs is intended to give you some background information to make your hot springs trips more enjoyable and to enable you to help preserve the fragile hot springs environment.

Where Are Hot Springs Found?

Throughout the world, hot springs are concentrated in geologically active areas. In North America, most springs occur along the western edge of the continent in the great mountain belt extending from Alaska into Central America. This belt is part of the "Ring of Fire" that circles much of the Pacific Ocean. Most hot springs in Canada occur in British Columbia, with the remainder in Yukon Territory, western Alberta, and the westernmost Northwest Territories: the areas with the youngest mountains, active volcanoes, and abundant earthquakes.

How does Canada compare in number of hot springs with the rest of the world? Not that well. Japan, which is about half the size of British Columbia, has about 4,500 springs, according to one report, whereas British Columbia has about 85. Little wonder that the Japanese are such lovers of hot springs. Idaho, which is less than half the size of British Columbia, has over 250.

What Makes the Water Hot?

Most people know that the earth gets hotter the deeper you go. Beneath western Canada, the temperature increases on average about 30°C (108°F) for each kilometre of depth, so rock 3 to 4 km (2 to 2.5 mi.) below the surface is above the boiling point of water. The earth's heat comes not from the cooling of a primordial body of molten rock but from the slow and constant decay of radioactive elements, particularly uranium, thorium, and potassium. Heat may also come from the cooling of buried bodies of molten rock; such molten rock probably exists beneath Mt. St. Helens in Washington and possibly beneath Mt. Meager in British Columbia. Because the heat for hot springs comes mostly from the decay of radioactive elements, hot springs are nuclear powered. The water is heated by essentially the same atomic processes that drive nuclear power plants, but in hot springs the radiation level is far too low to be a health hazard.

Almost all the water in hot springs comes from rain or snow. Water can circulate through rocks if they are permeable or if they are broken by fractures or faults. These networks of faults, fractures, and permeable rock form natural plumbing systems that allow water to penetrate several kilometres into the earth. Thus, rain falls on the mountains, percolates several kilometres into the earth, and then heats up (see Figure 1).

There are two processes that can drive the hot water to the surface and so form a hot spring. The first process works because water runs downhill. If cold water enters the underground plumbing system at a higher elevation than where the hot water exits the ground, the hot spring can be driven by this naturally occurring pressure (see Figure 1). This process is commonly called gravity feed or artesian flow. The second process, called thermal convection, occurs because hot water is less dense than cold water and thus tends to rise towards the surface. This difference in density sets up a giant convection cell, which is kept going by additional cold water percolating into the ground to keep the plumbing system filled with water. Most hot springs are probably driven by a combination of the two processes, artesian flow and thermal convection. But the fact that most Canadian hot springs are found in valleys and not high on mountains suggests that artesian flow is the primary mechanism.

Water temperature at the surface depends on how hot the rocks are that the water travels through, how long the water has to heat up, how fast the hot water rises to the surface, and how much the hot water mixes with groundwater on the way up to or at the surface. If the hot water ascends slowly, it will cool off, resulting in a cool spring. If it emerges into an area saturated with cold groundwater, it may become highly diluted, also producing a cool spring. If there is an unusually dry summer, not enough rain may fall to keep the system moving, resulting in a dried-up hot spring. Combinations of these factors explain the variations of temperature and rates of flow in different outlets at the same spring system from season to season and from year to year.

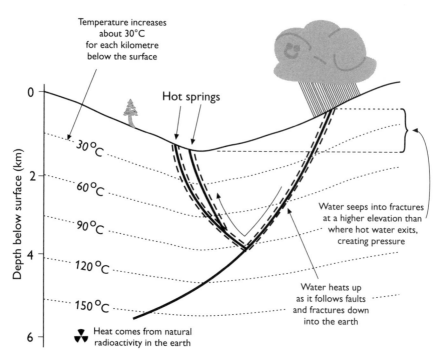

Figure 1. A schematic cross-section through the upper part of the earth's crust, illustrating how hot springs such as those at Banff are formed.

Hot Spring Water and Deposits

Hot water is a good solvent, and even rocks are soluble when hot water has time to act on them. Using methods similar to those used by archaeologists to date artifacts, geologists can determine the age of the water in hot springs. These tests show that it may take many decades to several thousand years from the time the water falls as rain until it emerges in a hot spring, plenty of time for it to pick up a load of dissolved minerals along the way. These dissolved minerals give many springs their tangy and distinctive soda or mineral taste.

As the hot, mineralized water reaches the surface, it cools, losing much of its dissolved gas and minerals. As a result, tiny mineral crystals are often deposited on the spring walls, nearby rocks, and any vegetation that grows too close. The resulting deposits may be crumbly and porous, in which case they are called tufa (rhymes with *roof-ah*), or hard and dense, in which case they are called sinter. Most tufa is made of calcite (calcium carbonate, the constituent of most seashells). Gypsum (calcium sulphate) and dolomite (magnesium carbonate) are other common constituents of tufa. Sinter may be composed of a form of calcium carbonate called travertine, similar to stalactites in many caves, or a form of silica that is chemically akin to opal. Tufa is common around many hot springs, where it often forms extensive terraces and benches. Good examples are found at Dewar Creek, Fairmont, Liard and Rabbitkettle hot springs. Sinter is less common than tufa, but it is abundant at Meager Creek and Dewar Creek.

Tufa deposits can be used to estimate the age of a hot spring, in other words, how long a spring has been active. For example, at Rabbitkettle, the tufa mounds are about 27 m (90 ft.) high, and about 2 mm (.07 in.) of tufa is deposited each year. Assuming no change in water chemistry or rate of flow, these figures suggest an age of very roughly 13,000 years for the Rabbitkettle tufa deposits. But geologists know that these deposits are built on glacial deposits that are about 10,000 years old, so it's probable that the tufa deposits began to form as the ice left the valley.

Studies at other springs show that individual hot springs have an age of no more than a few tens or hundreds of thousands of years. And, as hot springs are born, so they die (or the world would be overrun with hot springs). Mess Lake warm springs, for example, seem to be in the last decades of life. And anywhere you find old tufa deposits, you can be sure that there was once an active spring there, even though it may have dried

Extensive tufa deposits at Liard Hot Springs in northern B.C.

up long ago. The main reason that springs dry up is that the plumbing system of fractures, faults, and permeable rock slowly becomes clogged with minerals precipitated out of the water. Over the centuries minute deposits build up, until finally, fractures are blocked and the flow of hot water ceases.

Many hot springs have a distinctive sulphur odour that some people find offensive but that I rather enjoy if it's not too strong. This odour is hydrogen sulphide, the same as in rotten eggs. As noted above, much spring water is rich in sulphate. As the water nears the surface, special bacteria in some springs act on the dissolved sulphate, producing hydrogen sulphide gas. Some smelly springs, for example, the Middle springs at Banff, have a slightly milky colour from microscopic particles of sulphur suspended in the water. Leave your jewellery with your clothes when you jump into these springs, since there is enough sulphur to tarnish it badly.

Geologists have classified B.C. hot springs into three groups, based largely on the type and amount of dissolved material they contain and their geological associations. Different groups have slightly different origins and different potential for large-scale commercial development.

The first type of spring, which includes those in the Rocky Mountains, results from deeply circulating groundwater in layered sedimentary rocks such as limestones. Water in these springs tends to be rich in calcium and sulphate, and the springs often form extensive tufa deposits composed of calcium carbonate, perhaps with a bit of gypsum and very little dissolved silica.

Springs of the second type include almost all the springs in the Kootenays (west of Highway 95 between Golden and Cranbrook) and some springs on the B.C. coast. Many of these springs, for example, those around Nakusp, seem to get their heat by passing through rocks that are rich in radioactive elements and hence produce above-average amounts of heat. The chemistry of the spring waters is intermediate between the first type and the third type, described below. They tend to be rich either in calcium and bicarbonate or in sodium and chloride. Most of these springs don't form large tufa deposits, but Dewar Creek and Ainsworth are exceptions.

The third type of springs is associated with recent volcanic activity. Examples include Meager Creek and Pebble Creek (near the Mt. Meager volcanic complex, which last erupted 2400 years ago); Baker (near Mt. Baker, which was last active in the 1850s); and the springs near Mt.

Edziza, which last erupted about 1400 years ago. These springs tend to be high in sulphate or bicarbonate and rich in dissolved silica. Water in the springs tends to have only a mild taste or none at all.

Geothermal Energy and Commercial Uses of Hot Springs
Some hot springs have been used for cooking and heating on a small scale for hundreds of years. In this century, there has been much interest in using hot spring energy on a commercial scale. Large hot springs bring considerable heat to the surface, and much more heat remains below ground. This heat, known as geothermal energy, has recently been harnessed on a large scale, notably in Japan, New Zealand, California, Iceland, and Russia. Typically, a series of holes is drilled several kilometres into a body of hot rock, tapping either hot water or steam. Hot water has been used for space heating, the heating of greenhouses, agricultural irrigation, fish farming, and various industrial purposes.

If the holes tap steam or a mixture of steam and water, it may be possible to use the steam to generate electricity. The steam drives a series of turbines, which generate electrical power. The steam condenses to hot water, which is cooled and injected back into the hot rock through a separate series of holes (see Figure 2). Italy has been generating power in this fashion since the early 1900s, and the United States, Mexico, New Zealand, and Iceland also produce substantial amounts of electric power from hot springs.

To date, the only large-scale commercial uses of hot springs in British Columbia have been as resorts and as a source of bottled mineral water. Hot water doesn't travel far before cooling down, restricting the potential, non-electric use of geothermal energy to those few springs situated in agricultural areas or near towns.

As for using geothermal energy to generate electricity, not all areas of the province are suitable. Water in the Rocky Mountains springs (the first type of hot spring described in the previous section) probably doesn't get deep enough and hot enough to produce steam. Such springs may have some potential for agricultural use, but they have very little potential for the generation of electricity. The second type of springs, found in the Kootenays, may tap higher temperatures at lesser depths than the first type of springs. Some areas containing springs of this type may have modest potential for generating power, but no serious testing has been done in British Columbia.

The most determined testing for geothermal power in British Columbia has occurred at springs of the third variety, those related to the geologically young volcanic complexes such as the one at Mt. Meager. From 1975 to 1982, B.C. Hydro did extensive tests and drilling in the Meager area, culminating in the drilling of three holes that reached depths of up to 3500 m (11,500 ft.). The holes reached water-bearing rocks with temperatures of over 200°C (390°F), hot enough to produce steam (and power) at the surface.

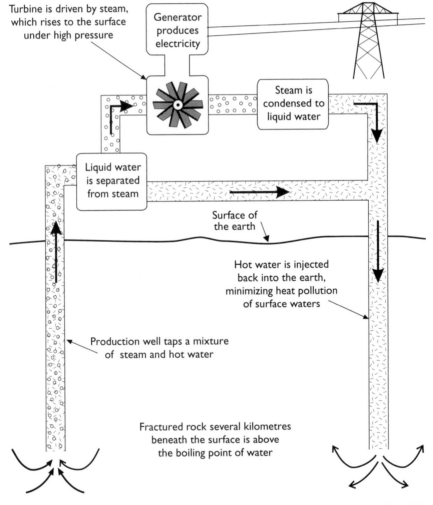

Turbine is driven by steam, which rises to the surface under high pressure

Generator produces electricity

Steam is condensed to liquid water

Liquid water is separated from steam

Surface of the earth

Hot water is injected back into the earth, minimizing heat pollution of surface waters

Production well taps a mixture of steam and hot water

Fractured rock several kilometres beneath the surface is above the boiling point of water

Figure 2. Systems such as this are used to produce electric power in some parts of the world and could possibly be used in the Meager Creek area.

From Hydro's point of view, the results were encouraging, but the project was shelved because of financial cutbacks. Since 1994, there has been renewed interest in the power potential of the Meager area. Drilling began early in 1995 to try to show the feasibility of supporting a 60 megawatt power plant, enough power for a city of 100,000 people. What effect, if any, such power production would have on Meager and Pebble hot springs remains unknown, but it's likely to be less than unchecked recreational use.

Therapeutic Uses of Hot Springs

For millennia, people in many parts of the world have used hot springs for their curative, restorative, and mystical powers. The hot springs at the Roman city of Tiberias on the Sea of Galilee were known as Hammath

A huge drill rig used in 1981 to test for the presence of high rock temperatures and hot water in the Meager Creek area.

("warm springs") in early biblical times; later the village was called Emmaus ("hot springs"). The springs in Bath, England, were the site of the Iron Age Celtic goddess Sul, who was thought to be the power behind the healing waters. Spas built around hot springs were popular in ancient Greece and Rome, and many Roman watering places continued as resorts into the modern era, including Bath (where Sul was crossed with the Roman goddess Minerva to produce the hybrid Sulis Minerva), Baden-Baden in Germany, Vichy in France (the source of Vichy water), and Spa in Belgium (our English word *spa* comes from here). In the 18th century, many of these spas underwent a revival, and it became fashionable to go to them to "take the cure" by soaking in the water, using mud baths, and drinking liberally of the spring water itself. Many of these resorts remain popular today.

The native people of North America made extensive use of hot springs. For example, on the west coast of British Columbia, the Nuu-chah-nulth used hot springs for treating chronic diseases such as arthritis. An 1873 report on the Fraser Valley by John Fannin reported:

> The Indians have, for a long time, been in the habit of using [hot spring water] in certain cases of sickness, and the plan they adopt is this:- A piece of cedar bark is placed on the ground at the edge of the spring from where the steam is rising, and the invalid, covered with a blanket, sits in a crouched position on this bark for hours at a time; and if they are to be believed, many cures have been effected.

In some cases, if a hot spring wasn't close by, its effects were simulated by steaming the patient over hot rocks covered with seaweed and salt water. Many native groups regard hot springs as sacred. Some springs are still used today by native peoples for healing and spiritual purposes.

Early visitors to Banff found the waters useful for treatment of rheumatism, syphilis, and gunshot wounds, not to mention mercury and lead poisoning. An early advertisement for St. Alice's Hotel (now Harrison Hot Springs) proclaimed the waters to be a sure cure for many ailments, including alcoholism, and to be excellent for the complexion. Springs high in lithium were said to be particularly beneficial for the kidneys and digestion.

The waters and gases in many hot springs are slightly radioactive because of the presence of minute amounts of radon, a naturally occurring radioactive gas. In the early years of this century, when radium was just beginning to be used for cancer treatment, slightly radioactive hot springs such as Radium and Fairmont were popular. Fairmont even advertised that radioactive water would be served with meals, not an advertising tactic that would attract many customers today. We now know that the level of radioactivity in Canadian hot springs is too low to be harmful.

Many people today still value spring water for therapeutic use, and at some undeveloped springs visitors bring bottles so that they can take some spring water home with them. Modern medicine tends to be skeptical of curative claims of hot springs, viewing any health benefits as temporary and as relieving symptoms rather than curing underlying problems. Nevertheless, most people find that nothing beats a good soak in a natural hot spring to make you feel more relaxed.

Elaborate spas built around hot springs, such as this one at St. Leon, were popular from the 1890s into the 1920s. By the time this photo was taken in the late 1940s, the popularity of these resorts had declined.

Biology and Ecology of Hot Springs

> *Green plants grow in the hot springs of Padua, frogs in those of Pisa,*
> *fishes at Vetulonia in Etruria near the sea.*
>
> Pliny the Elder, about AD 70

> *[Ainsworth] . . . is the only place in Canada where a frog concert can*
> *be heard every evening of the year. This is owing to the hot springs that*
> *bubble up on the townsite. The frogs keep under the houses, where the*
> *hot water oozes from the earth, and sing their solos and duets without*
> *any regard to, or interruption from, the iciest weather that the district*
> *can produce.*
>
> Robert Thornton Lowry, 1895

As these quotes show, hot springs often have special and remarkable eco-systems, a fact recognized for centuries. Air and water temperature, humidity, and water chemistry at a spring may be greatly different just a few metres away. If the flow and temperature of the spring is great enough, snow won't stick and the ground won't freeze, no matter how low the air temperature falls. These conditions arise because hot springs are an additional source of energy for life to use, beyond that provided by the sun, and allow some plants and animals to survive in surroundings that otherwise would be fatal.

Probably the most conspicuous life forms indigenous to hot springs are various kinds of algae and bacteria. Soft mats, films, and stringy filaments of white, grey, yellow, orange, purple, and green algae and bacteria cover some hot springs like a scab and make the pools unappealing for soaking. The colours arise from different pigments within the different kinds of algae. Blue-green material is algae, which can survive in very hot water. Brilliant yellow-orange material that forms a soft coating on rocks is usually sulphur-dependent bacteria. Ropy strands of white material are yet another kind of algae, often mixed with colonies of bacteria. These algae and bacteria are single-celled organisms that have adapted to hot water and require it to live. Blue-green algae can stand water up to 73°C (163°F); some species of bacteria can live in boiling water.

Some hot springs give off enough heat to allow flowers to bloom all year round. Where there are flowers there are insects, and where there are insects there are often animals such as frogs, mice, and snakes that feed on them. Thus, at some springs you may find a great deal of biological activity, even when the surrounding area is buried under many metres of snow. Other animals also like hot springs. Goats, sheep, and other animals use the salty spring deposits as natural salt licks. In winter, when their normal feed is covered by snow, some animals eat the algae and plants found at hot springs. As I've described for Dewar Creek, they probably appreciate the warmth, and carnivores probably appreciate the ready supply of herbivores. Fish too make use of the hot water. Although not indigenous, tropical fish live in the warm marshes below the Cave and Basin hot springs in Banff.

Few Canadian hot springs have been studied in any detail by biologists. Meager Creek, perhaps the best studied, gives us a glimpse of the special diversity of life at a hot spring. Some plants that are uncommon in the area grow abundantly at the hot springs. These include the snapdragon-like yellow monkey-flower (common at many hot springs); fleabane, with its pinkish, daisy-like flowers; and the beautiful mountain lady's-slipper orchid. Another equally interesting but less elegant plant is a species of sedge-grass, Olney's bullrush, that is known from only one other locality in western Canada. Biologists have also found two previously unknown species of mushrooms, several rare species of insects, and the rare and endangered Pacific rubber boa snake.

Unfortunately, the increasing use of Meager Creek hot springs has endangered its special community of life. Several rare plants have not been seen in recent years, and other species are present in greatly decreased numbers. Degradation of this ecosystem seems likely to continue unless conservation measures are implemented soon.

If this situation seems gloomy, it's not as bad as at some other springs. For example, the hot waters at Radium, Ainsworth, and Canyon were diverted or altered before any biological studies were done. The most recent disastrous loss of hot spring habitat occurred near Terrace, where the once-extensive hot springs at Lakelse (Mount Layton) were capped and pumped to a chlorinated swimming pool.

Each hot spring system has a different environment (water temperature, rate of flow, water chemistry) superimposed on terrain with different soil chemistry, bedrock geology, elevation, temperature and precipitation patterns, and so on. Therefore, each spring represents a unique ecosystem covering at most a few hectares. None of these ecosystems has been properly studied and few, if any, are properly protected. To me, these conclusions imply that there should be a moratorium on hot spring development until adequate studies are complete. For springs such as Meager that are endangered by too many visitors, public access must be severely restricted. This issue is discussed further in the Meager Creek section.

Environmental Responsibility

Probably the biggest threat to many delicate hot springs ecosystems is careless use by thoughtless visitors. The following suggestions will help preserve the undeveloped and partly developed springs for all to enjoy. They all stem from one principle: leave no trace of your visit.

- Camp only in established campsites. That way, the environmental damage is concentrated in a few spots rather than being spread over the whole area.

- Use stoves rather than campfires for cooking; they are more efficient and less damaging to the environment. If you do build a fire, build it in an existing fire ring and keep the fire small. Use only fallen, dead wood for fires.

- Avoid damaging the vegetation surrounding the springs. Stay on established trails and don't take shortcuts. Wildflowers are there to produce seeds; if you pick the flowers, there won't be new plants. Cut no live wood.

- If washrooms or outhouses are provided, use them. Otherwise, bury toilet paper after use, and bury waste at least 30 m (100 ft.) from streams or springs. This practice will help prevent the spread of giardia and other diseases.

- Keep dogs out of the pools. They can contaminate the water with the bacteria that cause leptospirosis, a potentially fatal disease.

- Do not use soap in the pools. Soap pollutes streams and can build up unattractive deposits on the pool walls, so it is best not to wash in the pools. Washing dishes in the hot springs is also unacceptable.

- Pack out all your garbage. While you are at it, why not pack out whatever garbage was left by previous visitors? Leave the spring in as good shape as you found it, or better.

- Educate others. Many people don't know how to treat the land and will be willing to change their behaviour if you tell them in a friendly, non-confrontational manner the right way to act. Peer pressure is powerful.

Some Health and Safety Warnings

Hot baths are highly pleasurable, but there are some precautions you should take to make your stay in the pool both satisfying and safe.

- If you have heart or circulatory problems, high or low blood pressure, diabetes, or are pregnant, you should check with your doctor before checking out the hot pools.

- Don't soak alone.

- Avoid overheating. If you feel dizzy or faint, get out and cool down.

- Keep a close eye on children, especially at springs such as Meager Creek that have fast-flowing creeks nearby.

- If you are pregnant, keep your hot soaks short.

- Do not soak while under the influence of alcohol or medications for cardiovascular problems. Combining drugs or alcohol with overheating can be fatal.

- Drink plenty of non-alcoholic fluid (not hot springs water) to counteract dehydration.

- Giardiasis ("beaver fever") is increasingly common throughout the guidebook area. Most hot springs are not hot enough to kill the *Giardia* cysts. In addition, some hot springs may contain potentially harmful amounts of heavy metals such as arsenic, and these metals are not removed by boiling or normal chemical treatment. Rather than drinking hot springs water, you may want to bring your own drinking water or boil or chemically treat water from nearby streams.

- Hot springs can harbour high concentrations of harmful bacteria, particularly coliform, meningitis, and *Leptospira* bacilli. These bacteria can enter the body through the nose. Therefore, it's advisable to keep your head above water at all times. This warning doesn't apply to the commercial pools, which are filtered and chemically treated.

- Poison ivy is common around some springs; watch where you put your clothes. Remember: "Leaves in three, let it be."

For the undeveloped springs, the following suggestions will increase your enjoyment:

- A pair of beach thongs or some old runners are handy around pools with sharp stones on the bottom or around them.

- Plastic garbage bags are great for keeping your clothes and towel dry on a wet day while you soak.

- Don't wear jewellery in the pools. The sulphur will tarnish it.

- Many people find night a special time for a dip in the pool. Candles give a magical light, but put them on a tin can lid or bit of aluminum foil to avoid unsightly wax buildup on the walls of the pool.

- Bathing suits are required at all commercial pools. For the rest, a general rule of thumb is that the degree of acceptable nudity increases with increasing distance from main roads. I've not indicated where skinny-dipping is acceptable and where it is not, because local custom at any pool may change from hour to hour, depending on the people present. At some popular spots, suits far outnumber skin during the day, but nudity is common after dark. At the remote pools, if you arrive and find another group, particularly a family with children, all suited, you should wear a suit or ask permission before skinny-dipping. In other words, use common sense and respect the sensitivities of others. If you arrive and find everyone nude, wear a suit if you feel more comfortable. No one will mind.

About This Guide

Each spring in the southern part of the guidebook area for which I have detailed, current information has a separate section in the book. Most of these descriptions are based on several visits within the last seven years. Most springs in the northern part of the region receive less detailed descriptions, mainly because I have less detailed information. The ends of some chapters give short notes on other hot and warm springs in the region, including ones I've never visited or haven't been to since I began keeping detailed notes. These sections also include whatever information is available on springs that are rumoured to exist or that are mentioned in old reports. These notes are a starting point if you wish to begin the rather addictive pastime of hunting for new and obscure hot springs. If you find any of these, I'd appreciate hearing about your trip. Write to me in care of the publisher (see copyright page).

Each long description begins with a short paragraph outlining the nature of the spring to help you pick the springs that interest you. What's the general access? Is the spring developed or wilderness? Is it an afternoon trip or an expedition? What special attractions or problems are there?

Best Time to Go

Many springs have a season when they are most enjoyable. Undeveloped springs on the banks of rivers, such as Sloquet and Halfway, are often flooded and inaccessible at high water (usually spring and late fall), and roads may be washed out then. Late summer and early fall, when river levels are lowest, are the best times for such springs. During winter, many back roads are closed by snow. If you can ski to the springs, you will probably have them all to yourself and you can enjoy the pleasure of a hot bath in snow-covered surroundings. Weekends, particularly in summer, bring large crowds to some springs. Visit these in mid-week or in the late fall for a quieter, more private trip.

Most commercial springs are open year-round; exceptions are noted. Some have restricted hours before mid-May and after Labour Day. Outdoor pools such as Nakusp and Ainsworth are excellent on a warm, spring day, but any time is just fine.

Most people think that late summer and fall are the best times for visiting hot springs. The weather is likely to be good, particularly if you hit one of our long, luxurious Indian summers. Days are still reasonably long, logging roads are in as good condition as they'll ever be, and mosquitoes and the like are finished for the season. Crowds and river levels are low, the leaves are turning, and there might be a nip in the air that gives a special zing to a hike and a soak.

Getting There

Estimates for the times required to reach the hot springs are averages from main population centres in the region. Times will vary depending on how fast you drive or walk, but most people should be able to do the trip in the time suggested.

You can reach all the springs with road access with an ordinary car. I used an elderly Volvo and a youthful Toyota to measure the distances in kilometres. Your odometer may be calibrated a bit differently, but I've given enough tie-in distances to bridges, junctions, and so on that you will have no trouble following the road logs. The road descriptions assume you have an ordinary car, but if you have a pickup truck and good road conditions, you may get farther up some roads than I've indicated. Gas up and check your oil and spare tire before heading out on any long backcountry road. Don't forget to take a good jack.

Logging roads tend to change from year to year and from day to day. Old roads are abandoned and wash out; new spurs and main lines appear where there were none last season. A good topographic map will help you follow the road systems even if they have changed. It's best to assume that all Forest Service roads are being actively used by loggers. When you are driving on such roads, always use headlights and watch for logging trucks. Loaded logging trucks have the right of way, take up most of the road, and can't stop quickly; pull off as far as you can if you see one coming. Wait until the dust cloud has cleared and you can see before pulling out; often there is another logging truck or a pickup following close behind.

If in doubt about road conditions and possible travel restrictions, check with the local district office of the Ministry of Forests (listed in all phone books).

For those hot springs that require a hike, many can be reached by almost anybody, and most are just short walks. Be sure to tell someone where you're going and when you expect to be back. For some springs, you need a topographic map and compass and the skills to use them. Unless otherwise indicated, ordinary walking shoes or light hiking boots are adequate. For the shorter hikes (less than an hour estimated time each way), take at least a spare sweater, a rain jacket, and some food and drinking water. A discussion of the equipment and wilderness skills needed for the longer and more remote hikes is beyond the scope of this book. Take appropriate equipment and safety precautions to ensure your safe return. A dry change of clothes left in the car is a welcome treat after a rainy hike.

Many hot springs on the B.C. coast are best reached by boat. A discussion of boating safety is beyond the scope of this book, but you should take the appropriate marine charts and the safety equipment recommended for your class of vessel by the Canadian Coast Guard. You also require the skill and experience to operate your boat safely in rough, open water.

Whether you go by foot, car, or boat, leave your itinerary with a reliable friend or relative.

The Springs

The Appendix lists all springs in this book in order of decreasing temperature. Water is considered hot if it has a temperature greater than 32°C (90°F) and warm if the temperature is less than 32°C but above an arbitrary 20°C (68°F). Under this definition some "hot" springs such as Canyon Hot Spring and Rabbitkettle Hotsprings are merely warm, but I've retained the established terminology. Springs cooler than 20°C but more than 5°C (41°F) warmer than the average annual air temperature in the region are cool springs; a few scenic and easily accessible cool springs have been included in the book. For comparison, body temperature is 37°C (99°F), and the hottest water that most people can stand to soak in is about 45°C (113°F). Most swimming pools are maintained at about 28°C (82°F).

Many hot springs vary slightly in temperature from season to season. They tend to be hottest in late summer and fall, because there is little dilution of the spring water with rainfall and runoff at those times. If you do a bit of exploring at a large spring such as Meager or Dewar Creek, you'll notice that the temperature varies from vent to vent. As a rule, I've given the highest reliable temperature and indicated the range, where known. For commercial pools, I've given the temperatures both of the pools and of the source of the spring itself.

In all the commercial hot springs, the water is filtered and treated with chlorine or ozone, as required by health regulations. At some commercial springs, the degree of chlorination varies from pool to pool, with the hottest pools often getting less chlorine. Temperatures in the pools are often controlled by adding cold water or by heating the water if it's too cool. Where possible, I've also described the natural state of the water, before treatment.

At the undeveloped springs, the bathing pools tend to change from season to season and year to year, depending on flooding, water level, and the degree of maintenance by volunteer groups. If you arrive early in the year at one of the remote pools, be prepared to do a little engineering before you have your bath.

Facilities, Rates, and Hours

For the commercial springs, this section describes the amenities you can expect to find at the spring (showers, snack bars, etc.) and gives information about campgrounds and motels. All commercial springs are accessible by wheelchair, and some have staff that are trained in assisting people who are physically handicapped. For the other springs, I've indicated which springs you might be able to reach in a wheelchair. If there's no comment you can assume that there is no wheelchair access.

The rates, hours of operation, and business addresses are current as of late 1996; they are, of course, subject to change. Group, family, and special package rates are available at some springs. Rates are in Canadian dollars in Canada and U.S. dollars in Washington.

History

Native use of most springs goes back thousands of years, and I suspect that almost all springs mentioned in this book were known to the native people. In the 1800s many of the best-known springs were "discovered," staked, and developed by Europeans with blatant disregard for the native people. The history of springs such as Skookumchuck and Halcyon, which were better known a hundred years ago than they are now, is fascinating and is outlined in the history sections for these springs.

Maps

For all the commercial pools and many of the rest, all you need is a road map and this book. For many of the springs, though, I've given National Topographic Series (NTS) map numbers for easy reference in case you wish to explore the nearby area. The 1:50,000 series of topographic maps published by the federal government covers the entire area in this guidebook except for Washington State and Alaska. The representation of logging roads is often badly out of date, but on the whole these maps are the ones to have for serious hikes. They are available from:

Geological Survey of Canada
101 – 605 Robson Street
Vancouver, BC V6B 5J3
604-666-0271
Fax: 604-666-1124

Mountain Equipment Co-op
130 West Broadway
Vancouver, BC V6J 1K1
604-876-6221
Fax: 604-876-6590

International Travel Maps & Books
552 Seymour Street
Vancouver, BC V6B 3J5
604-687-3320

The B.C. Ministry of the Environment publishes a series of maps at scales of 1:100,000 and 1:125,000 that cover most of the southern part of the area included in this book. I've given the map numbers where they are available and useful. These maps are available from World Wide Books & Maps, government agents in many communities, and:

Crown Publications
521 Fort Street
Victoria, BC V8W 1E7
250-386-4636
Fax: 250-386-0221

Most local government offices throughout British Columbia carry federal and provincial maps for their regions. The B.C. Forest Service offers maps showing up-to-date logging road and trail systems and Forest Service recreation sites for most forest districts in the province; these are available free at Forest Service offices throughout the province. Maps for Banff, Jasper, and Kootenay national parks are available at park entrances.

For springs on the B.C. coast, you will need the proper marine charts if you are kayaking or sailing there on your own. These are available from many marine-supply shops and from Crown Publications.

Washington State is covered by a standard series of U.S. Geological Survey maps at a scale of 1:24,000. Another popular series of maps is published by Green Trails. Both series are available in many outdoor stores in Washington; Mountain Equipment Co-op in Vancouver also carries a selection of these maps.

For many of the springs in Canada, I've included the Universal Transverse Mercator (UTM) grid coordinates. The system behind this six-digit number is explained on all federal and some provincial NTS maps.

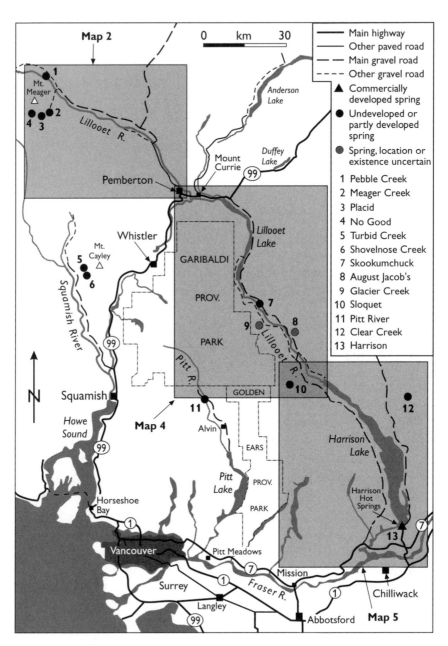

Map 1. Hot springs in the Lower Mainland of B.C.

CHAPTER 1

The Lower Mainland of B.C.

People living in the greater Vancouver area have some excellent hot springs to explore on weekends. These include the popular resort at Harrison Hot Springs, the very popular, partly developed Meager Creek hot springs, and several excellent springs that are less frequented. You can visit any of these springs on a day trip from Vancouver, but some of the remote ones deserve a weekend if you want to fully appreciate them and the surrounding region. If you head north to Pemberton, you can visit Meager, Skookumchuck, and Sloquet in a weekend.

Except for Pitt River hot springs, which requires a boat or plane, an ordinary car is the only vehicle you need. For all but Harrison Hot Springs, you'll have long drives on logging roads, so it helps if your car has decent tires and good clearance.

Given the large population of British Columbia's Lower Mainland, it is surprising that Harrison Hot Springs is the only one of these springs that is commercially developed. Surroundings at the other springs range from modestly developed to wilderness. Some springs are a short walk from a paved road; others require a moderate hike after a long drive on logging roads. It's your choice: there's a spring for everyone in this chapter.

Meager Creek Hot Springs

Partly developed

Maps 1, 2 & 3

Up to 59°C (138°F)

These springs, now part of Meager Creek Hotsprings Recreation Site, are about a four hour drive from Vancouver, the last hour on gravel. In September 1996, the hot springs were officially closed to bathing, and they remain closed as of April 1999. Possibilities are good that limited bathing may soon be permitted. Phone the Squamish Forest District, Ministry of Forests (604-898-2100), for the latest information.

Meager Creek is one of the most dangerous and unstable valleys in British Columbia. The valley was the site of large landslides or debris flows in 1931, 1947, 1975, and 1986 and there have been many other smaller slides. Four people were buried by the 1975 flow; their bodies were never found. Such slides are most likely to occur during and after periods of heavy rain; the water penetrates the rocks and weakens them and saturates the snow on the mountains above. Because of the possibility of slides and washouts, it is safest to avoid this area during and soon after periods of heavy rain.

Getting There

From Vancouver, follow Highway 99 north past Squamish and the Municipality of Whistler. It's about 160 km (100 mi.) and a 2½ hour scenic drive from downtown Vancouver to a major junction just before Pemberton, 33 km (20 mi.) past Whistler. Turn left and follow the paved road through Pemberton and into the pretty farming country of the Pemberton Valley. Pemberton is your last chance for gas, motels, and restaurants. At 25 km (15.5 mi.) from the junction, make a sharp right turn at the sign for the Gold Bridge road. To your left, way up the valley, you can see the spiky rock and glacier summits of Mt. Meager and Plinth Peak; the hot springs are in the valley at their feet. The pavement ends in 1.5 km (0.9 mi.), where the road crosses the Lillooet River. Watch for logging trucks from here on. If you see one approaching, pull off as far as you can, as they often take up the whole road.

In 7.8 km (4.8 mi.) from the bridge, there is an important junction: take the left (lower) fork. (The right fork, the Hurley River road, leads steeply uphill and over a pass to the old mining towns of Bralorne and Gold Bridge and then to Lillooet on the Fraser River.)

Follow the good gravel logging road along the Lillooet River valley floor. In winter, the road is gated just past the Gold Bridge turnoff. Go left at the first conspicuous left branch, about 1½ hours and 63.4 km (39.4 mi.) from the Pemberton junction. This is at the 37 km signpost and is the first really important-looking branch to the left past the Hurley turnoff. (The road going straight ahead continues up the Lillooet River towards Pebble Creek hot springs.)

Cross the bridge over the Lillooet River and follow the road along the west bank of Meager Creek. In 3.3 km (2.0 mi.) you cross the bridge over Capricorn Creek. The bare, devastated look here results from torrential debris flows that sweep down the creekbed once in a while. At 6.2 km (3.8 mi.) from the Lillooet River road, stay left (the road to some old geothermal drill sites is to the right). In another 0.6 km (0.4 mi.), you reach the parking area for the springs, just before the road drops down to the bridge across Meager Creek. This point is about 7.0 km (4.3 mi.) from the Lillooet River road and about 72 km (45 mi.) from Pemberton.

If you have visited Meager in the past, you probably remember driving across the bridge over Meager Creek and continuing up the road to a

Clear, hot water any time of year in the new, Japanese-style pool at Meager Creek.

large parking lot above the springs. Don't do this. Parking is now prohibited past the Meager Creek bridge, and the old parking lot is closed.
The Forest Service has warned that they may ticket those who disobey the
closure.

The Springs

From the parking area, walk across the Meager Creek bridge and follow a
good trail upstream to the springs and the soaking pools. This trail is sur-
faced with pumice and is easy to follow. The hike from the bridge to the
springs is less than 10 minutes.

There are more than 20 hot seeps and streams strung out on terraces
above the creek bank for a couple of hundred metres. The hot spring
waters are clear, odourless, and tasteless, and contain chloride, bicarbonate, sodium, and silica. The total rate of flow of the springs here is the
largest in southern British Columbia.

The main soaking pool was constructed in November 1998 and

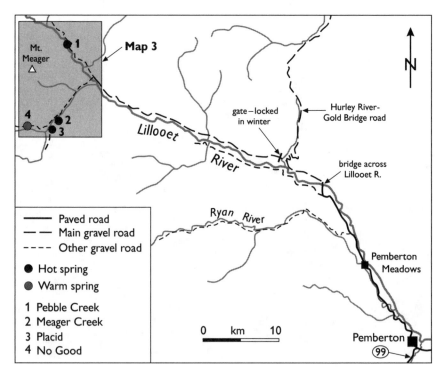

Map 2. Roads northwest of Pemberton

replaces the old cedar pool that stood in the same spot. The new rock pool is designed in the Japanese fashion to allow flow-through of water and to fit unobtrusively into its surroundings. It does so, beautifully. A new changing hut perches beside the pool, and a composting toilet is a short distance downstream.

An older, smaller pool is situated between the new pool and Meager Creek. It is made of river boulders and mortar, and holds about a dozen

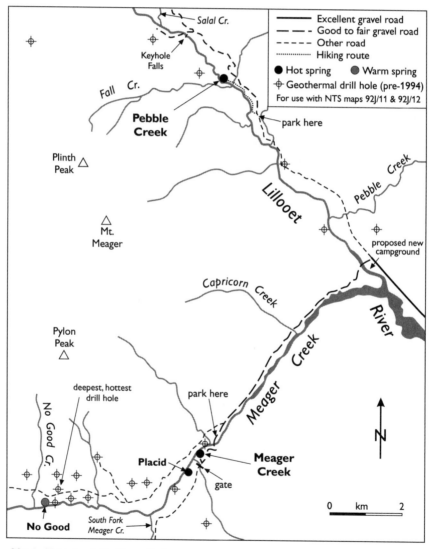

Map 3. Hot springs in the Meager Creek area

people. The cool air coming off the glaciers and down Meager Creek contrasts nicely with the warm, humid air rising from the pools. Under no circumstances should you bathe in or attempt to cross Meager Creek. It's very fast, turbulent, and cold, glacial, in fact. The muddy colour is largely due to silt carried down from the glaciers at the source of the creek.

From the pools, walk about 50 m (160 ft.) upstream, following trails along the sparsely vegetated bank of Meager Creek to a small geyser of hot water. In March 1974, the federal Department of Energy, Mines and Resources drilled a hole to test the potential of the area for geothermal energy. At a depth of 10 m (33 ft.), the hole hit hot water; the little geyser spouts from the drill hole. The water has a temperature of about 59°C (138°F), making it the hottest water at Meager.

From the geyser, trails lead up and away from the creek. Just before a boardwalk, you may be able to see remains of a large cedar pool, recently dismantled. The area above the trail is off-limits to visitors: it is ecologically fragile and the Forest Service is attempting to restore it to its original state. The boardwalk leads across a marshy area and loops back downstream to the new Japanese-style pool.

Facilities and Comments
Meager Creek Hotsprings Recreation Site is maintained and supervised by the B.C. Forest Service. The Forest Service intends to actively supervise the site to stop the excesses and environmental damage that have occurred in the past. A supervisor will be on-site in the summer months. In general, bathing will only be permitted in the lower (downstream) part of the hot spring system, and then only if the pools meet basic health standards. The upper parts of the spring system are to be preserved in their natural state. The campsite above the springs is restricted to walk-in campers (park before crossing the Meager Creek bridge). An overnight fee will be charged. Camping, fires, tree-cutting, and pets are absolutely forbidden on the gravel flats in the vicinity of the hot springs. Stay on the trails, and don't divert spring water to make new soaking pools.

There is plenty of good, free camping available along the Lillooet River both upstream and down from the Meager Creek turnoff. Future plans call for development of a new tent and RV campground on the flats by the junction of Meager Creek and the Lillooet River. When it is open, the present campsite at the springs will probably be closed.

History and Future Outlook

Beginning in the early years of this century, trappers ran their winter traplines up the valley. There was a cabin, "Headquarters," on the Lillooet River not far downstream from Meager junction, and a smaller cabin, "Hotsprings," at the springs. These cabins were home to the trappers during the winter months. The Hotsprings cabin with its naturally hot baths was probably particularly appreciated after an overnight trip on snowshoes to check the trapline. But one old-timer records that the cabin had a drawback. Because of the high humidity, items left in the cabin would rust or be attacked by mildew. Before they left the area in the spring, the trappers hung everything in the surrounding trees, under cover, so that air could circulate around the items.

Until 1973, the springs were little known outside the Pemberton Valley and were visited mainly by trappers, prospectors, and mountaineers. In 1973, spurred by the energy crisis of the day, the federal Department of Energy, Mines and Resources and B.C. Hydro began serious exploration of the Meager Creek and upper Lillooet River valleys for geothermal energy (see the Introduction). In addition to much geological work, nearly 30 holes were drilled between 1974 and 1981 to test how quickly tem-

Water gushing from a drill hole at Meager Creek hot springs, winter 1974. Until recently, a small sauna surrounded this geyser.

perature increases with depth and how much hot water might be found (see photo, p. 41). The deepest holes, on the north side of Meager Creek upstream from Meager Creek hot springs, reached about 3500 m (11,500 ft.) and encountered temperatures up to 264°C (507°F). Tentative plans for a 50 megawatt power plant were shelved in 1984.

During the period of geothermal exploration, logging roads advanced up the Lillooet River and Meager Creek, making the area easily accessible to a larger public. The wooden pools and boardwalks were built, and maintenance of the facilities was taken over by the B.C. Forest Service. The Meager Creek Hotsprings Natural History Society, a now-defunct non-profit group, studied the biology of the hot springs and publicized the unique and fragile nature of the hot springs ecosystems (see the Introduction).

In 1994 the springs received over 30,000 visitors. Crowds, rowdy behaviour, loud music, and a party atmosphere spoiled the springs for many people. The rate of damage to the unique and fragile hot springs ecosystem continued to accelerate. Also in 1994, geothermal exploration was renewed by the geothermal leaseholders, who hoped to find enough energy to support a 60 megawatt power plant, but exploration stopped in 1997.

In 1995, the B.C. Forest Service began to limit the number of vehicles allowed on the site, imposed a camping fee, and hired an on-site supervisor for the summer. These policies helped curtail some of the problems, but in 1996, the pools were officially closed to bathing because of unacceptably high levels of coliform bacteria.

A public review begun in 1997 concluded that changes were needed in how the site was used by visitors and how it was managed by the Forest Service. It is clear that the hot springs support an irreplaceable, unique ecosystem and that the main cause of damage to the ecosystem is too many people. It is also clear that the area is subject to landslides, debris flows, and flooding. The measures being implemented by the Forest Service are a good start towards restoring and preserving the springs, but responsible behaviour by all visitors is equally necessary.

Pebble Creek Hot Springs

Undeveloped

Maps 1, 2 & 3

Up to 60°C (140°F)

This is an undeveloped spring in a wild setting not far from Meager Creek. The rate of flow is small and there are no soaking pools. This special spot is only for experienced wilderness travellers.

Because of possible danger from flooding, rockfall, and mudslides, you should consider doing this trip only when the river is at its lowest level. Generally, this means in dry weather, from mid-summer until the first heavy autumn rains.

Getting There

Round-trip driving time from Vancouver is about nine hours, and there is a long hour's walk each way. Follow the approach route for Meager Creek hot springs to the Meager Creek turnoff at 63.4 km (39.4 mi.) from the Pemberton junction. Instead of heading left and across the Lillooet River to Meager Creek, continue straight ahead up the Lillooet River valley. In 1.5 km (0.9 mi.) you cross Pebble Creek. In another 1.4 km (0.8 mi.) the main road drops down to the river; stay left on the road. For the next 1.3 to 1.9 km (0.8 to 1.2 mi.), the road is cut into a steep bank beside the Lillooet River, and washouts are a good possibility. When you've gone 5.4 km (3.3 mi.) from the Meager Creek junction, park on a flat stretch about 0.5 km (0.3 mi.) before the road begins to climb steeply uphill away from the creek. Driving time is about 1½ hours from Pemberton.

You'll need good hiking boots from here. Follow an old, overgrown skid road that runs along the west edge of the logging slash. From the edge of the embankment above the river, drop down the steep slope on a sketchy trail to the gravel bars along the Lillooet River. Avoid the temptation to stay high on the benches, because it gets very difficult and dangerous to drop down to river level the farther upstream you go. When you reach the river bank, hike upstream, passing an attractive waterfall on your right. About five to 10 minutes past the waterfall, cross a steep, rushing stream. Cross this creek very carefully, because it is tricky and, at high water, difficult and dangerous.

At low water, continue upstream along the river bed to where the valley narrows and the columnar cliffs on the far side of the river are near the river. Where the river makes a sharp bend to the right, you will have to scramble over a large outcropping of white granite. Head around the corner; you'll find warm water about 100 m (300 ft.) upstream.

If the Lillooet River is at all high, it is impractical to travel along the river upstream of the creek crossing. Instead, climb the bank into big timber and follow benches for 10 to 15 minutes to the springs. Hiking time for the roughly 1.5 km (0.9 mi.) from the car to the springs is about an hour each way.

The Springs

Hot water seeps from fractures in the bedrock near the river and from the overlying gravel and loose volcanic deposits for roughly 100 m (300 ft.) along the river bank. The spring that is farthest downstream bubbles up from sand on the river bank, and it's hot. This is a good place to scoop out a shallow bathing pool; the sand is easy digging, particularly if you've brought a small folding shovel. The Lillooet River is only a few steps away, allowing you to adjust the water temperature to your liking. The river will soon wash away your pools, leaving the area as you found it.

The largest and hottest spring issues from several vents near the back of the gently sloping wooded bench about 50 m (160 ft.) above the Lillooet River. You can climb up to the spring from the river bank. Be very careful, especially coming down, since the rock is steep and slippery. The hot water (up to 60°C (140°F)) forms several shallow pools on the forest floor and then joins a small, cold creek. The mixed, tepid water flows over the bank below into the Lillooet River. The water is clear and colourless, with a faint sulphur smell and mineral taste. Chemically, it is similar to Meager spring water but is lower in chloride and higher in sulphate. The soft yellow iron oxide deposits and red and blue-green algae that coat the pools make a colourful and rather charming sight in the shade of the old-growth conifers. You will probably find numerous deer tracks in the mud of the pools, because deer seek out the white minerals deposited around the springs. It's salty and serves as a natural salt lick. One person who visited these springs in the heart of winter found the spring area free of snow and the pool swarming with tadpoles and breeding frogs. Please tread carefully on the vegetation, and don't try to make bathing pools here. You can do that at the river's edge.

Comments

The springs aren't marked on most maps, and you don't really need a map to find them. They are at UTM grid reference 676127 on NTS map 92J/11. The name Pebble Creek for these springs is a bit misleading, since they are about 5 km (3 mi.) upstream past Pebble Creek, much closer to Salal Creek, but the name has stuck.

Some people find the setting here, a narrow gorge with waterfalls and cliffs all around and high peaks above, spectacular; others find it claustrophobic. The approach to Pebble Creek hot springs, more than any other in this book, gives the feeling of walking in a geologically active and unstable world. And here it *is* active, young, and unstable. On a clear day from the car park area, you can often see what looks like smoke or mist high up on Plinth Peak, the conspicuous, rugged peak south of the river. It's not smoke or cloud; it's dust from the constant rockfall from the rotting walls of Plinth.

On the hike in, you pass some large cliffs on your right before you get to the rushing creek. These cliffs are composed of volcanic ash and blocks of volcanic rock, products of an eruption that occurred millenia ago high on the north side of Plinth Peak. As you continue your hike past the cliffs, look on the river bank for white, porous bits of volcanic rock produced by the eruption. This is pumice, so light it floats on water.

If you look carefully along the base of the cliffs, you can see charred tree trunks that were buried by some 150 m (500 ft.) of volcanic debris. The trees are upright, still standing where they were growing. Geologists have used samples of charcoal from these trees and radiocarbon dating to put the eruption at about 410 BC. This catastrophic explosion probably dwarfed the 1981 eruption of Mt. St. Helens in pure explosive power. Ash from the Plinth eruption was blown high into the stratosphere and has been found as far east as Edmonton. No doubt the ancient Greeks, whose classical civilization was flourishing then, enjoyed several years of spectacular sunsets as a result of the ash circulating high in the atmosphere. This explosion was only the most recent in a series of volcanic eruptions extending back several million years that built up the Mt. Meager and Plinth Peak edifice.

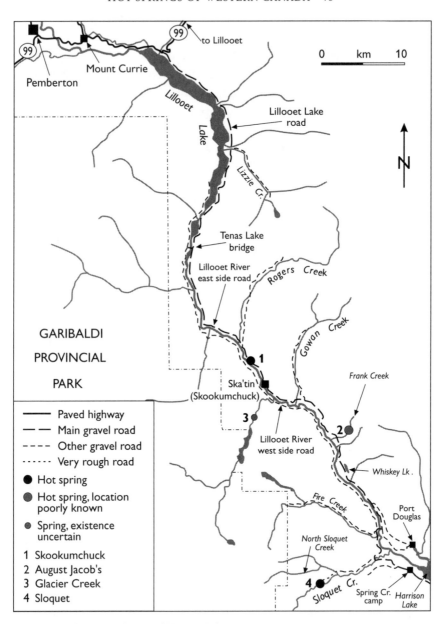

Map 4. Roads between Pemberton and Harrison Lake

St. Agnes Well (Skookumchuck Hot Springs)

Partly developed

Maps 1 & 4

54°C (129°F)

Facilities at these historically important springs southeast of Pemberton have been much improved recently. You can drive right to the springs, where there is good camping, and the new pools offer rather good soaking. Until recently, this site tended to be muddy and unkempt but the springs are now worth a visit. The nine hour round-trip drive makes a visit a long day from Vancouver.

For many years these springs were generally known as Skookumchuck hot springs. Recent usage seems to be reverting to the original European name of St. Agnes Well.

Getting There

From Vancouver, follow Highway 99 north past Squamish and Whistler. It's about 160 km (100 mi.) and a 2½ hour scenic drive from downtown Vancouver to the Petro-Canada station at the junction just before Pemberton, 33 km (20.5 mi.) past Whistler. Follow Highway 99 for 7.3 km (4.5 mi.) to the turnoff to Lillooet at the church in the village of Mount Currie. This is your last chance for gas, motels, and restaurants.

Follow Highway 99 through Lil'wat land. It's flat, good land, and in the fall you can sometimes see people drying fish near Lillooet Lake. At 10.0 km (6.2 mi.) turn right onto the In-SHUK-ch (Lillooet Lake) Forest Service road; the sign for Lillooet Lake Lodge is conspicuous here. Watch for logging trucks and use your headlights.

The excellent gravel road follows the east side of Lillooet Lake south past several attractive B.C. Forest Service campsites and then continues downstream along Lillooet River. It's a scenic drive, especially on a clear day in the fall when the leaves are turning and there's fresh snow on the mountains. About 31 km (19.2 mi.) from Highway 99, just after the 30 km marker, there is an obvious junction. Stay left; the right road leads to the Tenas Lake steel span across the Lillooet River and provides one possible route to Sloquet hot springs. The drive from Mount Currie to this junction takes about an hour.

About 14.7 km (9.1 mi.) from the Tenas junction, you cross the bridge over Rogers Creek (the first large creek south of Lillooet Lake). In another 3.4 km (2.1 mi.) there is a turnoff to the right that leads to the spring. The turnoff is marked by a large, carved sign that reads "St. Agnes Well /

T'Sik / Skookumchuck Hot Springs." Follow the road downriver for a few hundred metres to the camping area. The hot springs are near the south end of the large camping area, on your left between the access road and the main highway. The 60 km (38 mi.) drive from Mount Currie to the springs takes a bit less than 1½ hours.

If you are coming from Sloquet Creek or Harrison Lake, use the directions for Sloquet Creek hot springs given in the next section.

The Springs

A wooden walkway leads from the road to the pools. A small flow of hot water issues from the base of a large pool dug out of gravel a few metres behind the bathhouse. The water is clear with a very slight sulphur odour. Dissolved minerals are mainly sulphate, chloride, sodium, and calcium. Hot water is piped a few metres from this pool to the bathing tubs.

The main tub is half of a septic tank, large enough for several people, enclosed in an attractive, A-frame bathhouse. The hut has nice wooden floors and benches, and convenient spots to hang towels and clothing. Excellent ventilation helps it avoid that closed-in, humid, sauna feel common to many bathhouses. This new hut, built by the owners in 1996, is a big improvement on the old, rather squalid hut that stood here for years. Taps on the hot and cold water pipes let you adjust soaking temperature to suit yourself, and the tub can be drained for easy cleaning. With a push from a friend, people in wheelchairs should be able to get right to this pool.

There are two other tubs, one close to the road and the other to the right of the main bathhouse. Both have wooden walkways around them, with benches for clothes and towels. Both are open to the skies, but the benches are sheltered by steeply pitched roofs.

Comments

The springs are on private property. Signs read, "Welcome to St. Agnes Well. You are guests here of the Tretheway family. Contrary to what you may have read, there is no government or forestry money here. All improvements are by the owners, who have held title for 45 years." The facilities and campsites are maintained by the owners and users. There are outhouses and abundant space for tents and RVs. The spots near the river among the large fir trees remain pleasantly cool on a hot summer's evening. A box for donations is near the pools.

These springs are a reasonable day's outing from Whistler (about five or six hours round trip) and are something to visit when it's raining all the way to the top of the ski lifts and you're bored with life in the village. Because of the easy access, the pools are often crowded, and the camping area tends to be packed during the summer months. You may want to visit in the middle of the week or in the winter or spring months, or camp nearby and soak in the early morning.

The road along Lillooet Lake can be blocked by snow, floods, or washouts during the fall and winter, but in most years the road is open all year round as far as the Lil'wat village of Ska'tin (Skookumchuck), just past the springs. The B.C. Forest Service in Squamish (phone 604-898-9671) may know the current road conditions.

For one worthwhile side trip, drive south along the main road for 3.7 km (2.3 mi.) to Ska'tin (Skookumchuck). What you'll see is completely unexpected: a large Gothic church dominates the village. This superb building, the Church of the Holy Cross, was completed in 1906 and restored a few years ago. It is the third church to have been built on this site. Go and have a look at the interior of the church, which is as elaborate as the outside.

The new bathhouse and old, outdoor tubs at Skookumchuck, fall 1996.

On your way back to Pemberton, you can stop and see some of the remnants of the old wagon road, the history of which is described in the following paragraphs. One such remnant is by Rogers Creek, 3.2 km (2.0 mi.) north of the hot springs. Park just before the bridge; hike about 20 m (65 ft.) uphill, and you will see the road, much as it was a hundred years ago. There are other well-preserved sections, but this is one of the most accessible and makes a relaxing end to your day.

History

These springs were once far better known than the now-famous spa at Harrison Lake. In 1858, the gold miners in the interior of the province needed food and supplies for the winter, but there was no good trail from the coast to the gold fields. Governor James Douglas chose a route that went by steamer to the head of Harrison Lake and then by trail and lake to Pemberton and on into the interior. The trail was built by five hundred miners, who worked not for wages but for groceries. Their main incentive was to be the first to reach the interior by the new trail and have several weeks to prospect before the next flood of miners arrived. The route was badly laid out and the work poorly done, however, and much of the trail had to be rebuilt by the Royal Engineers and others over the next few years.

From 1859 to 1863, a steady flow of miners, prospectors, merchants, and entrepreneurs followed the Douglas Trail to the interior. Freight was carried on wagons, mules, and camels at $0.18 a pound. The camels were imported from California, where they had been used as pack animals. They were not a great success, since the alternately rocky and wet ground didn't agree with the sand-loving animals, and their smell terrorized the horses and mules. The hot springs, which had been used for thousands of years by the St'at'imc, were taken over by entrepreneurs (without permission of the native people or any compensation). A wayside house, one of several along the trail, was built at the springs, which were about a day's journey from Harrison Lake. The wooden tubs at the springs were understandably popular with travellers: one miner described the baths as the only cheap comfort in British Columbia. Judge Matthew Begbie and his assistant, Arthur Bushby, travelled the route in April 1859. In his journal, Bushby wrote:

We got that afternoon to the Hot Springs where we camped–
it is a very pretty spot the rock from which the spring emme-
nates is in the midst of a cedar wood and each side of the Hot
springs are two cold ones. An Irishman is building a modern
Hotel and a bath House over it–we bathed of course, the first
time I have been really clean since I left S. Francisco.

Begbie and Bushby named the springs St. Agnes' Well, after Agnes
Douglas, the eighteen-year-old daughter of Governor Douglas, "a stunning girl. black eye & hair & larky like the devil" whom Bushby was later
to marry.

Another visitor that year, Captain Richard Mayne (for whom Mayne
Island is named) wrote that the

> . . . very curious hot spring . . . runs in a small stream out of a
> mass of conglomerate into a natural basin at its foot, overflow-
> ing which it finds its way into the Lilloett River. Here have
> been built a restaurant and bath-house. On my first visit I
> stopped to bathe, and found the water in the basin hotter than
> I could bear. Unfortunately my thermometer was only marked
> to 120°, up to which the mercury flew instantly.

By 1864, most traffic to the interior had switched to the new and supe-
rior route up the Fraser Canyon. The wayside houses were abandoned
when the government stopped maintaining the trail, and the hot springs
were left to the native people and the occasional trader and oblate mis-
sionary. Today the old restaurant site is an open meadow near the springs,
and you can still camp there among wild mint and ancient apple trees
where, quite possibly, the camels used to graze.

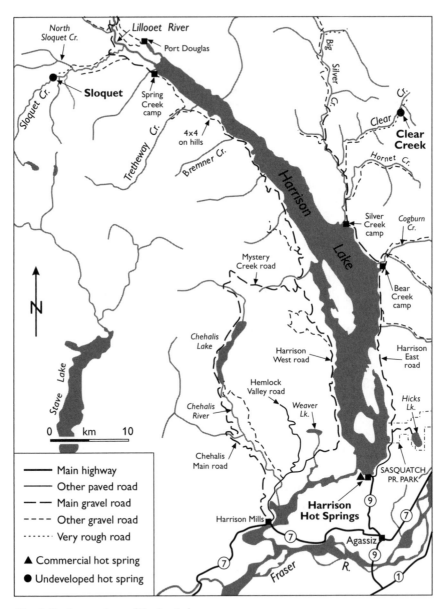

Map 5. Roads east and west of Harrison Lake

Sloquet Hot Springs

Undeveloped

Maps 1, 4 & 5 · Colour photos, pages 194 & 195

Up to 68°C (154°F)

These springs are perhaps the best in the chain of springs stretching from Harrison Lake to Meager Creek. They are an undeveloped spot right beside clear, cold, mountain-fed Sloquet Creek. Because there is a long drive, they escape much of the drive-in traffic and rowdy behaviour that has tended to spoil St. Agnes Well (Skookumchuck) and Meager. With recent improvements to the road up Sloquet Creek, the springs have become increasingly popular but are still among the most attractive of the major springs in southern British Columbia.

The 12 hour round-trip drive and hike from Vancouver makes Sloquet best as a weekend trip, perhaps combined with St. Agnes Well (Skookumchuck) hot springs.

Getting There

You can reach these springs either by good gravel road from Pemberton or by a very rough road from the Fraser Valley. The approach from Pemberton is the most popular, since any vehicle can make the trip. Don't forget to gas up in Pemberton or Mount Currie. The approach from the Fraser Valley up the west side of Harrison Lake is suitable for 4×4s only. The two approaches converge at the bridge over Sloquet Creek.

If you have a 4×4, you can make a weekend-long circle trip by approaching Sloquet from the Fraser Valley and then continuing north to St. Agnes Well (Skookumchuck) and Meager Creek hot springs before returning on pavement via Whistler and Squamish.

From Pemberton to Sloquet Creek bridge (*Map 4*)   Follow directions in the previous section and drive to St. Agnes Well (Skookumchuck) hot springs, 60 km (37 mi.) from the village of Mount Currie. Continue south past Ska'tin (Skookumchuck) village, with its incredible triple-spired Gothic church. About 8 km (5 mi.) south of the hot springs, the road crosses the bridge over Gowan Creek, and in another 18.3 km (11.3 mi.) you reach a junction; stay right. (The left fork leads to Port Douglas at the head of Harrison Lake.) The road soon descends to the Lillooet River and crosses it, 3.8 km (2.3 mi.) from the Port Douglas turnoff. In 0.6 km (0.4 mi.) the road joins the Lillooet River West Side road at a wide T-junction.

An alternative way to reach this junction is to follow roads down the west side of the Lillooet River. At 30.2 km (18.7 mi.) from the Duffey Lake road, turn right and cross the Lillooet River on the Tenas Lake bridge. Turn left at the large junction just past the bridge and follow the main road south to the junction with the east side road (48 km (30 mi.) from the Tenas bridge). This less scenic route is rougher than the east side road and is subject to washouts.

From the T junction, drive 4.2 km (2.6 mi.) south along the main road to the bridge over Sloquet Creek. Driving time from Pemberton to here is about 2½ hours by either road.

From Fraser Valley to Sloquet Creek bridge (Map 5)   If you have a four-wheel-drive vehicle with high clearance, you can reach the spring from the Fraser Valley by rough gravel roads west of Harrison Lake.

Follow Highway 7 east from Mission or west from Agassiz to Harrison Mills, just west of where the highway crosses the Harrison River. Turn north at the Sasquatch Inn onto the road to the Hemlock Valley ski area, which is well marked. Follow the main road; stay left at the Chehalis Café and turn right at the Hemlock Valley turnoff. The pavement ends about 10.6 km (6.6 mi.) from Highway 7. In another 2 km (1.2 mi.), continue straight ahead on the Harrison West Forest Service road (the Weaver Lake road branches left). Now follow the main road for another 29 km (18 mi.) to a large junction. Go right (the Chehalis-Mystery Creek road branches left). Cross the bridge over Bremner Creek in another 26 km (16 mi.). This far, the road is suitable for most cars, but it is much rougher from here on and not suitable for most two-wheel-drive vehicles. Follow the main road to the Spring Creek logging camp at the mouth of Tipella Creek near the head of Harrison Lake (about 76 km (47 mi.) from the Sasquatch Inn). Check in at the camp, and watch for logging trucks on the road beyond. Continue north past the camp for 5 km (3 mi.) to the bridge across Sloquet Creek. Driving time from the Sasquatch Inn on Highway 7 to here is about four hours, depending on road conditions, your vehicle, and your driving skills.

From Sloquet Creek bridge to the hot springs   The Sloquet Creek road starts 50 m (160 ft.) north of the bridge. The road forks in 50 m (160 ft.); take the left fork. In another 6.1 km (3.8 mi.), stay left and take the bridge over North Sloquet Creek. From the bridge, the road is nearly level for a ways and then climbs a long hill to an open area and large turnaround 3.1 km (1.9 mi.) from the bridge. There are plenty of good campsites here. From the far side of the clearing, a very rough road drops steeply for 100 m (300 ft.) or so to a large clearing on the bank of Sloquet Creek; this clearing makes a pretty campsite.

The Springs

From the downstream end of the clearing, a well-worn trail leads into the woods and along a log to the base of a scalding hot waterfall. The waterfall is about 10 m (30 ft.) high, and the hot cascade is beautifully framed by lush moss and ferns. The water temperature at the source of the springs, a few metres above the waterfall, reaches 68°C (154°F), making this (with Harrison) one of the two hottest springs in southwestern British Columbia. The water, clear and tasteless, has a slight sulphur smell. Mineral content is quite low, consisting mainly of sulphate, sodium, calcium, and silica. At the base of the waterfall, the water collects into a hot creek that parallels Sloquet Creek for about 30 m (100 ft.) to the bathing area.

The main bathing pools are right beside Sloquet Creek. Depending on the level of the river and the enthusiasm of recent visitors, you may find one, several, or possibly no pools. Generally there are about three, with built-up retaining walls of stream-bed cobbles and perhaps some plastic sheet. Each soaker is 30 to 100 cm (1 to 3 ft.) deep and holds several people. Water flows from the highest into successively lower pools. The highest is far too hot for all but the most asbestos-skinned individuals, but the lower ones are just right. The lowest bath mixes hot spring water with the icy, clear Sloquet Creek. You can lie in hot water and dangle your legs over the retaining wall in the creek as mixed hot and cold water swirls around you, a great experience.

If you prowl around, both upstream and down, you will find other small seeps along the creek bank. There are at least a dozen, but none are as hot as the main ones or large enough for bathing. One of the vents has deposited small amounts of tufa.

Comments

Sloquet is best in summer and early fall. Most years, snow blocks the Lillooet River and Sloquet Creek roads from about November to March.

Sloquet Creek was once known as Spring Creek, no doubt for the hot springs, and the old name survives in the Spring Creek logging camp. The

Steam rising from the rocky bed of the hot creek at Sloquet hot springs.

springs aren't shown on most maps, but they are at UTM grid reference 489088 on NTS map 92G/9. There is plenty of space for tents, both in the clearing by the creek and at the top of the hill, and there is good camping along the Lillooet River and Lillooet Lake roads. Many people drink the water from Sloquet Creek; others bring water from home.

The springs are on public land, although timber rights to the area are privately held. The hot springs escaped the logging that devastated the watershed years ago, and there are many large cedars around the pool. New logging roads run up the south side of Sloquet Creek, and I've heard rumours that logging may soon start again on the north side. These springs need protection as an ecological reserve.

Harrison Hot Springs

Commercial resort

Maps 1 & 5 · Colour photos, page 196

62°, 68°C (144°, 154°F) at source

These springs are the centrepiece of a luxury hotel in a popular resort town east of Vancouver. Water is pumped to pools at the hotel, which are reserved for those staying at the resort. Overflow water is piped to a public swimming pool a few blocks away. The resort operates all year round, but the peak season (and prices) is from June through September. Summer weekends are especially crowded.

Getting There

You can visit Harrison as a day trip from Vancouver. From Vancouver, take Highway 1 east to exit 135 east of Chilliwack and then take Highway 9 through Agassiz to the town of Harrison Hot Springs (about 1½ to 2 hours and 130 km (80 mi.) from downtown Vancouver). Alternatively, take Highway 7 along the north side of the Fraser River to intersect Highway 9. This more scenic approach is about the same distance but takes half an hour longer. After you reach Harrison Hot Springs, turn left along the waterfront and go a couple of blocks to the hotel.

If you are coming from Seattle, follow Interstate 5 to Bellingham. Take the Meridian/Lynden exit and Highway 539 to Lynden. Continue north to the border and Highway 1 and follow the directions above (about three hours from Seattle).

The Springs

From the lake shore in front of the hotel, an excellent path (suitable for wheelchairs) leads in five minutes past the end of the lake and along the west shore to a yellow cement-block edifice at lake level. Spring water bubbles up from below and is contained in a large concrete pool to prevent dilution with the lake water. There's a faint sulphur smell in the air, and a little shell-shaped drinking fountain where you can feel the water with your hand and drink a bit of it; it has a mild mineral taste. A bronze plaque tells a bit of the history of the springs. Many who went to Harrison as small children remember this spot forever.

There are actually two springs issuing from the lake shore. The one you see bubbling up in the pool is slightly hotter (about 68°C (154°F)) than the covered-over spring (about 62°C (144°F)). The main dissolved mineral constituents are sulphate, sodium, chloride, calcium, and silica. The water is moderately radioactive but, like all B.C. springs, not enough to do you the slightest harm. Water from the combined springs is piped to the resort. As you walk back along the path, you'll see a water tank on the slope above you. This holds the hot water on its way to the hotel; if you climb up to the tank, you can feel the heat radiating from it.

Facilities

The pools at the hotel are for guests only. There are three outside pools: one for swimming laps (29°C (85°F)), a family pool (about 32°C (90°F)), and an adult pool (35°C (95°F)). Indoors are a large swimming pool (35°C (95°F), a smaller hot pool (40°C (104°F), and separate saunas for men and women. All pools are filtered and chlorinated.

The public pool is one block east of the hotel, in a plain cement-block building opposite Hot Springs Plaza. The pool is about 1 m (4 ft.) deep and has a temperature of about 40°C (104°F). The facilities are plain and utilitarian, but they are clean and include lockers and showers with soap.

The village of Harrison Hot Springs has a good selection of restaurants, motels, and campgrounds, and there's a public campground at Sasquatch Provincial Park on the east side of town. The sandy beach and playground are public and offer a fine view north up the lake, where steamboats travelled in gold rush days and well into the twentieth century. The lake offers cold swimming and is popular with windsurfers and boaters. A public boat launch is just east of town.

For maps and information on the many activities in town, stop at the tourist information office, on your left just as you enter the town.

Rates, Hours, and Address

Harrison Hot Springs Hotel is open year-round. Room rates begin at $120–$145 plus tax, depending on the season, and include full use of the pools. Several cottages in the garden behind the pool are also available; pets are allowed in the cottages but not the hotel. Special package deals are frequently offered. For more information, contact:

Harrison Hot Springs Hotel
Harrison Hot Springs, BC V0M 1K0
604-521-8888 (toll-free from Vancouver)
1-800-663-2266 (toll-free from elsewhere in Canada and United States)
604-796-2244
Fax: 604-796-3682

Two early photos of the St. Alice Hotel at Harrison Hot Springs. The top photo was taken about 1887, shortly after the hotel opened. The bottom photo was taken about 1901. Trips on sternwheelers such as this one, possibly the Delaware, *were popular with the guests.*

The public swimming pool is open from 8:00 AM to 9:00 PM daily. Admission is $7.00 for adults and $5.00 for children and seniors. Family and group rates are available. Phone 604-796-2244 for more information.

History

The springs were known and used for millennia by the Stó:lo people. Judge Matthew Begbie was the first European to mention the springs. Although he didn't visit them, in 1859 he made note of the "very curious hot wells" and named them St. Alice's Well, for Governor James Douglas's younger daughter. No doubt he wished to avoid the appearance of favouritism after he and Arthur Bushby had named the better-known springs at Skookumchuck for her sister, Agnes.

In those days, the springs were off the main travel routes and were almost unknown compared with St. Agnes' Well. But in 1873 the land surrounding the springs was purchased (for $40!), and the timbered, country-style St. Alice Hotel and its baths opened late in 1886. An 1889 advertisement called it "the Baden Baden of America . . . absolutely free from Malaria. These springs are warranted to cure Venereal, Skin, Rheumatic and similar diseases." Not a bad deal, even if rates *were* an expensive $1.50 to $3 a day.

In July 1920, the old hotel burned to the ground, and it wasn't until May 1926 that a new hotel (brick this time) was opened. The new resort was called the Harrison Hot Springs Hotel, and the name St. Alice faded into history. The hotel boasted a ballroom, a billiard room, tennis courts, and, most novel of all, a golf course. The resort prospered as a holiday destination, with a break during World War II when it served as a hospital.

In 1949–1950, the resort changed hands and underwent extensive renovations. A large pub was one of the new attractions, not surprisingly, since the new owner was United Distillers Ltd. Another distillery, the House of Seagram, bought the hotel in 1953; over the next 19 years Seagram's modernized, renovated, and added on to the hotel.

In 1987, ownership of the hotel complex passed to Japanese banking interests, who added a large new tower to the hotel. In 1997 the property was sold to an American company, and further expansion and renovation seem likely. Today the resort has a distinctly international flavour and attracts visitors from all over the world.

Clear Creek (Ruth Larsen) Hot Springs

Partly developed

Maps 1 & 5 · Colour photo, page 195

Up to 43°C (109°F)

These springs are a popular, pleasant soak northeast of Harrison Lake, about a four hour drive from Vancouver (the last two hours on logging roads), followed by an hour's hike. The pools are maintained by volunteers, and there's a nice cabin nearby. It's a popular destination with the 4×4 crowd. From late spring to early fall, you can drive most of the way in for a long day trip from Vancouver. In winter, some parties ski the last part of the road to the springs.

Getting There

From Vancouver, take Highway 1 east to exit 135 east of Chilliwack and then follow Highway 9 to the town of Harrison Hot Springs (about 1½ to 2 hours and 130 km (80 mi.) from downtown Vancouver). Harrison Hot Springs is your last chance for gas, motels, and restaurants.

Follow the road, which is paved at first, as it swings up the east side of Harrison Lake. At 7.4 km (4.6 mi.) from the turnoff to Sasquatch Provincial Park, there's a major junction; bear left onto the Harrison East Forest Service road. Use your headlights and watch for oncoming logging trucks. In another 22.7 km (14.1 mi.) you reach the Bear Creek logging camp; stay right and don't go into the camp. In 1.3 km (0.8 mi.), angle left at a large, open junction. In another 0.5 km (0.3 mi.), go left after crossing the large bridge over Cogburn Creek. Follow the logging road along Harrison Lake to the logging camp and log dump area at the mouth of Big Silver Creek (39 km (24 mi.) and a bit over an hour from Harrison Hot Springs). It's a good idea to stop at the camp office during working hours (dawn to dusk) so that the radio-controlled logging trucks on the road ahead will know that you're coming.

The road now swings away from Harrison Lake and follows Big Silver Creek past a flat, straight stretch that doubles as a landing strip for small planes. In 3.3 km (2.0 mi.) you cross the Hornet Creek bridge; make a careful note of your mileage here. In another 2.2 km (1.3 mi.), the Clear Creek road branches sharply right.

Some two-wheel-drive vehicles may be able to negotiate the next 7 km (4 mi.), but others may not. The road is fairly steep for a kilometre and then it levels off and swings into the Clear Creek valley. At about 2.5 km

(1.5 mi.) and 4.7 km (2.9 mi.) there are steep, rough sections. If you make it past these, it's easy driving through large clearcuts to a good turn-around, 7 km (4.3 mi.) from the Big Silver main road. The turnaround is just before the end of navigation for all two-wheel- and most four-wheel-drive vehicles. The drive to this point is about 45 minutes from the Silver Creek logging camp.

From the turnaround, it's about 5 km (3 mi.) to the springs, a very rough trip for 4×4s or about a 1½ hour hike. After the vehicle turnaround, there aren't any more clearcuts and the hike into the springs is pretty. The vegetation is lush and green, Clear Creek bubbles away nearby, and it's pleasantly cool even on a hot day. The road drops steeply down to Clear Creek and then generally parallels the creek. Follow the ancient track, staying on the south side of the creek. At one point, where the road has been thoroughly washed out, you have to take a bit of a trail through the bush. For much of the last kilometre, the road climbs steeply and in places is little more than a boulder-strewn stream bed. When the road levels off again you're just about there. You won't miss the cabin, right on the trail between Clear Creek and the springs.

The Springs

From the cabin, walk past a large, silt-filled pool to the soaking pools. Spring water issues from several tiny, plant-filled grottos in the boulders and clay above the pool. The hottest spring is about 43°C (109°F). The water is clear and odourless, with only a slight mineral taste.

The pools were thoroughly renovated in 1991. Plastic hoses and pipes collect the water and carry it to the two main bathing pools. The larger one, a large plastic tub, holds about six people and is a good all-day soaking temperature. The other is a hot-tub-style cistern made from tongue-and-groove cedar boards with cedar benches to sit on while you relax. It's hotter than the plastic, often too hot for me to stay in for very long, but just right for many. There's a wooden deck surrounding both tubs for sitting on when you get too warm.

The tubs drain into the large, silt-filled pool, now unused except by large numbers of frogs. Years ago, someone brought a couple of porcelain bathtubs to the site, imitating the fishermen who brought such luxuries to hot springs along the B.C. coast. The tubs aren't hooked up to the present plumbing system and are usually ignored.

Comments

The logging companies that control the roads often restrict public traffic to weekends and evenings. If you are going during working hours or during periods of high forest fire risk, phone Lineham Logging Company at 604-796-9166 or 604-792-3394 for information.

The pools are on public land, and the site is maintained by volunteers. It's in a clearing in old-growth forest. Large, first-growth cedar trees surround the spring site, shading the pools for all but an hour or so each day. You will see some monster trees on the last kilometre or so of your hike in.

Some local people call the site Ruth's Reach or Ruth Larsen hot springs, after a prospector who had mineral claims in the area years ago. She used the ancient, rusting bulldozer you pass just before the springs to build part of the road and scoop out the large, silt-filled swimming pool, which must have been a big hit with her young children.

The log cabin is clean and has a wood stove and loft. You are welcome to use the cabin as long as you leave it in as good as or better shape than you found it. The cabin sleeps at least a dozen people comfortably. Even if you aren't staying overnight, it's an excellent place to change in wet weather or wait out a rain shower before heading home. Firewood is scarce; use only dead wood lying around or scrounged from the surrounding bush. Take your garbage out with you. If you arrive by vehicle, you might spend a few minutes collecting trash left by others to take out so that all can continue to enjoy this special spot.

If the cabin is full or is too claustrophobic for you, camp at one of the lovely small spots on the banks of Clear Creek. Most people quite happily drink Clear Creek water, but it is more prudent to bring water from home.

Pitt River Hot Springs

Undeveloped

Map 1

57°C (135°F)

This tiny gem is set in a canyon on the banks of the Pitt River. It is the closest spring to Vancouver and one of the least visited, because you need a boat or plane to reach it. The springs are covered by the Pitt River for much of the year. Late winter through May before the river starts to rise and late summer into fall are the best times to visit. If you can solve the problem of getting there, you will have an enjoyable day trip from Vancouver and you won't be disappointed.

Getting There

The main access problems are getting to the dock at the head of Pitt Lake and getting 22 km (13 mi.) up the logging road from the dock. For the first problem, you need a boat or a plane. If you don't have your own boat, you might be able to rent one at the marina where Highway 7 crosses the Pitt River.

The expensive alternative is to charter a plane. Altair Aviation will fly two people to the dock at the head of the lake for about $120 (picking you up will be another flight and another $120). The very scenic flight takes about 30 minutes. For information, contact:

Altair Aviation
Pitt Meadows Airport
#7 - 11465 Baynes Road South
Pitt Meadows, BC V3Y 2E6
604-465-5414 or 1-800-665-0596

From the dock at the head of Pitt Lake it is about 22 km (13 mi.) on logging roads to the springs. You may be able to hitch a ride with a logging truck, but cycling up the road is probably the most reliable and enjoyable method. If you are flying to the head of the lake, the plane will take two bicycles if you remove the wheels and handlebars. Check with Altair when you make your reservation.

The gravel road is wide and has an excellent surface. Around 7 km (4 mi.), you pass the little community of Alvin. The road is shady, with good views of Mamquam Mountain near the head of the Pitt River. Continue up the main road past Alvin. Until the 15 km sign, the road is flat. From there to the 21 km marker, the road has gentle ups and downs. At the 21 km sign, fork left and drop about 0.5 km (0.3 mi.) to the log bridge over the Pitt River. The bike ride will take a little over an hour, depending on how fast you cycle.

From the bridge, the springs can be seen in the spectacular canyon upstream, if you know exactly where to look. About 20 m (65 ft.) past the bridge, a faint trail takes off into the bush. Leave your bikes and follow the trail upstream. In about 80 m (260 ft.), continue steeply uphill and upstream on the main trail, ignoring a side trail that drops steeply down to the river and a sand bar. In another 40 m (130 ft.) the trail descends to the edge of a sharp drop to the river, from where you can see the pool

Looking down the steep bank to the hot pool beside Pitt River.

below. Reach the pool by carefully descending 10 m of steep rock. There is often a rope hanging down the rock, but it may be rotten.

The Springs

Hot water issues from a crack in the cliff about 4 m (13 ft.) above the main pool and drops in a tiny waterfall. The flow is small, but the water is clear, tasteless, and odourless, and has a low dissolved mineral content.

The main pool is about 3 m (10 ft.) across and about knee-deep. There is a concrete retaining wall on the river side; the other sides are natural granitic bedrock that has been smoothed by the river. The bottom of the pool is good sand, free of scum and algae. It's a wonderful spot, right on the bank of the unlogged canyon of the Pitt River, which is about 20 m (65 ft.) wide here. The river itself is a deep green; the water flows silently but boils with eddies and turbulence.

Contemplating this scene, with the bridge downstream being the only sign of civilization, it's hard to realize you are less than 60 km (37 mi.) from downtown Vancouver. The springs are well known to the loggers and residents of Alvin, but you are likely to have them all to yourself. If you do have company, ask them if they know of any other springs nearby. I've heard rumours of another spring in the area.

The soaking pool at Pitt River hot springs.

Other Springs in the Lower Mainland

Several other springs exist in the Lower Mainland. Most are too small, too cool, and too hard to find to interest most people. I've included them for those who want to hunt down every last trickle of warm water.

Placid and No Good Springs

Undeveloped

Maps 1, 2 & 3   45°C (113°F) for Placid; up to 35°C (95°F) for No Good

During the geothermal exploration at Meager Creek, two other small hot springs were discovered. Both are cooler than Meager Creek hot springs and much smaller in volume. The only recreational interest is in the challenge of trying to find them.

Placid hot springs issue from the gravelly south bank of Meager Creek about 600 m (0.4 mi.) upstream from Meager Creek hot springs, at UTM grid reference 666019 on NTS map 92J/11. The best way to find them is to hike up the gravel bars past Meager Creek hot springs (best in late summer or winter), watching for warm water. The several small vents have a temperature of about 45°C (113°F). There are no soaking pools.

No Good warm springs are on the north bank of Meager Creek, about 5 km (3 mi.) upstream from Meager Creek hot springs. To reach them, backtrack along the Meager Creek road from Meager Creek hot springs, cross the bridge across Meager Creek, and continue downstream for several hundred metres until you can turn hard left onto the old logging road that follows the north bank of Meager Creek. There may be a locked gate about 1 km (0.6 mi.) along this road. Continue along the road for another 5 km (3 mi.). The springs issue from a grassy bank above a gravel bar on the north side of Meager Creek, at UTM grid reference 635010 on NTS map 92J/12. There are about six small vents spread out along the creek; water temperatures range from 20° to 35°C (68° to 95°F). The name, No Good, aptly describes the soaking possibilities here.

August Jacob's Hot Spring

Undeveloped

Maps 1 & 4

51.5°C (125°F)

This spring was mentioned in geological reports in the 1920s but was then "lost" for many years. It was found again during airborne infra-red prospecting for geothermal sources in the 1970s but was not visited at that time. It has recently been rediscovered by hikers, but I don't have detailed information.

The spring is probably located at about 600 m (2000 ft.) elevation on Frank Creek south of Ska'tin (Skookumchuck) village. Water temperature reaches about 51.5°C (125°F). Take map 92G/16 and be prepared for steep, bushy travel.

There are rumours of a hot spring on Glacier Creek west of the Lillooet River.

Turbid and Shovelnose Warm Springs

Undeveloped

Map 1

29°C (84°F) for Turbid; 27°C (81°F) for Shovelnose

Two tiny groups of warm seeps were found by geologists in 1980 on the very rugged south side of Mt. Cayley. The Turbid Creek springs are at an elevation of about 800 m (2600 ft.) on the north side of Turbid Creek. Temperature is about 29°C (84°F), and the rate of flow is little more than a trickle. The Shovelnose spring is at an elevation of about 975 m (3200 ft.) in Shovelnose Creek. This tiny seep is about 27°C (81°F).

Both of these springs are in very rugged, steep valleys that are prone to mud and rock slides and avalanches. There are no bathing possibilities at either site. Access is from the Squamish River road and then by foot up Turbid and Shovelnose creeks. I do not recommend visiting these springs, but if you do go, take hard hats, mountaineering boots, and NTS map 92J/3.

Many years ago a member of the Squamish band told me that his father saw steam rising from the south side of Mt. Cayley one winter while he was hunting on ridges west of the Squamish River. At the time I put the story down to legends of volcanic activity on Mt. Cayley, but I think it is more likely that the hunter saw a plume of steam from the warm springs or dust from nearly constant rockfall from the cliffs above.

Rumours persist of two springs, one warm and one hot, west of Mt. Cayley and Tricouni Peak. If they exist, they are well hidden.

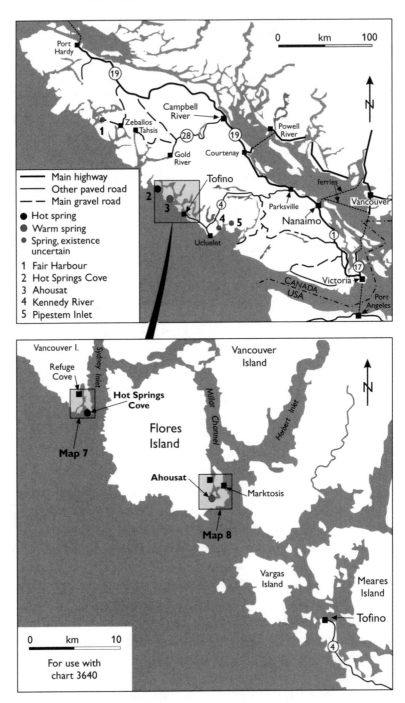

Map 6. Vancouver Island (top) and Tofino area (bottom)

CHAPTER 2

Vancouver Island

Although Vancouver Island has few hot springs, many people consider one of them, Hot Springs Cove, to be the finest in Canada. The springs on Vancouver Island have no resorts or swimming pools, and visiting them can be an adventure. Unlike most undeveloped springs in British Columbia, these don't require lengthy drives on logging roads, although you do need boat or a plane, either one of your own or one of many for charter. You also need a bit of luck with the weather. But it's all in the cause of a great soak, so if you haven't been to Vancouver Island for a while, it's time to go.

You can reach Nanaimo on Vancouver Island from Victoria (a two hour drive), by ferry from Tsawwassen (best if you are coming from the United States) or Horseshoe Bay. Phone B.C. Ferry Corporation (604-669-1211) for current rates and schedules on all ferries. The Horseshoe Bay-Nanaimo ferry runs about every two hours, and the crossing takes about an hour and 35 minutes.

Hot Springs Cove (Sharp Point, Refuge Cove)   Undeveloped

Maps 6 & 7 · Colour photo, page 193   51°C (124°F)

Whether you go by power boat, kayak, or airplane, the trip to Hot Springs Cove is a wilderness adventure with all the scenery, marine life, and uncertain weather for which the west coast of Vancouver Island is famous. This unspoiled but increasingly crowded spot on the edge of the open Pacific offers possibly the best soak in Canada, good at any time of the year.

Getting There

This trip can be done as a long day outing from Vancouver, if all goes well with ferries and your plane or boat transport. But you will get far more pleasure if you take a few extra days and combine a trip to the springs with a visit to Pacific Rim National Park or another special place on the island.

From Nanaimo, drive north on Highway 19 to Parksville and take Highway 4 towards Port Alberni, Tofino, and Pacific Rim National Park. It's about 35 km (22 mi.) to Parksville and another 180 km (112 mi.) to the town of Tofino, all on pavement. Allow about 2½ hours for the drive, more if the traffic is heavy.

Hot Springs Cove is about 37 km (23 mi.) northwest of Tofino. You can reach it by boat (an hour) or plane (20 minutes). Tofino Air Lines (250-725-4454), based at the government wharf at the foot of First Street, will fly you and your gear there in either a three-passenger Cessna 180 or a six-passenger Beaver. The cost per planeload is $140 (Cessna) or $196 (Beaver), regardless of how many are in your party. You'll have to double these figures for a round trip. The 20 minute flight gives a spectacular, sweeping view of deserted white sand beaches and surging waves on cliff faces. A single vista may encompass Tofino, the many islands with solitary houses or tiny communities, and boats of all sorts: pleasure boats, fishing boats, tugboats, and deep sea ships. You might see some whales or colonies of sea lions.

The main street in Tofino is lined with offices advertising whale-watching excursions. Some of these also offer trips to Hot Springs Cove combined with whale or sea lion watching, at a cost of about $50 a person for the afternoon outing. Some companies have covered, solid-hull boats (nice in rainy weather). Others use large inflatable boats and will supply you with the necessary wet-weather gear. Most are operated by people who have a good knowledge of the local area, its history, and the whales. The Tofino Chamber of Commerce can provide a list of companies currently in operation (see address under "Maps and More Information"). Note also that many companies require at least four people before they will make the trip. If you get to Tofino and find that no one else wants to go to Hot Springs that day, you may be out of luck. Confirm your reservations the night before you leave for Tofino. Charter boats and water taxis in Tofino are most plentiful from May through September. Many charter operators close for the winter.

The Nuu-chah-nulth people run regularly scheduled trips to Hot Springs Cove. Phone 1-800-665-9425 or 250-725-2888 for rates and information.

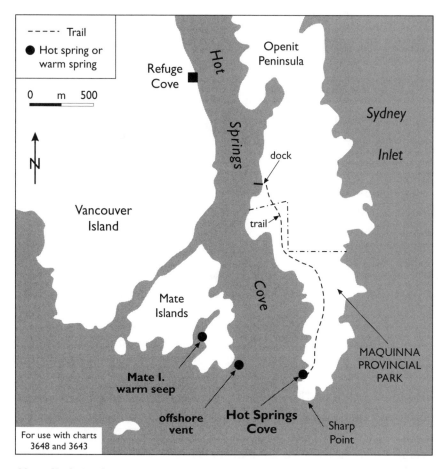

Map 7. Hot Springs Cove

If you have your own boat, you aren't restricted by the schedules of the commercial operators. The shortest route to Hot Springs Cove, around the west side of Flores Island, is about 40 km (25 mi.), much of it in open water. The route around the east and north sides of Flores is longer but more sheltered. The west coast of Vancouver Island is serious boating country: weather can turn bad and water whip up very quickly. You shouldn't attempt this trip unless you are properly equipped and know what you are doing.

The trip from Tofino to Hot Springs Cove is popular with kayakers. Again, only experienced and properly equipped parties should consider this paddle. Don't try to put ashore right at the springs; go around the corner into Hot Springs Cove and take out at the government dock. Tofino Sea Kayaking offers guided kayak expeditions to Hot Springs for those who are fit and adventurous. Phone 250-725-4222 for information.

From the government dock, follow the obvious forest path to the spring. The 1.5 km (0.9 mi.) walk along a split-cedar boardwalk takes about half an hour, and a very pleasant half-hour it is. The boardwalk is well maintained and winds gently over little hummocks and hollows to the springs. Many of the split boards are carved with the names of boats, girlfriends, and patron saints. Some of the carvings have been inlaid with rope that has been well varnished to resist the damp; take time to admire them. The forest has that primeval, land-that-time-forgot feel that so many people associate with the West Coast rain forest. Salal, ferns, and blueberry bushes are taller than people but are dwarfed by the huge western red cedar, spruce, and Douglas fir trees that form the overhead canopy. Near the springs, the vegetation opens out and you might catch a whiff of sulphur in the air or see steam rising from the pools.

The Springs

Hot water and gas bubble from a crack in bedrock beneath large fir trees. It's very hot (51°C (124°F)) and the temperature has not changed significantly since 1898, when it was first measured. The water is clear, with a faint sulphur taste and smell. Dissolved mineral content, mainly chloride and sodium, is low. The hot creek runs about 30 m (100 ft.) past several small pools and an old enamelled bathtub that seems totally incongruous in this setting. These pools are too hot for bathing except in very cold or wet weather. The stream pours 3 m (10 ft.) in a curtain-like waterfall to the tidal zone and main soaking pools.

The split-cedar boardwalk that leads through old-growth forest to the pools at Hot Springs Cove.

The main pools are in a little canyon between the waterfall and the open ocean. The number, size, and temperature of the pools depend on the tide. The pools are irregular and entirely natural: no plastic pipe, cement, or plastic sheet here. They are surprisingly comfortable, but it's not a bad idea to wear an old pair of sneakers to avoid cuts. Above the pools on the south side is a nice open area, good for sunning, reading, picnicking, and watching the ocean, birds, and boats. You might spot a curious harbour seal or two and, if you are very lucky, a pod of killer whales.

Most hot springs vary somewhat from season to season and year to year. One of the enchanting things about this spring is that it changes from hour to hour. At high tide, you are confined to near the waterfall. As the tide falls, you can follow it down to where you are swimming among the seaweed, starfish, sea anemones, and whatever other sea life drifts in to join you. As you watch the swells roll in from the Pacific, you have the weird feeling that you are sitting at the edge of the world looking *up* at the ocean. My favourite time is during an incoming tide: sit in the cool end of one of the pools and wait for a large wave to wash over you. The cold salt water is denser than the hot water and sinks to the bottom of your pool, leaving the surface warm and toasty. When the water gets too cool, just migrate upstream to a warmer pool. Float on your back and let the tidal swell rock you back and forth. This is serious, hours-at-a-time recreation.

The tidal action means that the pools are flushed twice daily, so they are always very clean. Most bathers prefer the afternoon for the sun, and an incoming tide for best water temperature and variety.

Maps and More Information

You don't need any maps if you are taking the plane, a water taxi, or a charter boat. If you have your boat or kayak, you need the proper marine charts published by the federal Hydrographic Service. Chart 3640 covers the region; charts 3648 and 3643 provide more detail.

For information on charter boat operators and tour companies and accommodation in Tofino, contact:

Tofino Chamber of Commerce
P.O. Box 476
Tofino, BC V0R 2Z0
250-725-3414

The hot waterfall at Hot Springs Cove.

Comments

There isn't a *best* time to visit Hot Springs Cove; every season has its charms. The driest, warmest months are June through September (although fog can be a problem on some days). Late March through May are the best months for watching the migration of the great gray whales, but Tofino and the surrounding area can be packed with tourists then. Many of the whale-watching tour companies run trips to the hot springs. If your visit coincides with a tour, the pools will be packed. During the winter, the short days and often rainy weather discourage most visitors. This time is preferred by those who want several days of uninterrupted solitude and reflection.

Camping is allowed in the park, but there are no formal or maintained campsites. Some people camp in campsites near the government dock. Ask at the native village across the inlet for permission and rates. Camping is not permitted near the springs. You will find outhouses near the springs.

An old-fashioned hand pump at the government dock emits slightly sulphurous but good drinking water. At the springs, there is no fresh water other than the spring water itself.

History

These springs have been in continuous use by the Nuu-chah-nulth since before anyone can remember. They may have shown the springs to the early Spanish explorers; if so, they were probably the first hot springs in Canada visited by Europeans. In the late 1890s the area was pre-empted for a resort, but fortunately the proposal came to nothing and the claims were allowed to lapse. Today the springs and most of the approach trail are in Maquinna Provincial Park, established in 1955 to prevent commercial development. A large area of Openit Peninsula adjoining the park is being developed as a subdivision, which will probably make the springs even more popular than they are now.

Ahousat (Flores Island) Warm Springs

Undeveloped

Maps 6 & 8

Up to 25°C (77°F)

These springs are in Gibson Provincial Marine Park, about halfway between Tofino and Hot Springs Cove. The lukewarm water flowing into a cement tub is no substitute for Hot Springs Cove, and access can be awkward if you don't have your own boat. But if you have some extra time in the area, you might want to check this one out. Any time of the year with clear, dry weather and calm water is suitable for this trip. The hike from Ahousat or Marktosis and back again is best at low tide and is bushy and muddy.

Getting There

Like Hot Springs Cove, this spring can be visited in a long day from Vancouver, but it's not worth a separate visit. It's an easy day return from Tofino by boat or plane. You can reach the native villages of Ahousat and Marktosis on Flores Island by regularly scheduled flights, charter flights, and water taxi from Tofino. Regular trips run from Tofino, so you shouldn't need to charter a boat. The springs are at the head of Matilda Inlet, south of the villages. You can hike to the springs from either village, about 1.5 km (0.9 mi.) from Ahousat and 2.5 km (1.5 mi.) from Marktosis.

From Marktosis, follow a sketchy trail south towards an old power line on the shore of Matilda Inlet. If the tide is low, you can cut across the tidal flats to reach the springs; otherwise, follow the shoreline. From Ahousat, follow vague trails and the old power line south to the springs. At low tide, you can cut across a small inlet at about the halfway point, but at high tide you will have to go around.

If you have your own boat, head down Matilda Inlet past Ahousat until you see a large concrete pool at the high-tide line, near the east end of the extensive tidal flats at the south end of the inlet. If the water is calm, another approach is to land on the beach in Whitesand Cove in Gibson Marine Park on the south side of Flores Island. Then take the good, kilometre-long trail and boardwalk through the timber to Matilda Inlet and the springs.

The Springs

The warm springs are just above the high-tide mark. The water issues from the bottom of a concrete pool about 2 m by 6 m (6 ft. by 20 ft.) and about a metre deep. Another spring forms a warm streamlet about 5 m (15 ft.) to the south. The water is clear and tasteless, has a faint sulphur smell, and has a maximum reported temperature of 25°C (77°F). The mineral content, mainly chloride, sodium, and silica, is one of the lowest of any spring described in this book. Bathing isn't the best: often you will have to share the tub with a prolific crop of ropy algae, and besides, the water is too cool for an extended dip.

Comments

Chart 3640 covers the entire region, and charts 3648 and 3643 provide more detail. The hiking map for the area is 92E/8, but the springs aren't shown. Gibson Marine Park was established in 1967. The main attractions of this park are the beautiful sandy beaches of Whitesand Cove and the warm springs. There is good camping on the beach here, but you will have to bring your own water.

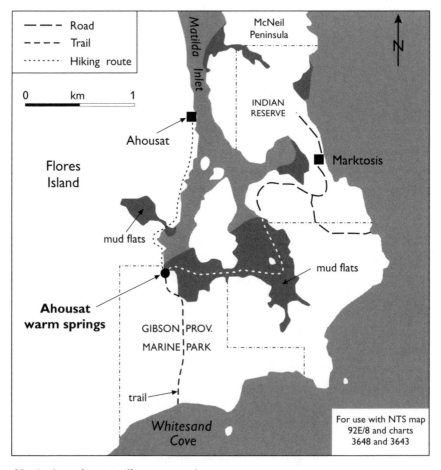

Map 8. Approach routes to Ahousat warm springs

OTHER SPRINGS ON VANCOUVER ISLAND

A few other springs have been reported from Vancouver Island, but little reliable data exists for most of them.

Mate Islands Warm Seep

Undeveloped

Map 7

25°C (77°F)

Mate Islands are the small islands visible across Hot Springs Cove from the springs. There is a warm seep in a small, rocky inlet on the south side of the island. The seep is on the east side of the inlet near its head; water temperature is 25°C (77°F). It is covered except at low tide, and the ground is too rocky for soaking. And, for scuba divers only, there is a hot vent off the southwest tip of Mate Islands in about 15 m (50 ft.) of water.

Fair Harbour

Existence uncertain

Map 6

The author of a 1913 geological report on Hot Springs Cove mentioned that he had heard of this spring but not visited it. Hot water was reported to issue from several sources about 1.5 km (0.9 mi.) from Fair Harbour in Kyuquot Sound. There is a logging road from Zeballos to Fair Harbour; map 92L/3 covers the area. The spring could not be found during infra-red scanning of the area a few years ago. Maybe it dried up, or maybe it never existed.

Kennedy River

Existence uncertain

Map 6

There have been rumours of hot springs near the lower rapids, about 1.5 to 2 km (0.9 to 1.2 mi.) around the mouth of Kennedy River where it empties into Kennedy Cove in Tofino Inlet. The springs are said to be on the north bank of the river and are flooded during high water. Nothing else is known. Map 92F/4 covers the area.

Pipestem Inlet

Existence uncertain

Map 6

This small, shallow inlet is north of the Broken Islands in Pacific Rim National Park. The spring is allegedly on the north shore of the head of the inlet. No other information is available, but water in the inlet is reported to be unusually warm. Map 92F/3 might be useful.

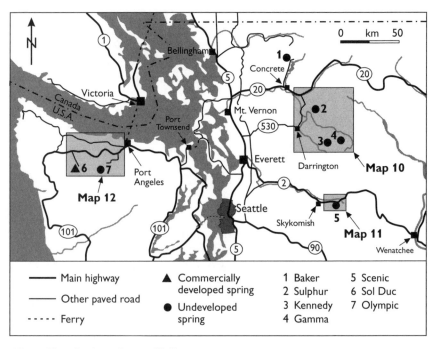

Map 9. Hot springs in northwestern Washington

CHAPTER 3

Northwestern Washington

Compared with the other western states, Washington is not richly endowed with hot springs. Nonetheless, there are over 20 hot springs in Washington, mostly in and west of the Cascade Range. This chapter describes springs west of the crest of the Cascades and north of Highway 2 (Scenic hot springs are just south of Highway 2, but the approach is from the highway). Most of these springs are excellent and well worth a visit.

An ordinary car is the only vehicle you need. For Baker and Sol Duc, little or no walking is required. Olympic and Scenic springs require moderate hikes, and Kennedy Hot Spring is a moderately long hike on a good trail. Sol Duc is the only commercially developed spring. If you live in Vancouver, you can visit any of these springs as a day trip from Vancouver, although Sol Duc and Olympic are very long days. If you live in Seattle, Scenic is the closest hot spring with good soaking pools.

Baker Hot Spring

Map 9

This easily reached mudhole southeast of Mt. Baker is a five minute walk from the car on an excellent trail. Even though the pool is unattractive, this spot is popular with Washington and B.C. residents. The nearby area has good camping, hiking, and boating.

It seems that everybody knows about these springs. If you can, schedule your visit for mid-week or early morning to avoid the crush. Except in deep winter, you can drive to the start of the footpath. When there is enough snow, the last part of the road makes an excellent, easy cross-country ski trip.

Getting There

Baker Hot Spring can be done as a day's outing from Vancouver, if you don't mind the five hour round-trip drive and the possibility of long border waits. From Vancouver, drive south to the Canada-U.S. border near Blaine and then take Interstate 5 south to the North Cascades Highway (Highway 20) exit at Burlington. (You can also reach Highway 20 by following Highway 9 south from Sumas or the Mt. Baker ski area.) Drive east on Highway 20 for about 37 km (23 mi.) and turn left onto the Baker Lake road just after the Mile 82 roadside marker and just before the town of Concrete (your last chance for gas and food).

Turn left off the pavement onto Forest Road 1144 opposite Baker Lake Resort, about 32.8 km (20.4 mi.) from Highway 20. Follow the rough gravel road for 5.1 km (3.1 mi.) to a wide parking area on both sides of the road. Driving time from Interstate 5 is about 1 to 1½ hours, depending on traffic.

From the uphill end of the parking lot, a five minute walk along an excellent, gentle trail leads to the spring. You might be able to get a wheelchair along this path with some work and assistance.

In winter it's wise to check with the Forest Service in Sedro Woolley (360-856-5700) for current road conditions.

The Springs

There is one large mudhole of a pool here, dug out of the gravelly bank at one end and blocked with rocks and dirt at the other. It comfortably holds a dozen or more people. There are a few convenient logs nearby for clothes, and the dirt bank slopes down to give easy access to the pool. The hot water, up to 44°C (111°F), spurts up from several spots in the bottom of the pool. The water has a strong sulphur odour and a low dissolved mineral content (mainly sodium, bicarbonate, chloride, and silica).

The temperature of the pool is usually less than the maximum because it is cooled by surface water and, in the spring, a little streamlet that overflows into the pool. Many people enjoy spending hours in the pool; others consider it a mud-wallow and refuse to use it. The water is often very murky because the pool is dug into dirt and because forest debris inevitably finds its way into the pool.

Comments

If you have clear weather for the drive, you'll see a sharp, glacier-hung peak from about 12 km (7.5 mi.) up the Baker Lake road. This is not Mt. Baker but Mt. Shuksan. Mt. Baker itself first appears at 22 km (13 mi.). This impressive peak, visible from much of Vancouver, is a dormant volcano that erupted about six times in the 19th century and has shown some signs of life in recent decades. Baker Hot Spring, like Meager hot springs, probably has its origins in the volcanic activity.

The soaking pool at Baker is muddy and unattractive but is a popular spot with many people.

The short trail to the hot spring passes through lovely, largely un-logged forest and its carpet of small, inconspicuous plants. The biggest trees are red cedars; there is a particularly large one just above the pool. The man-sized shrub with large broad leaves and a brown stem bristling with spines is devil's club. In late summer this pretty shrub has masses of showy red berries. They aren't edible, but you may find ripe blueberries and huckleberries nearby, if other hikers and the squirrels haven't beaten you to them.

The forest is quiet, except for birdsong, running water, and wind in the trees. Many trees have woodpecker holes and, if you are alone and quiet for a while, you may be lucky and see a woodpecker or two. You can pic-nic in the shade of the cedars a few metres above the pool; bring your own beverages and don't drink the nearby creek water. From the picnic spot you can admire some nice old broadleaf maples nearby that have moss and ferns growing up their trunks for many metres.

There is much to do in this area besides sit in a hot mud pond. Numer-ous Forest Service campgrounds line the shores of Baker Lake. If you bring a boat, you can launch it at Shannon Creek campground, a few kilometres past Baker Lake Lodge. There are many summer hiking trails, and in winter many of the forestry roads have good cross-country skiing. Ask at the Forest Service office for maps showing the hiking trails and other recreation possibilities.

History
Baker Hot Spring was once known as Morovitz hot spring. Joe Morovits (also spelled Morovitz) was a prospector, mountaineer, and gentleman who lived near the spring from 1891 to 1917. During that time, he and a partner dug a hole at the springs and lined it with logs, making a good bathtub for one person. In the 1970s, there was a large cedar tub at the springs, and there was even a split-cedar screen surrounding the pool. The cedar pool tub was removed for health reasons (bacteria tended to accu-mulate in the cedar), and today the pool is muddy but safe. Until a few years ago, a cedar boardwalk led from the parking area to the spring, but it too was removed because it was rotting and very slippery.

Kennedy Hot Spring
Undeveloped

Maps 9 & 10
35°C (?) (95°F)

A 9 km (5.5 mi.) hike on an excellent trail leads to a very nice pool deep in the Glacier Peak Wilderness. This is one of the more popular hikes in the North Cascades and is well worth the effort. May through October are the best months for this trip.

Getting There

People living in Vancouver can do this trip in a long day return (including about six hours of driving). It's a slightly shorter trip from Seattle. From Interstate 5, take exit 208 (Arlington-Darrington-Sylvania). Follow Highway 530 east to Darrington, about 50 km (31 mi.) from Interstate 5. Driving time is a little over two hours from Vancouver and a bit under two hours from Seattle. From Darrington, follow the paved Mountain Loop Highway south. In 15 km (9 mi.), turn left onto Road 23 (gravel). At 9 km (5.5 mi.), the road crosses a large bridge over the White Chuck River; in another 0.6 km (0.4 mi.), go straight ahead. The road end, campground, and parking lot are 8 km (5 mi.) from the large bridge. Driving time from Darrington is about half an hour.

The unusual soaking box at Kennedy is about 2 m (6 ft.) deep and is fed from the bottom.

The trail leaves the parking lot to the right of the notice board. The first part of the hike is through lovely old-growth forest well above White Chuck River. Shortly after the second footbridge, the trail makes several switchbacks up the hill to bypass a steep, washed-out section along the river. In another half an hour, the trail breaks out of the forest into an open gravel area by the river. In five more minutes, you reach a large tributary, Kennedy Creek. Head onto the gravel bars and cross Kennedy Creek on a footbridge. Pick up the trail on the far bank; in a couple of minutes you'll see a Forest Service ranger cabin.

Cross White Chuck River on the footbridge by the cabin, go left on the trail, and in 50 m (160 ft.) you'll reach the springs. The hike from the road to the springs is about 9 km (5.5 mi.) and will take most parties about two hours (and about the same time back).

The Springs

The soaking pool here is unusual: a box about 1.5 m (5 ft.) square and nearly 2 m (6 ft.) deep set in the flat ground above the river. Hot water and gas stream up from the base of the hot tub, swirling around and creating a very relaxing whirlpool effect. The water is slightly yellow and turbid, with a mild sulphur smell and strong iron oxide taste. The dissolved mineral content, mainly bicarbonate, sodium, and chloride, is high.

Maximum temperature is about 35°C (95°F), but temperatures up to 39°C (102°F) were reported in the past. Some guidebooks suggest that the spring is cooling down at the rate of about half a degree a year, but I talked with one regular visitor who claimed that it is hotter now than it was five years ago.

The hot tub is deep, over your head if you are short. The whirlpool effect helps buoy you up, and there are a couple of logs to sit on. There is a sturdy wooden platform around the tub and some wooden railings for clothes and towels. Overflow from the hot tub forms a small stream that is coating the rocks and gravel below with brilliant, rust-coloured tufa.

About 50 m (160 ft.) upstream from the hot tub is a large cliff coated in yellow, orange, and brown tufa. Some large logs are being incorporated into the deposits. Warm water seeps from the top of the cliffs and trickles down, depositing minerals as it goes. The spring looks spectacular, but there are no soaking possibilities.

Comments

The topographic maps for the area are the Glacier Peak West USGS quad and the Green Trails Glacier Peak (number 112) map. The springs are marked on both maps.

The Forest Service is trying to re-establish the natural vegetation around the springs and has banned camping at the springs. If you want to camp nearby, check the map posted at the ranger station.

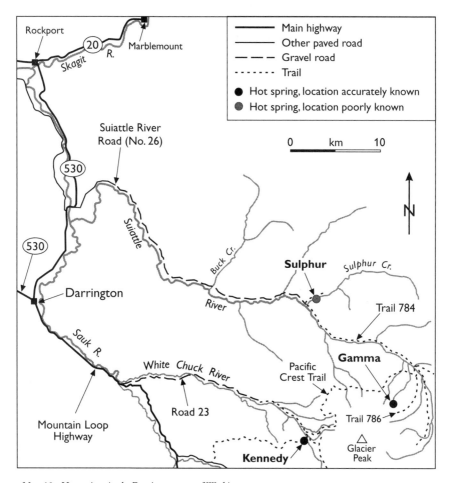

Map 10. Hot springs in the Darrington area of Washington

Scenic Hot Springs

Formerly developed, now partly developed

Maps 9 & 11 · Colour photo, page 197

53°C (?) (127°F)

These popular springs east of Everett, not far from Stevens Pass, are about a 3½ hour drive from Vancouver (not counting the border wait). The springs are about an hour's hike from the car on a steep trail. The pools are perched on a steep hillside far above the valley, and the water is excellent. These appropriately named springs are becoming increasingly popular, and with good reason.

People visit Scenic hot springs throughout the year, but spring through fall is the best time for a visit. If you can, schedule your visit for mid-week or early morning to be certain you will have the springs to yourself.

Getting There

If you live in Vancouver, a trip to Scenic requires too much driving (seven hours, round trip) to make it attractive as a day excursion. Instead, take this one in during a hiking or camping trip in the Cascades, or take a break from driving and traffic if you are travelling along Highway 2. From

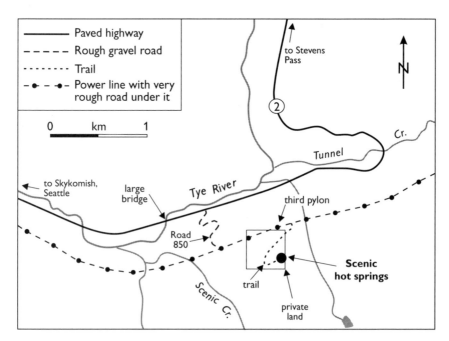

Map 11. Scenic hot springs

Vancouver, drive south to the Canada-U.S. border near Blaine and then take Interstate 5 south to the Highway 2 (Stevens Pass) exit in Everett. Drive east on Highway 2 for about 80 km (50 mi.) to the town of Skykomish (last stop for gas, food, and motels). Continue east for 16.9 km (10.5 mi.) to where you cross a large bridge over the Tye River and valley. In another 0.3 km (0.2 mi.), you will see a dirt road (Forest Service Road 850) that heads steeply uphill on your right. This point is about 3½ hours from Vancouver and about 1½ hours from Seattle.

If your car has low clearance, you should park here. Hike or drive up the road for 0.8 km (0.5 mi.) until you reach a power line; you'll know it when you're there. Keep hiking up the road under the power line. At the top of a long, steep stretch, you'll see a well-worn trail branching sharply and steeply right up the hill. This point is about midway between the third and fourth power pylons that you pass (the third has a conspicuous missing arm, in case you lose count).

The trail leads up and right through shady, second-growth timber. You'll probably want sturdy shoes, since the track can be muddy in places. Where it makes a sharp turn to the left and levels out, you are just a couple of minutes from the springs. The hour-and-a-bit hike from the pavement to the springs involves an elevation gain of about 340 m (1100 ft.).

The Springs

The springs are on a steep slope with a view out over the valley below. Hot water flows from two spots in gravel and feeds three main pools. There is some disagreement about the temperature of the springs. Some guidebooks give the water temperature as 42°C (108°F), but the temperatures of 47° to 53°C (117° to 127°F) found in the scientific literature are probably more accurate. Whatever the temperature, you'll find that one of the pools offers the perfect soaking temperature for you. The main spring feeds a well-constructed wooden pool that is 2 m (6 ft.) square. This pool, the hottest of the three, has a wooden floor and wooden walkway around it, suitable for sitting and changing. The pool is sheltered under a large, overhanging cedar tree. If this pool is too hot for you, there is a second, slightly cooler and larger pool just below. This one is also made of wood and has comfortable places to sit and enjoy the view. This pool overflows into a third, cooler and smaller pool. The spring water is clear, odourless, tasteless, and very low in dissolved minerals, mainly bicarbonate and sodium.

Comments

This is a lovely spot, clean and well maintained. Maybe it's the view out over the valley, with the highway far below, that makes it so special. The approach trail above the power line and the springs are on private land. There are a few flat, cleared areas beside the trail near the springs where people have camped.

History

The springs were once called Great Northern hot springs, after the Great Northern Railroad that runs through the valley below. After completion of the rail line in the 1920s, a health resort known as Scenic Hot Springs operated in the valley for many years, using water piped from the springs to the resort. It was a long distance, and the water cooled off enough so that it had to be reheated at the resort. Today there is little left of the resort and it is hard to believe that the springs were once commercially developed.

Olympic Hot Springs

Formerly developed, now undeveloped

Maps 9 & 12

27°–52°C (81°–126°F)

Some seven rustic pools of varying temperatures hide in the rain forest along Boulder Creek in Olympic National Park. The springs are about a 45 minute hike along an excellent trail from your car, and there is a good backcountry campground nearby. The forest setting and pleasant access make this one of the most popular springs in Washington.

These springs are pleasant at all times of the year. During the summer, campsites, trails, and pools can be crowded, especially on weekends. During the winter, you will probably have the springs to yourself.

Getting There

For Vancouver residents, the driving and ferry time makes this excursion too long for a relaxed day trip. It's best done as part of a weekend outing, perhaps combined with a visit to Sol Duc or a hike. If you live in Victoria, the ferry between Victoria and Port Angeles makes this a feasible day trip. Seattle residents can visit these springs in a longish day trip.

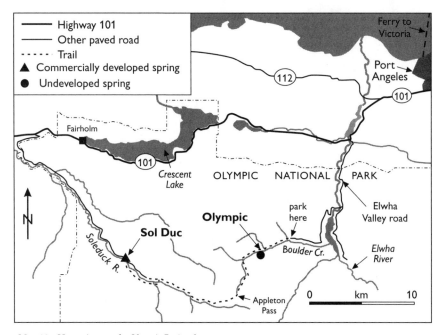

Map 12. Hot springs on the Olympic Peninsula

From Vancouver, drive south to the Canada-U.S. border near Blaine and then take Interstate 5 south to the Highway 20 (west) exit at Burlington. Follow Highway 20 to the Keystone ferry terminal on Whidbey Island, about 76 km (47 mi.) from Interstate 5. The drive from Vancouver to the ferry terminal takes about 2½ to three hours, depending on the wait at the border. The ferry to Port Townsend runs about every 90 minutes, and there is often a wait. Phone 206-464-6400 (1-800-84-FERRY in Washington) for current schedules and rates. The ferry crossing takes

One of many small pools in the forest at Olympic Hot Springs.

about 30 minutes. In good weather you get spectacular views of the Olympics and Port Townsend ahead, with Mt. Baker dominating the sky-line behind. From Port Townsend, follow Highways 20 and 101 to Port Angeles, about one to 1½ hours from the ferry terminal.

From Seattle, take the ferry to Bainbridge Island and then follow the main highways to Port Angeles. Depending on the ferries and traffic, allow about 2½ hours from Seattle to Port Angeles.

From Victoria, take the Black Ball ferry to Port Angeles. Phone 250-386-2202 for current rates and ferry schedules.

From Port Angeles, drive west on Highway 101 for 14.1 km (8.7 mi.). Turn left onto the Elwha Valley road, just before the bridge over the Elwha River. You will have to stop at the toll booth and pay $5 for a per-mit, good for seven days anywhere in the park. It's money well spent. Drive up the paved road for 16.5 km (10.2 mi.) to the roadblock and parking area high above Boulder Creek.

The 3.5 km (2.2 mi.), 45 minute hike to the springs follows the old road through the old-growth forest. Any footwear will do, since the road is paved. The grade is gentle, except for the last roller-coaster hill. When you reach a large bridge over Boulder Creek, you have arrived. The camp-site is five minutes farther, on your right. To reach the hot springs, cross the bridge and follow the well-worn trail 50 m (160 ft.) downstream to the first pool.

The Springs

There are some 20 seeps and springs and about seven soaking pools strung out for 200 m (650 ft.) along Boulder Creek. Most pools are on the uphill side of the main trail, but there are a couple of overflow pools between the trail and the creek. Pools have been scooped out of the dirt and gravel hillside and dammed with rocks, logs, and gravel. Water tem-perature ranges from about 27° to 52°C (81° to 126°F). The water is clear and has a slight mineral taste and sulphur smell. It is moderately alkaline with a slightly soapy feel.

The first pool you reach is in a lovely open spot. Hot water and gas bubble up from the bottom of the pool, which is one of the hottest and which is big enough for two to four people. Stop here for a bit, or con-tinue down the trail past three mediocre pools to the largest pool, a dou-ble one that is about 6 m (20 ft.) across, knee-deep, and a good tempera-ture for hours of relaxing. There are good logs to sit on beside the pool.

This is the most popular pool, and it's not unusual for it to be packed with 20 or more people on a nice summer day.

There's one hidden gem that most people miss. Follow a trail that climbs up the steep hillside above the main pond to a small soaker about 30 m (100 ft.) above the big pool. It's hot but bearable, has a nice gravel bottom, and holds four to six people.

Comments

This is a very popular spot. The hike through the rain forest is easy and attractive. The area is regularly patrolled by park rangers, who keep it clean and fresh. Park policy is that swimwear must be worn, but apparently this is seldom enforced unless the rangers receive complaints of nudity. Use discretion if you are skinny dipping.

The nearby campground is a popular overnight stop for backpackers, but backcountry use permits are required for all overnight stays in the park. If you have an extra day in the area, you can follow the excellent trail past the campsite to Appleton Pass, about 9 km (5.6 mi.) each way. There is an excellent viewpoint along the divide just east of the pass. From the pass you can take the trail down to Soleduck River and hike out to Sol Duc Hot Springs. For this hike you should take the Mount Currie USGS map or the Green Trails Mount Olympus map.

History

These hot springs were once developed as a resort but have reverted to a more natural state. By 1907 there was a cabin and cedar bathhouse at the springs, and by the 1920s a posh lodge had been built. In the early 1930s, the road to the springs was completed. Room rates were $4.50 per day, including meals; mud baths were extra.

In 1940, the lodge burned to the ground. In the same year, President Roosevelt added much heavily forested land to the park, including Boulder Creek and the hot springs. Parks authorities leased the springs back to the former owners, who built a new lodge, a concrete swimming pool, and a small group of cabins. In 1955, health officials forced the operators to chlorinate the water, and business soon dropped by 50 percent. The lodge closed forever in December 1966, and the remains of the buildings and pools were dismantled. In 1983, the road was closed to vehicles at its present point.

Sol Duc Hot Springs

Commercial resort

Maps 9 & 12

Up to 56°C (133°F) at source

This fully developed commercial resort is in Olympic National Park. It's nicely done and worth a visit if you are passing through the area or if you've been camping and want to clean up. The resort is open from mid-May through September, and the pools only are open in April and October as well.

Getting There

If you live in Vancouver, Victoria, or Seattle and want a bit of a luxury weekend getaway, Sol Duc (pronounced *sole-duck*) is a good destination. It's too far to be an enjoyable day trip from Vancouver, but the ferry between Victoria and Port Angeles makes it a feasible day trip for Victoria residents. Seattleites can also visit this spring as a day trip. From Port Angeles (see Olympic Hot Springs), drive west along Highway 101 and turn left onto the Soleduck River road 3.1 km (1.9 mi.) past Fairholm (47 km (29 mi.) from Port Angeles). If you don't already have a permit, you will have to pay $10 per vehicle at the toll booth just off the highway (only between Memorial Day and Labour Day). Follow the paved Soleduck road for 19.8 km (12.3 mi.) to the hot springs; it's about an hour's drive from Port Angeles.

The Springs

Three main springs with temperatures up to 56°C (133°F) are piped into the soaking and swimming pools. The main pool is a large swimming pool, chlorinated and kept around 26°C (79°F) with heavy infusions of river water. More interesting to hot spring lovers are the three small, circular pools at one end of the swimming pool. These are not chlorinated and are maintained at temperatures of about 36° to 41°C (97° to 106°F). Each circular pool holds several dozen people, and there are benches to sit on. One of these pools is shallow and suitable for toddlers. The hottest pool has a little geyser spouting out of its centre. As at Olympic Hot Springs, the water has a faint sulphur odour and a slightly soapy feel.

Facilities
The swimming pool and the round pool with the geyser are wheelchair accessible. Showers have plenty of hot and cold water, and the premises are very clean. A poolside snack bar and deli is a nice touch; you can have a bite to eat without the bother of getting changed. It's not cheap, though. Massage therapy is available in the resort.

The lodge is built of cedar and in the summer is decorated with cheerful hanging baskets. Both the lodge and the restaurant are wheelchair accessible. Cabins are available ($92 and up), and RV hookups are $16 a night.

There are plenty of good hiking trails nearby, and in the summer the park naturalists lead nature walks and host evening campfire talks. There are good campgrounds in Olympic National Park and a variety of motels and restaurants in Port Angeles.

Rates, Hours, and Address
The resort is open daily from mid-May through September, and the pools are open from April to October. Admission to the pools for day use is $6.75 a person. Children under four are free, and seniors are $5.75. Swimsuits and lockers are available for rent. For more information, contact:

Sol Duc Resort
P.O. Box 2169
Port Angeles, WA 98362
360-327-3583
Fax: 360-327-3593

History
Like Olympic Hot Springs, Sol Duc has a long history. The first European to see the springs was probably a settler, Theodore Moritz, in the 1880s. He promptly staked the springs and attempted to exploit them, with little financial success. One of his guests in 1903 was a seriously ill logging baron, Mike Earles, who became convinced that the waters cured his illness. In 1909, Earles purchased the land and built an access road, followed by an elaborate resort that included 165 bedrooms, a one hundred-patient sanatorium, medical staff, X-ray equipment, and an operating room. At the peak of its popularity in 1915, up to 10,000 people a year stayed here, some drawn by claims that the water cured gout, rheu-

matism, alcoholism, and other ailments. But most were attracted by the golf, billiards, croquet, motion pictures, and horseback riding at this palatial resort in the rain forest. High-stakes poker games that ran all night attracted others.

In 1916, the resort burned down. It was soon rebuilt, but it never attained its former splendour and popularity. More fires damaged the resort in the 1920s and 1930s. In 1966, the National Park Service bought the property, intending to return it to its natural state. Costs were prohibitive, though, and in 1987 the Park Service sold the resort to private interests. The new owners built the present facilities, which now attract about 65,000 visitors a year.

One of the small, hot pools and the lodge at Sol Duc Hot Springs.

OTHER SPRINGS IN NORTHWESTERN WASHINGTON

Washington State has two other springs north of Highway 2, neither of which I have visited. Another spring is listed in some guidebooks: Doe Bay Resort on Orcas Island in the San Juan Islands. The spring water, however, is cold; it is heated by electricity and piped to several pools. Phone 360-376-2291 for more details. The guidebooks by Evie Litton, Bill Kaysing, and Marjorie Gersh-Young (see References) contain descriptions of many springs in Washington south of the area covered here.

Sulphur Hot Springs
Undeveloped

Maps 9 & 10   37°C (?) (99°F)

These springs are shown on the USGS Downey Mountain map and the Green Trails Cascade Pass map around the 1920-foot contour. The Forest Service describes them as being 1.8 miles (2.9 km) up the trail, but a U.S. Geological Survey report puts them 0.75 mile (1.2 km) up the trail. Temperature is variously given as 27°, 30°, and 37°C (81°, 86°, 99°F). Rate of flow is given as "seep" in one report and 4 to 8 litres a minute in another. Possibly there is more than one spring here.

From Highway 530, 12 km (7.5 mi.) north of Darrington and 19 km (12 mi.) south of Concrete, turn east onto the Suiattle River road (No. 26). Follow this excellent road for 35 km (22 mi.) to the Sulphur Creek campground just past the 22 mile sign. The Sulphur Creek trail (No. 793) starts 100 m (330 ft.) back along the main road. It climbs steeply for a ways before dropping down into Sulphur Creek. There is a strong sulphur odour in the air along the creek, but I never did find the springs. Judging by comments on the notice board in the campground, many other people have also failed to find them. Go late in the fall, when Sulphur Creek is low, and be prepared for bushy, difficult travel.

Gamma Hot Springs
Undeveloped

Maps 9 & 10
65°C (149°F)

Gamma is the hottest spring known in the North Cascades. This one is for experienced mountaineers only. Access is very difficult; allow at least three days for the round trip from your car. Take the USGS Lime Mountain and Gamma Peak maps or the Green Trails Glacier Peak map.

From Sulphur Creek campground, follow trail 784 up the Suiattle River for about 20 km (12 mi.). Cross the river on the Skyline Bridge and follow the Pacific Crest Trail for about 700 m (0.4 mi.) to where the old Gamma Ridge trail (trail 786) branches east. Follow this trail until you are high on Gamma Ridge and can find a safe way to drop about 460 m (1500 ft.) into the headwaters of Gamma Creek. The springs have also been reached by thrashing directly up Gamma Creek from the Pacific Crest Trail, but unpleasant bush and waterfalls abound. The springs flow from several cracks in bedrock on the east side of the creek, more or less in the creek, at an elevation of about 1500 m (5000 ft.).

These springs were discovered by geologist Rowland Tabor while mapping the area in 1962. They are popular with mountain goats but are seldom visited by humans.

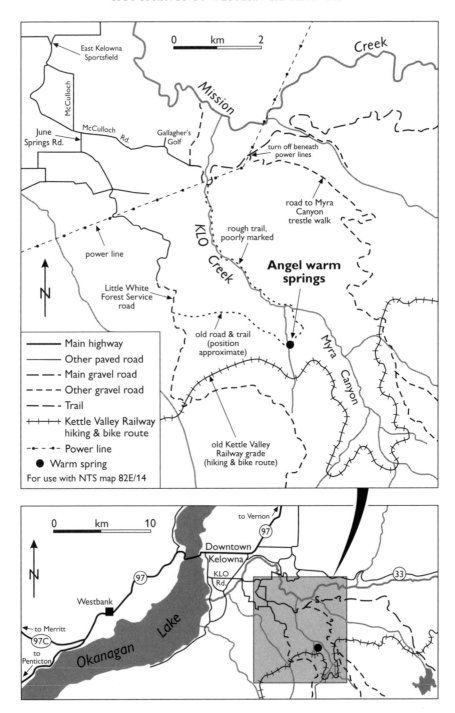

Map 13. Angel warm springs in the Okanagan valley

CHAPTER 4

The Okanagan Valley

The area around Kelowna in the Okanagan is well known for many things, such as wine, orchards, sunshine, but not for hot springs. The only "hot spring" that was ever widely advertised was really a cold creek. There are, however, several obscure warm springs.

Kelowna is 400 km (250 mi.) (a four hour drive) from Vancouver. The fastest route is by the Coquihalla Highway (Highway 5) to Merritt; then take Highways 97C and 97. Vernon is another 120 km (75 mi.) north of Kelowna on Highway 97. There are abundant tourist facilities throughout the area.

For some years, "Cedar Hot Springs" near Vernon was featured in some U.S. hot springs guides. Although advertised as a hot spring, the pools used cold creek water that was artificially heated to about 42°C (108°F). This facility is now closed.

Angel (Kelowna) Warm Springs   Undeveloped

Map 13   21°–29°C (70°–84°F)

These little-known springs are southeast of Kelowna, not far from some of the most spectacular parts of the old Kettle Valley Railway. A moderately rugged hike leads to a small, lukewarm stream. It's too cool, small, and unattractive for soaking. Because the springs themselves aren't much to see, you might make a full day by combining your visit with a hike along the Myra Canyon section of the railway. Go in autumn, when the water in KLO Creek is low and you can enjoy the fall colours.

Getting There

From Highway 97 in Kelowna just east of the bridge across Okanagan Lake, drive 2.5 km (1.5 mi.) south on Pandosy Street and then turn left at the traffic light onto KLO Road. In 5.3 km (3.3 mi.) bear right onto McCulloch Road at East Kelowna Sportsfield. In 1.8 km (1.1 mi.) continue right on McCulloch and follow the signs for Gallagher's Canyon Golf Course. In another 1.5 km (0.9 mi.), just after a sharp left turn, June Springs Road takes off to the right.

June Springs Road gives possibly the easiest access to the springs (another route is described below). Drive up June Springs Road and turn left in 0.5 km (0.3 mi.). The pavement ends about 6.3 km (3.9 mi.) from McCulloch Road. Continue up the Little White Forest Service road and park at the 1 km sign. The trail to the springs starts on the east side of the logging road. According to John Greenough in the guidebook *Geology of the Kelowna Area and Origin of the Okanagan Valley, British Columbia* by Murray Roed (Kelowna: Kelowna Geology Committee, 1995), you reach the springs after hiking for about an hour and 3 km (2 mi.) on an old road and trail.

There is another approach route, suitable in late summer and autumn for moderately experienced hikers. Continue east on McCulloch Road past the June Springs turnoff. 2.1 km (1.3 mi.) from June Springs Road you pass the turnoff to Gallagher's Canyon Golf Course. Pavement ends in another 1.1 km (0.7 mi.), and in another few hundred metres the road bends right into KLO Creek valley and crosses the creek. Park here.

Follow a series of old roads and trails up the canyon of KLO Creek, which takes its unusual name from the Kelowna Land and Orchard Company, formed in 1904. Start just east of the creek; an old road leads through a quarry and soon crosses to the west side of the creek. From here on, the track degenerates to a trail, spotty in places, that crosses and recrosses the creek in the narrow canyon. In about an hour, you might see a wooden sign that points right to Angel Springs. Continue straight ahead on the KLO trail on the east side of KLO Creek. In about another 10 minutes, the trail crosses to the west side of the creek. It climbs continuously and fairly steeply but is well marked and easy to follow. Soon you see a few mossy, overgrown cliffs of tufa and some small cold springs. About 30 minutes after leaving KLO Creek, you reach the spring. Total hiking distance is about 4 km (2.5 mi.), with an elevation gain of 420 m (1400 ft.).

The Springs

The springs are easy to recognize: they are a brilliant orange-rust colour and are right beside the trail in deep forest. The water itself is slightly cloudy; the orange comes from algae and the rust-coloured iron minerals that are being deposited. Temperature of the main spring is about 21° to 25°C (70° to 77°F), too cool for pleasant soaking. The warmest (29°C (84°F)) water seeps from the ground a few hundred metres uphill from the main springs. The water is odourless and has a strong iron taste. The extensive tufa deposits in the area point to the past existence of other, larger springs. The springs are at about UTM grid reference 316180 on NTS map 82E/14, at an elevation of about 960 m (3150 ft.).

Comments

The main recreational feature in this area isn't the warm springs but rather the old Kettle Valley Railway. To reach the most spectacular and popular stretch, the Myra Canyon section, continue east on McCulloch Road from where it crosses KLO Creek.

In less than a kilometre, the road passes beneath some power lines and a side road branches steeply right; take this road. It is steep but suitable for most cars; in about 5 km (3 mi.) you reach a huge, open, flat area with a long, large parking area on your right. Park and walk west. The round trip to the largest trestles takes several hours and offers absolutely breathtaking views into the KLO canyon. Alternatively, you can drive up June Springs Road to where it intersects the railway grade, but the hike to the trestles is less spectacular than from the other end.

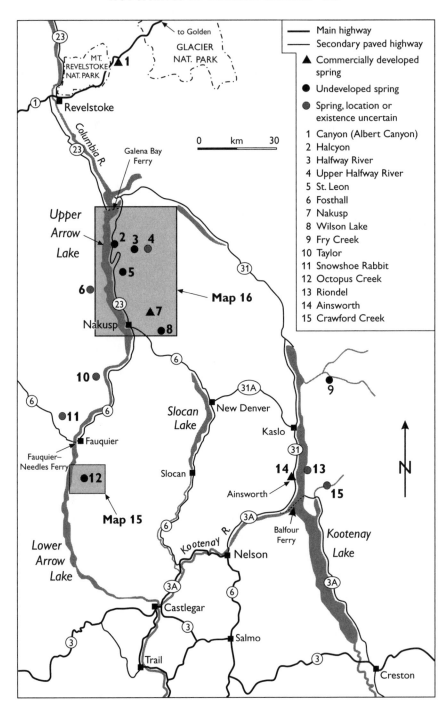

Map 14. Hot springs in the West Kootenays

CHAPTER 5

The West Kootenays

The West Kootenays are a geographically complex corner of British Columbia. The Selkirk Mountains dominate the high country, and large lakes such as Slocan, Kootenay, and Upper and Lower Arrow lakes fill many of the valley bottoms. This is an area of old mining towns, giant hydro-electric projects, and small ethnic communities scattered in unlikely places. The region is well known for its excellent downhill and backcountry skiing, hiking, climbing, fishing, boating, old ghost towns, and its general historical interest.

The West Kootenays have a wonderful variety of hot springs ranging from well-known commercial springs to the almost unknown. On Kootenay Lake, Ainsworth Hot Springs is a popular and interesting commercial spring. The area around Nakusp on Upper Arrow Lake has a varied suite of springs ranging in style from low-key commercial (Nakusp) to truly obscure (Octopus Creek) and including the popular undeveloped St. Leon, Halfway River, and Halcyon. Nakusp could be called the hot spring capital of British Columbia, because no other town has such a good selection of readily accessible springs.

The area is well served by paved highways connecting Highway 3, which crosses southern British Columbia, with Highway 1 farther north. The largest community, Nelson, is a scenic town with good tourist accommodation and many lovely old Victorian and Edwardian buildings. Nakusp on Highway 6 makes a good base for visiting nearby hot springs and has adequate tourist services. The villages of Kaslo and New Denver also have a reasonable selection of motels. If you are camping, there are many private campgrounds, Forest Service campsites, and opportunities for wilderness camping. Rosebery Provincial Park on Highway 6 between Nakusp and New Denver has 36 rustic campsites in an attractive setting relatively close to most of the hot springs.

The important springs described in this chapter are on or close to paved highways or good gravel roads. A few involve hikes of 15 minutes or less on good trails. If you have even a few hours, it's worth hitting one of these springs. Better yet, stay a few days around Nakusp and visit several. You can easily do Nakusp, St. Leon, Halfway, and Halcyon in one day.

Ainsworth Hot Springs
Commercial resort

Map 14 · Colour photo, page 198

Up to 47.5°C (118°F) at source

This resort includes a fully developed pool and hotel overlooking Kootenay Lake. For many people, Ainsworth is the best commercial hot spring in B.C. The main attractions are the "caves": old mine workings dug into the hillside. Ainsworth is popular with families and local residents. It's definitely worth a visit, especially if you are in the Nelson area or are exploring the old mining towns of Kaslo or Silverton. This resort operates all year round and any time is good for a visit. Summer is the peak season; weekends are often crowded. A clear winter day is an ideal time for a visit. The warm, humid atmosphere of the caves contrasts nicely with the cold, crisp outside air, and the view across the lake is lovely.

Getting There
Ainsworth is on Highway 31 between Kaslo and Balfour. From Nakusp, follow Highway 6 to New Denver, 31A to Kaslo and then 31 to Ainsworth; total distance is about 115 km (71 mi.). From Nelson, follow Highways 3A to Balfour and 31 to Ainsworth, a total of 48 km (30 mi.). Driving time is about 40 minutes from Nelson and about 1½ hours from Nakusp.

If you are coming from the East Kootenays, take Highway 3/95 to Creston, where you have a choice. The quickest and most scenic route is up Highway 3A along the east side of Kootenay Lake to the ferry terminal at Kootenay Bay (80 km (50 mi.)). Take the world's longest free ferry ride

(40 minutes) across the lake and drive 14 km (9 mi.) to Ainsworth. The alternative route, which doesn't put you at the mercy of ferry schedules, follows Highways 3 and 6 to Nelson and continues to Ainsworth (total distance of 170 km (105 mi.)).

The Springs
The resort is centred on the so-called caves: the old mine tunnels that were carved by miners trying to improve the flow of hot water from the springs. The water (45° to 47.5°C (113° to 118°F)) gushes from near the back of the caves and is also piped into the caves from several sources above the resort. From the caves the outflow is filtered twice and lightly chlorinated before flowing into the outdoor pools. The water is naturally rich in bicarbonate, sodium, calcium, silica, and lithium.

The main pool (about 12 m by 15 m (40 ft. by 50 ft.) and 1 m (3 ft.) deep) is a free-form shape with several little bays, giving the feel of several smaller pools. Even when it is full of people, it doesn't feel like a crowded swimming pool. The temperature is about 35°C (95°F). At the entrance to the caves are two small, circular pools. One is nice and hot: 40° to 44°C (104° to 111°F). Wide ledges line the pool walls and are good places to sit and admire the view across Kootenay Lake to the Purcell Mountains. The other pool, straight from a cold spring, is 4°C (39°F), good for a brief and very refreshing dip after the hot pool and the steamy atmosphere of the caves. All the pools have a tough vinyl lining that is very comfortable and easy on the skin.

The caves are the most interesting feature at Ainsworth. Originally there were two parallel tunnels, more properly called adits. These have been connected by a cross-tunnel, forming an H-shaped structure. From the hot pool, you enter them through either of two modern, tiled entrances. If you wear glasses, leave them in little niches just outside the caves, because they will instantly steam up inside and it will be harder for you to see than without them. The two tunnels join to form a horseshoe-shaped structure, and branch tunnels continue for up to 30 m (100 ft.) from the opening. About 3 m (10 ft.) inside, you can see the original wooden beams, now largely coated with deposits of minerals. Temperature in the caves ranges from hot to unbearable.

Hot water drips from the ceiling, and in one place there's a natural hot shower you can sit under. At the back of the caves, in a sauna-like spot close to the main source, there is a rock ledge, quite hot, to sit on. Tufa is constantly being deposited on the cave walls and ceilings, forming multi-coloured stalactites and ringed, layered deposits that resemble ancient fungus growths on old trees. Maintenance crews periodically remove the deposits to prevent the caves from completely filling in.

If you walk along the lane that runs behind the pool complex, you can see several hot springs that emerge from tufa just above the road. This water is piped into the pools and caves. It's slightly fizzy as a result of dissolved gas, and like the water in the caves, it is odourless. Outflow from the pool complex has formed an extensive tufa bench just above the highway.

Facilities

The main pool deck and adjoining hotel are wheelchair accessible, but the hot pool and caves are not. The pool deck is heated so that it doesn't get icy in winter. Changing rooms are clean, with warm showers and electric outlets. There is a snack bar adjoining the pool. The hotel offers a massage service, gift shop, restaurant and lounge, and banquet and meeting rooms.

There are several other motels in Ainsworth, a good selection in Kaslo, about 16 km (10 mi.) north on Highway 31, and a large number in Nelson. There are private campgrounds in Balfour south of the springs, at Mirror Lake 10 km (6 mi.) north of the springs, and in Kaslo.

Rates, Hours, and Address

The pools and caves are open year-round from 10:00 AM to 9:00 PM. Rates

The "caves," old mine tunnels filled with hot water and coated with tufa, at Ainsworth Hot Springs.

for a single swim are $6.50 for adults, $5.50 for seniors, $6.00 for children aged 13 to 15, and $4.50 for children aged three to 12, GST included. All-day passes are available. Towels are available for rent. Rooms in the hotel start at $81–$139, depending on the season, including the unrestricted use of the pools. For more information, contact:

Ainsworth Hot Springs
P.O. Box 1268
Ainsworth, BC V0G 1A0
250-229-4212
Fax: 250-229-5600

History
Ainsworth was the first white settlement on Kootenay Lake and, for a brief time, the largest. In 1882, prospectors established "Hot Springs Camp" on the shore of Kootenay Lake and staked 65 ha (160 acres), including the hot springs. The following year George Ainsworth, a promoter from California, bought the camp and renamed it after himself.

The town quickly grew, serving as a centre for intense prospecting throughout the region. At its peak, it had nearly 3000 people and five hotels. But by the end of 1891, most of the miners had moved on to Kaslo and Slocan, chasing the rich deposits of silver discovered there. In 1896 a large fire destroyed most buildings; the town was rebuilt but was never the same, even though mining continued on a small scale into the 1960s.

The caves were created by miners in 1906. Bathing facilities have been rebuilt several times over the years, and the present hotel and pool date from 1986–1987. Today Ainsworth has fewer than one hundred permanent residents and no mining. Unlike some other mining communities in the area, Ainsworth has a modest but secure future, because over 200,000 visitors come to visit the springs each year.

Other Activities in the Area
The Ainsworth region has good fishing, boating, golf, hiking, and cross-country skiing. Undeveloped Kokanee Glacier Provincial Park, well known for great hiking in summer and alpine skiing in winter, is nearby. Cody Caves Provincial Park has 800 m (0.5 mi.) of excellent natural caverns. You can begin to explore the rich mining history of the area at Kaslo, where the *Moyie,* the last of the Kootenay Lake sternwheelers, is berthed. Sandon, west of Kaslo, is slowly being restored to its 1890s state, and Nelson has over 350 heritage buildings, many lovingly restored.

Octopus Creek Hot Springs

Undeveloped

Maps 14 & 15

Up to 49°C (120°F)

This is a lone warm pool at the end of a long hike. Finding it is a challenge for experienced wilderness hikers with a taste for the obscure, but the soak is only mediocre. Most people can safely give this one a miss. Hikers with little wilderness experience or without strong map and compass skills should not attempt this trip.

Getting There
A round trip from Fauquier will take at least five hours. Reach Fauquier on Highway 6 by driving 60 km (37 mi.) south of Nakusp, or by driving 135 km (84 mi.) east from Vernon on Highway 6 and taking the ferry from Needles. From Fauquier, drive south on Applegrove Road, which soon becomes gravel. In 10.2 km (6.3 mi.) from Fauquier, the road is

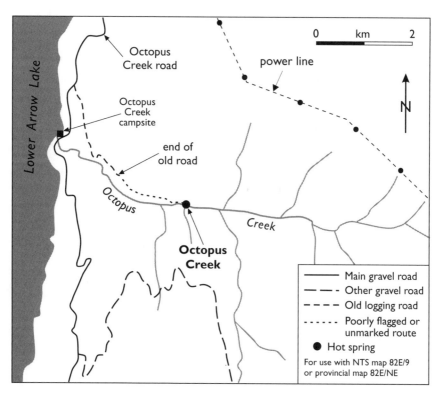

Octopus
Creek road

power line

Octopus
Creek
campsite

end of
old road

Lower Arrow Lake

Octopus

Creek

**Octopus
Creek**

0   km   2

N

———— Main gravel road
— — - Other gravel road
— — — Old logging road
· · · · · · Poorly flagged or
         unmarked route
● Hot spring
For use with NTS map 82E/9
or provincial map 82E/NE

Map 15. Octopus Creek hot springs

marked Octopus Creek Forest Service Road. Continue for another 5.8 km (3.6 mi.) on good gravel to where an old logging spur branches left and the main road goes downhill. This spur is the road you want. If you miss it, the Octopus Creek recreation site on the shore of Lower Arrow Lake is just 1.2 km (0.7 mi.) down the road; backtrack from there.

Park here and start hiking (if you have a 4×4, you can drive up the road for a bit, but it will be hard on your nice new paint job). After walking for about 25 minutes, the road becomes very bushy, little more than a trail. Keep on the road for another 15 minutes until it drops down a bit and peters out.

From here to the springs you're pretty much on your own. A compass and topographical map (and the skills to use them) are essential. The springs are at UTM grid reference 227096 on NTS map 82E/9. The provincial government map 82E/NE shows the springs about 200 m (650 ft.) too far west. An altimeter is useful. There is a bit of a route sporadically flagged out, but it's hard to follow and you will probably lose it. The bush beneath the large Ponderosa pines and Douglas firs is light, though, and the walking quite easy. Follow the hillside at about the same elevation as the road for roughly a kilometre until you are about opposite the first side valley on the south side of Octopus Creek. Drop down the steep slope to the creek where you can and then walk up Octopus Creek. Shortly after a steep, cliffy area on the north side of the creek, the north bank opens out and the angle of the bank decreases. The springs are in this area, on the north bank of the creek. You might catch a whiff of sulphur not far below the springs. They are about an hour's hike from the end of the ancient road and about two hours from the parking area.

The main problem on the return is finding the old logging road. One method is to climb until you are sure you are above the maximum elevation of the road and then head west, staying at the same elevation until you see stumps from the old selective logging. Angle gradually down until you hit the road. The return trip should be a bit faster than the walk in.

The Springs
The springs issue from gravel around the high-water level of Octopus Creek. The sole soaking pool is dug into the river gravel and rimmed with boulders. Colourless hot water with a faint sulphur smell and mild mineral taste issues from the upstream end of the pool along with a small amount of gas; the rate of flow is small. The maximum reported temper-

ature is 49°C (120°F), but the water was cooler, about 40°C (104°F), at the time of my visit. The spring water is low in dissolved solids but is distinguished by the highest fluoride content in the province. The small pool has a good gravel bottom and very little algae. It's a so-so pool in an unspoiled setting, and most people will not find it worth the hike.

Comments

If you do make this trip, save it for dry weather when the bush is dry and the water is at its warmest. Late summer and fall are probably the best times to visit. The springs might be flooded by the creek in spring. People have camped near the springs, but it's best to make this a day trip and camp at the Octopus Creek recreation site or elsewhere; see "Facilities" under Nakusp Hot Springs.

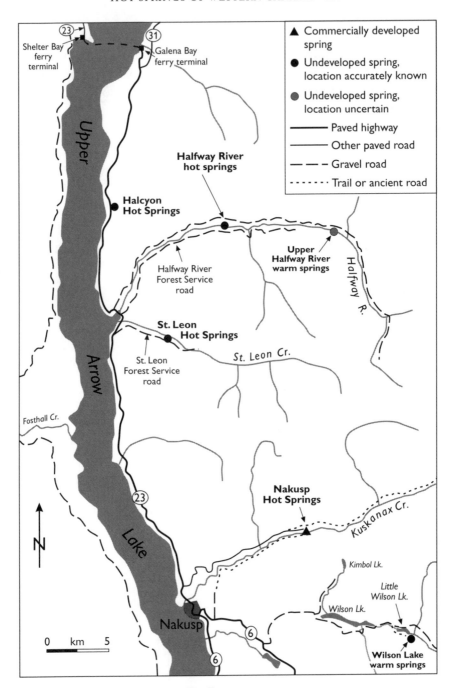

Map 16. Hot springs in the Nakusp area, West Kootenays

Nakusp Hot Springs

Commercial pool

Maps 14 & 16 · Colour photo, page 200

Up to 54.5°C (130°F) at source

Located just outside Nakusp, these are small, attractively developed, and easily accessible springs. They are among the least visited of the commercial pools in this book, but they are perhaps the best. A short, good trail to the source of the springs adds interest. The pools are very popular with local families and are open all year. Because they are not as crowded as the other commercial pools, any time is good for a visit. Summer is the peak season, when about 350 people visit each day. In winter, daily traffic averages about one hundred visitors.

Getting There

The village of Nakusp is on Upper Arrow Lake, about halfway between Nelson and Revelstoke. Driving time from Castlegar or Nelson is about two hours (150 km (93 mi.)) on Highways 3A and 6 and about 1½ hours (115 km (71 mi.)) from Ainsworth. From Revelstoke it's about 100 km (60 mi.) plus a short ferry trip south on Highway 23. Driving time from Vancouver to Nakusp is about 10 hours via Castlegar and about eight hours via the Coquihalla Highway and Vernon.

Nakusp Hot Springs.

From Nakusp, drive 2.5 km (1.5 mi.) north on Highway 23 to the well-marked turnoff to the hot springs. If you are coming from Revelstoke, the turnoff is about 54 km (33 mi.) south of the Galena Bay ferry terminal. It's 12 km (7.5 mi.) on pavement from the highway to the hot springs. Driving time from Nakusp is about 20 minutes.

The Springs

Hot water issues from several sources along Kuskanax Creek and is piped about 1 km (0.6 mi.) to the bathing pools. The water is chlorinated and filtered. The flow-through water system ensures that water in the large pool completely changes every day and that the water in the small pool turns over about seven times per day.

The circular pool is about 8 m (25 ft.) across and divided in two by a cement walkway. The smaller section of the pool is hotter (about 42°C (108°F)) than the larger (about 38°C (100°F)). Both are everywhere less than 1.5 m (5 ft.) deep and are open to the sky. The smaller pool has wide ledges for sitting. In summer, planters full of flowers ring the poolside, the big forest trees seem very close, the view down the valley is good, and you can hear the gentle roar of Kuskanax Creek.

Before or after soaking, take the 20 minute walk to the source of the hot springs. From the entrance to the pool building, an excellent, well-marked trail heads upstream along Kuskanax Creek. Along the way, especially from the bridge across the creek, you get good views down into the canyon. The several spring sources are in an open, meadowed area on the south side of Kuskanax Creek. Poison ivy is abundant here; a sign illustrates what the plant looks like. The hot spring water is colourless and tasteless, has a mild sulphur odour, and reaches about 54.5°C (130°F). The water is low in dissolved solids; sulphate, sodium, and calcium are the most abundant constituents.

Spring water is collected and funnelled into a rectangular cement box in the lower part of the meadow, and insulated pipes carry it from the box to the bathhouse. Several old cement pools and structures in the meadows are reminders of earlier developments. Overflow water from the cement box and nearby sources collects in several pools down by Kuskanax Creek. Depending on how much water is available, it is possible to soak in these pools. I've always found them very muddy though pleasantly warm, but other people have given them rave reviews. If you do get too muddy, have a shower and a soak in the commercial pools back by your car.

Steam-filled meadows at the source of Nakusp Hot Springs.

Facilities

The pools, building, and change rooms are wheelchair accessible. The changing rooms are very clean and well equipped, with hot showers, soap, blow-dryers, and lockers. Bathing suits and towels are available for rent. Snacks and light meals are available in the large, bright lobby overlooking the pool. A massage therapist is available by appointment. Staff members are consistently very friendly and helpful. This is a friendly, low-pressure operation, run by the village of Nakusp, which clearly is working hard to get your return business.

Housekeeping units and camping are available just down the road from the hot springs, and the town of Nakusp has an adequate selection of motels, bed-and-breakfast places, private campgrounds, and restaurants. A village-run bus makes regular trips between Nakusp and the springs. There are many Forest Service campsites in the area, particularly east of Nakusp; pick up a map at the Tourist Information or Forest Service office in Nakusp. Other camping possibilities are at Halfway hot springs and at various places along the many logging roads in the area.

Rates, Hours, and Address

The hot springs are open year-round, except for a few days in April or May when they are closed for maintenance. Hours are 11:00 AM to 9:30 PM from October through May and 9:30 AM to 10:00 PM from June through September. Admission for a single swim is $5.50 for adults, $4.50 for seniors over 65 and students six to 18, GST included; children under six are free. Day passes and special group rates are available. For more information contact:

Nakusp Hot Springs
P.O. Box 280
Nakusp, BC V0G 1R0
250-265-4528
Fax: 250-265-3788

History

Nakusp was settled during the mining rush that flooded the West Kootenays with prospectors in the 1890s. The mining interest soon centred on Slocan Lake, but Nakusp grew slowly as a logging, sawmilling, and farming town.

Like many other hot springs in British Columbia, these were staked by private individuals (in this case in the mid-1890s). Strong protests from residents of Nakusp resulted in cancellation of the claims by the provincial government. Other staking efforts and ensuing legal battles prodded the government into creating Nakusp Hot Springs Park Reserve in 1925 to ensure that the springs were preserved for use by everyone. The surviving mineral claims were purchased by the Leary family in 1928, and in 1955 the family donated 4 ha (10 acres), which included the springs, for a park to be supervised by the town. The park was made a Class A provincial park in 1964.

The present facilities were built in 1974. The provincial park status was cancelled in late 1990, and ownership and administration of the land was totally assumed by the village of Nakusp. More than 20 years after the present facilities opened, they remain the only community-owned springs in British Columbia.

Other Activities in the Area

Nakusp makes a good base for exploring other hot springs in the area; St. Leon, Halfway and Halcyon are especially popular. The region offers good golfing, cycling, boating, and fishing, and heli-skiing is popular in the winter. Some commercial heli-ski trips finish with a visit to the springs, where you can warm up in the hot pool.

St. Leon Hot Springs

Formerly developed, now partly developed

Maps 14 & 16

50°C (120°F)

This guitar-shaped concrete pool on a deeply wooded hillside is only a short drive on a logging road and a short but steep hike from the highway. It's one of my favourites, and it's also popular with local residents. The pool is most popular in spring, summer, and fall.

Getting There

These springs are about a 35 minute drive from Nakusp followed by a 10 minute hike, making this an easy afternoon outing. If you are coming from Nakusp, drive north on Highway 23 up the east side of Upper Arrow Lake. About 21.2 km (13.1 mi.) from the stop sign at the north end of downtown Nakusp, you pass a roadside rest area on the right with a picturesque waterfall. In another 2.5 km (1.5 mi.), the St. Leon Forest Service road branches right; it's clearly marked.

If you are coming from the north, cross the bridge over St. Leon Creek 23.1 km (14.3 mi.) from the Galena Bay ferry terminal and about 0.5 km (0.3 mi.) from the Halfway hot springs turnoff. The St. Leon Forest Service road branches left 1.7 km (1.0 mi.) south of St. Leon Creek.

Drive up the logging road, always staying on the main road. There are a few rough spots, but most cars will have little difficulty. At 3.6 km (2.2 mi.) from the highway, there is a pullout on the right, on a level stretch at the top of a long hill. Park here. There's a good turnaround 0.5 km (0.3 mi.) farther up the logging road.

The trail drops steeply down the bank from the parking area. It's about a 10 to 15 minute hike down the trail through big timber to the hot springs and about the same for the hike back up. There is a loss in elevation of about 60 m (200 ft.). The trail is steep but in good shape and easy to follow.

A longer but gentler approach, often used in winter, begins where an old spur road branches left about 2.8 km (1.7 mi.) from the highway. Don't drive down it unless you have a 4×4, because you might not get back up. Hike down this old road to its end, drop down on a trail to a lower road, and hike to the hot springs, about 1 km (0.6 mi.) from the main St. Leon road.

An alternative approach is to hike in from Highway 23. The old wagon road up St. Leon Creek begins about 200 m (650 ft.) south of the bridge over St. Leon Creek. It's a bit difficult to find; look for it near the north end of some small cliffs. The trail is fairly steep to begin with and then flattens out. Allow about two hours to reach the springs.

The Springs
Unlike many springs, these aren't in the valley bottom but on a steep hillside about halfway from the road to the creek. The graceful main pool is

The cement-lined pool at St. Leon, in a clearing in old-growth forest.

cement, with a guitar-shaped outline and a smooth, curved bottom and sides. It's about 6 m by 3 m (20 ft. by 10 ft.) and up to 1 m (3 ft.) deep. A few boulders are cemented into place in strategic spots for sitting. Beside the pool a wooden platform with a bit of a roof offers a good place to park clothes. Hot and cold water is piped into this pool; the temperature can easily be regulated by adjusting the hoses. It's all tastefully done, and there is a welcome lack of algae.

The main pool is fed by two springs. The left and larger source flows from cracks in bedrock at the back of a low cave a couple of metres deep. The right-hand system is at the top of a rock slab. Water issues from cracks at the base of a small cliff. Someone has artfully used concrete and stones to build a retaining wall and small V-shaped pool to catch the water. This pool is hot, but is very comfortable for one person. Overflow is piped down the slab to the main pool.

The water is clear and colourless, with a faint mineral taste and a very faint sulphur smell. Sulphate, calcium, and sodium are the main dissolved minerals.

Comments

The springs are deep in the forest; if you want sunlight, be there at noon or early in the afternoon. People have camped on the old wagon road about 30 m (100 ft.) west of the springs, but I suggest camping at Halfway River hot springs or one of the Forest Service campgrounds in the area. The springs are privately owned; please treat the site with respect.

History

St. Leon Hot Springs were once far better known than they are today. At the turn of the century, the resort at Halcyon hot springs farther north on Upper Arrow Lake was thriving. Mike Grady, an Irish prospector who had become wealthy through his claims at Silverton, decided that a resort built around the hot springs at St. Leon would do equally well. Grady spent $750,000, a fortune even today, building a three-storey cedar hotel on the lake shore. The hotel and its well-stocked bar opened in 1902. Hot water was piped from the springs to the hotel, where it was reheated in a large boiler.

The resort did very well for some years. Sternwheelers made regular stops there, and the resort (and its well-stocked bar) was also popular with loggers from the camps up and down the lake. Business dropped off

St. Leon Hot Springs.

sharply with World War I and prohibition, and it never recovered. Completion of the Kettle Valley Railway led to decreased sternwheeler traffic on the lake, which further isolated the resort. Grady stayed with the hotel through the depression, eccentric and reclusive, and died in 1945.

That year, the property was purchased from Grady's estate by an American engineer, Edwin Gates. He refurbished the hotel, renaming it the Gates of St. Leon (see photo, p. 23). The Gates family operated it as a hunting and fishing resort and health spa, but poor access hampered the operation. The hotel was expropriated in the early 1960s under terms of the Columbia River Treaty and stood empty, awaiting drowning by the rising lake, until it burned down in November 1968.

Ed Gates died in Nakusp in 1973. Today nothing remains of the resort. The hot springs themselves remain privately owned, and the pool is maintained by volunteers from Nakusp.

Halfway River Hot Springs

Partly developed

Maps 14 & 16

Up to 60.5°C (141°F)

Halfway River hot springs are the only popular springs in the Nakusp area that escaped commercial development. You reach the springs after a 12 km (7 mi.) drive on a logging road and a short, steep hike. The pools are in a lovely setting beside the Halfway River and seem to be slightly less frequented than nearby St. Leon or Halcyon. During spring runoff one of the best pools is often flooded or only lukewarm. Snow closes the logging road in winter, but the hot springs make a good cross-country ski destination.

Getting There

In spring, summer, and fall these springs are an afternoon's outing from Nakusp. From Nakusp, drive north on Highway 23. About 21.2 km (13.1 mi.) from the stop sign at the north end of downtown Nakusp, there is an attractive rest area on the right at Ione Falls. In 2.5 km (1.5 mi.) the St. Leon Forest Service road branches right; in 1.7 km (1.0 mi.) you cross the large bridge over St. Leon Creek. In another 0.5 km (0.3 mi.), turn right onto the Halfway River Forest Service road.

If you are coming from Revelstoke, the large steel bridge over the Halfway River is 22.2 km (13.8 mi.) south of the Galena Bay ferry terminal and 10 km (6 mi.) south of the Halcyon turnoff. The Halfway Forest Service road branches left 0.4 km (0.2 mi.) farther south.

The gravel road is in good shape, and the drive to the springs should take about 15 minutes. A 10 km sign is 10.5 km (6.5 mi.) from the highway, just after a large gravelled area beside the road. At 11.2 km (7.0 mi.), you pass a very rough road dropping steeply left. At 11.6 km (7.2 mi.) and the 11 km sign, another road branches left and down. Park here, or drive a hundred metres down the side road to a good parking area.

From the 11 km sign, walk about 70 m (230 ft.) down the branch road and then look for a trail dropping steeply over the bank. The trail is steep but good; it leads to a flat area on an old road. From the upriver end of the flat area, pick up another trail that heads steeply down to the river. When you reach the flats along the river, follow the trail for about 100 m (330 ft.) downstream to the pools. Hiking time from the main logging road is about 10 to 15 minutes, with an elevation loss of about 70 m (230 ft.).

Halfway River hot springs, which are in a forest, are a good choice on a hot day.

An alternative, less popular approach starts from 11.2 km (7.0 mi.) on the logging road. Hike about 300 m (1000 ft.) down the ancient road, which is very steep at first and then becomes more level, to its end at the flat area described above. This route avoids the steep, upper hill on the main trail but takes longer to hike.

The Springs

Several springs percolate from gravels along and near the river bank. The temperature and characteristics of the water are not well known, but the maximum recorded temperature is 60.5°C (141°F). The water has a slight sulphur smell and mineral taste; like other springs in the area, it probably has a low mineral content. There is very little algae in these springs.

The main spring bubbles from the base of a 5 m (16 ft.) high cliff. Water is piped about 20 m (65 ft.) to the pools. The main pool is a sturdy, wooden structure, about 2 m (6 ft.) across and less than 1 m (3 ft.) deep. An adjoining, smaller wooden pool is hotter. Both are good soaking temperatures. There is also a covered changing shelter.

From the main pool, a good trail leads about 50 m (160 ft.) downstream to a secluded pool at the base of a bluff by the edge of the river.

Very hot water emerging from gravel at the base of the cliff feeds a 2 m by 3 m (6 ft. by 10 ft.) pool lined with plastic and rocks. This pool is likely to be flooded during spring runoff. Several other springs percolate through the gravel in and near the river; these are smaller and cooler than the two main ones.

Facilities

The river flats upstream of the pools are lovely, open, and parklike. There are several picnic tables, an outhouse, and campsites with fire rings. Watch where you camp: as the sign near the outhouse informs you, poison ivy seems to be everywhere here. A signboard points out that this spot has been protected from commercial development since 1974. The site is beautifully maintained by volunteers from Nakusp.

You can camp by one of the fire rings along the flat old road halfway up to the logging road, away from the poison ivy. Car-campers will find a good open area at the end of the spur road just off the logging road, where the main approach trail begins.

A very hot pool at Halfway River hot springs, downstream from the main soaking tubs, is next to the river, so it's easy to cool the pool down before you get in.

Halcyon Hot Springs   Commercial resort

Maps 14 & 16 · Colour photo, page 199   46.5°–51°C (116°–124°F)

Like St. Leon, Halcyon Hot Springs were once the focus of a thriving resort. From 1955 to 1999, the springs had a reputation for excellent, free soaking in rustic tubs. Now these springs have been redeveloped and are the site of Canada's newest commercial hot springs resort. Development is not yet complete, but the resort will probably complement rather than compete with Nakusp Hot Springs. It is definitely worth a visit.

Getting There

Driving time is less than 30 minutes from Nakusp and less than 1½ hours from Revelstoke. From downtown Nakusp, drive north on Highway 23. The turnoff to the resort is 35.3 km (21.9 mi.) from Nakusp. If you are coming from Revelstoke, take Highway 23 south to the Shelter Bay ferry terminal. The ferry is free and runs every hour; crossing time is 20 minutes. The turnoff to the resort is 13.9 km (8.6 mi.) south of the Galena Bay terminal. The turnoff is well marked in both directions. Go down the driveway to the parking area by the new resort.

The Springs

Hot water is piped to the resort from several springs above the highway. No chlorine is used in the water treatment; instead, it is filtered and treated with ozone before reaching the pools. A large warm pool at 37.7°C (100°F) holds about 100 people, and a smaller hot pool (40.5°C (105°F)) seats 40. There is a small cold plunge (23.9°C (75°F)) that is fed by water from a local creek. A "sprinkler pool" for children and a large swimming pool should be open by the summer of 1999. All pools are of the flow-through variety in which new spring water is constantly being added to maintain heat and cleanliness.

To see the source of the springs, drive or walk north along the highway for 1.3 km (0.8 mi.) from the turnoff to the resort. Look for a side road (usually gated) that branches uphill; the turnoff is conspicuous and is marked by a large Private Property sign. Hike up the road to where it makes a sharp bend. Take the upper of two nearly level roads that cut sharply back south. The source of the springs and the old soaking pools are just a few steps above the end of the road. The water in the several springs has a moderate sulphur smell and a very strong, tangy mineral taste. Sulphate and sodium are the main constituents of the water, and fluoride is also high. Some visitors used to take bottles of the water home with them.

Two of the main springs are piped to the resort. Until very recently, another spring was piped to some rustic soaking tubs. If you have visited Halcyon before, you probably enjoyed lying in these pools and enjoying the wonderful views of Upper Arrow Lake. As of spring 1999, the tubs are empty, pending decisions by the owners and the Ministry of Health.

Facilities

The new pools at the resort are outdoors and have spectacular views of Upper Arrow Lake and the Monashee Mountains beyond (the high peak you can see is Mt. Odin). The adjoining, brand-new lodge houses the changing rooms, showers, and washrooms; the facilities are wheelchair-accessible. Also in the lodge are a licensed bistro, a gift shop, and a tiny grocery store.

Accommodation is available in one- and two-bedroom chalets and rustic cabins scattered in the forest near the lodge. There is also a fully serviced RV park and area for tent camping on the property.

The new lodge and pools at Halcyon, March 1999.

All that remains of the pre-1955 hotel and resort is a little chapel, reached by a short trail from the lodge. The chapel has been restored to close to its original condition, and it contains some of its original furnishings. Tentative plans are that it will be turned into a small museum illustrating the history of the springs.

Rates, Hours, and Address
The pools are open every day all year from 9:30 AM to 10:00 PM. Admission for a single swim is $6.00 for adults. There are reduced rates for seniors and children, and families, and day and weekend passes are available. The chalets rent from $110 per night and the cabins from $60, depending on the season. RV sites are $22.50 per night, and tent camping is $15. For more information, contact:

Halcyon Hot Springs
P.O. Box 37
Nakusp, BC V0G 1R0
250-265-3554
1-888-689-4699 (toll-free from Canada and United States)
Fax: 250-265-3887

History
Like St. Leon, this property has a long, colourful, and somewhat melancholy history. It was developed in 1890, when the first sanatorium was built by a Captain Robert Sanderson. He built wooden pipes to carry the hot water to the building, which also had a well-supplied bar. The sanatorium was called Halcyon, signifying health and happiness. The facilities were greatly enlarged in the late 1890s under new owners, the Halcyon Hot Springs Sanitarium Company. A wharf was built by the provincial government, and sternwheelers stopped twice a day at Halcyon. A special plant bottled water for shipment to the United States and England.

Like St. Leon, Halcyon fell out of favour during World War I and prohibition, but unlike St. Leon it recovered in the mid-1920s. The hotel complex was acquired in 1924 by the White Cross society, under the direction of General Frederick E. Burnham. Burnham and his society emphasized healing over partying. The bar was shut, and smoking and drinking were prohibited on the premises. He and his family completely renovated the structure, furnished it with antiques and works of art, and built cottages and new hot baths. The four-storey hotel, built on the lakefront, was an imposing structure, but over the years the flow of visitors slowly and steadily declined.

The general stayed on, even after the death of his wife. But disaster hit in 1955. Someone spilled oil while lighting the stove, and the hotel, the art, and the general went up in flames. With construction of the dams on the Columbia, all ruins but the chapel disappeared in 1969 beneath the rising waters of Arrow Lakes.

From 1955 to 1997, the pools above the road were a popular bathing and camping spot, in spite of periodic bouts of rowdyism and vandalism. In 1997, the property was sold to new owners (from the Nakusp area) who began the present period of redevelopment. The new resort opened to the public on March 5, 1999.

Halcyon Hot Springs as it appeared about 1925. The cordwood piled on the shore was fuel for steam-powered sternwheelers, which made regular stops at the springs.

Canyon (Albert Canyon) Hot Springs

Commercial pool

Map 14

27°C (81°F) at source

These springs are on the Trans-Canada Highway east of Revelstoke, halfway to Rogers Pass. At 27°C (81°F), they feed two heated outdoor pools, one hot and the other a good temperature for swimming. There is much to do nearby: camping, hiking, horseback riding, river rafting, train watching, and exploring the small ghost town of Albert Canyon. The pool is open from late May through September.

Getting There

The resort is just off Highway 1, 35 km (22 mi.) west of Rogers Pass and 35 km (22 mi.) east of Revelstoke. Large, stylized red umbrellas (the company logo) on the south side of the highway mark the two entrances.

The Springs

The source of the springs is on private land south of the Canadian Pacific Railway and is off limits to the public. The water is odourless and tasteless and has a relatively low mineral content; bicarbonate, calcium, and sodium are the main constituents. The old pools that once existed at the source are boarded up, and all the water is piped about 2.5 km (1.5 mi.) to the resort.

At the resort, unheated or slightly heated water is fed into a swimming pool about 12 m by 20 m (40 ft. by 65 ft.). At 27°C (81°F), this pool is a good temperature for swimming. Spring water in the hot pool is heated to about 40°C (104°F). This pool is about 1 m (3 ft.) deep and has comfortable ledges for sitting. Both pools are chlorinated and are outdoors, affording a good view down the valley to the mountains of Mount Revelstoke National Park. Recorded music or FM radio is piped into the pools and the pool area.

Facilities

The pools are wheelchair accessible. The changing rooms are clean, with hot showers, soap, electrical outlets, and blow dryers (a nice touch). A cafe serving light meals has an open-air patio and can be reached without leaving the pool area, and you can eat on picnic tables in a grassy area beside the pool before resuming your soak.

A campground and RV park adjoin the pools and are operated by the same people. The complex also has laundry facilities, a gift shop, and a small store. There is a good selection of motels, campgrounds, and restaurants in Revelstoke. Glacier National Park has several good campsites (they fill up fast in the summer) and excellent backcountry camping.

The hot pool and, behind it, the swimming pool at Canyon Hot Springs.

Rates, Hours, and Address

The resort complex and pools are open daily from 9:00 AM until 9:00 PM in May, June, and September, and until 10 PM in July and August. Admission is $5.00 for adults, $4.50 for seniors, and $4.00 for children aged three to 14, plus GST. There is a special family rate of $15 for four people. Suits and towels are available for rent. For more information contact:

Canyon Hot Springs
P.O. Box 2400
Revelstoke, BC V0E 2S0
250-837-2420
Fax: 250-837-6160

History

The building of the Canadian Pacific Railway permeates the history of this area. The springs were originally known as Albert Canyon Hot Springs, because they are close to the little section house and village of Albert Canyon. In 1892, four railway men blasted a large pool at the source of the springs. Surveyor A.O. Wheeler visited the springs in 1901 and wrote:

> A path, opened out through giant fir and cedar, devil's club, skunk cabbage and other tropical undergrowth, leads up one of the slopes for about half a mile from the clearing; here, a large spring bubbles from the ground, said to contain mineral properties. A bath-tub of cedar slabs has been made by the inhabitants, so arranged that it can be filled or emptied in about 10 minutes; when not in use, the overflow from the spring passes through along the bottom. The water has a temperature of about 78 or 80 degrees. During the strike, the section men employed their leisure hours in enlarging the tub.... Judging by the quantities of soap lying around, the inhabitants are of a cleanly disposition.

Today a road leads from the resort down to the remains of the old town and farms beside the railway. The houses and orchards are all long abandoned and overgrown.

OTHER SPRINGS IN THE WEST KOOTENAYS

Other hot springs have been reported from the West Kootenay region. Most aren't well known and I haven't visited them. These notes are starting points for those wishing to track them down.

Snowshoe Rabbit Warm (?) Spring   Existence uncertain
Map 14

The *Geothermal Resources of British Columbia* map (see References) shows a spring of this name at 49°55′N, 118°11′W. No temperatures or other details are available. Map 82E/16 shows Snowshoe Lake at this locality, which looks like a good place to start searching.

Taylor Warm Spring   Undeveloped
Map 14   25°C (77°F)

Warm water discharges at a rate of about a litre per second from a diamond drill hole. The spring is on the west side of Upper Arrow Lake, probably somewhere around Dixon Creek (see map 82K/4). From a large sand dune, walk about 300 m (1000 ft.) uphill and follow an old road south for another 220 m (720 ft.). Cross the spring outlet creek and walk uphill to the source.

Fosthall Springs   Existence uncertain
Map 14

An 1896 geological report mentions two springs on Mt. Baldur, on the west side of Upper Arrow Lake between Fosthall and Pingston creeks. No temperatures or location data are available. People I've talked to who know the area well have not heard of these springs. It's possible that they no longer exist or were flooded by Upper Arrow Lake.

Upper Halfway River Warm Springs   Undeveloped
Maps 14 & 16   About 28°C (82°F)

These aren't the well-known springs described in this chapter but smaller springs that were found by the Forest Service around 1973. They are some

20 km (12 mi.) up the river in a rocky canyon on the south side of the river. Temperature is about 28°C (82°F) and the soaking is reported to be poor. The Forest Service office in Nakusp might be a good place to ask for information.

Wilson Lake Warm Springs   Undeveloped

Maps 14 & 16   About 35°C (95°F)

Be prepared for bushy hiking for this one. From Rosebery, a few kilometres north of New Denver on Highway 6, take the East Wilson Creek road just south of the Rosebery Park sign. Follow the excellent gravel road to Little Wilson Lake Forest Service campground, about 33 km (20 mi.) from the highway. You can also reach this point by a rougher road (okay for most cars) from Nakusp: 6.3 km (3.9 mi.) south of Nakusp on Highway 6, take the Wilson Lake turnoff. Follow the rough road for about 18 km (11 mi.) to the campsite. Pick up a Forest Service map in Nakusp to navigate this complex of roads.

The springs are on the south side of the valley, about 1 km (0.6 mi.) east of Little Wilson Lake. The best approach might be to hike the overgrown road along the south side of Little Wilson Lake; this road starts about 2.2 km (1.3 mi.) west of the recreation site. The springs seep from talus a short distance up a small side creek. Provincial government map 82K/SW shows the springs at UTM grid reference 606633 and an elevation of 950 m (3100 ft.). The 1:50,000 map for the area is 82K/4, but the springs aren't shown. Water temperature is about 35°C (95°F) and the volume is small.

Fry Creek Hot (?) Springs   Undeveloped

Map 14

From Argenta on the northeast corner of Kootenay Lake, drive 12 km (7 mi.) south on a gravel road to Johnsons Landing. Hike south on a good trail to the Fry Creek Canyon Provincial Recreation Area. Follow old trails and logging roads for about 9 km (5.6 mi.) up the north side of Fry Creek to Carney Creek. Cross Carney Creek and continue up Fry Creek. There are apparently two springs up Fry Creek on its north side a few kilometres apart. Map 82K/2 and experience in wilderness travel are essential.

Riondel Hot Spring
Inaccessible

Map 14
40°C (104°F)

The *Geothermal Resources of British Columbia* map (see References) shows a hot spring near the town of Riondel, about 10 km (6 mi.) north of the Kootenay Bay ferry terminal. The spring is totally inaccessible because it's deep in one of the many old mine shafts in the area.

Crawford Creek Warm Springs
Undeveloped

Map 14
31.5°C (89°F)

You can reach the settlement of Crawford Bay on the east shore of Kootenay Lake by the ferry from Balfour (see the section on Ainsworth Hot Springs) or by following Highway 3A from Creston. Two small warm springs have been reported along the north side of Crawford Creek about 2.5 km (1.5 mi.) upstream from Crawford Bay. The reported temperature is 31.5°C (89°F). According to a visitor to the springs in the early 1970s, the route takes the road up the north side of Crawford Creek past the garbage dump to a rusty quarry or road cut on the left side of the road. The short trail to the springs begins about 50 m (160 ft.) farther up the road and heads down towards the creek.

Some years ago I heard a rumour of a hot spring near Rose Pass at the head of Crawford Creek. Topographic maps show suspiciously named Spring Creek about two-thirds of the way from Crawford Creek to Rose Pass, suggesting the rumour may have some substance to it. The main road up Crawford Creek intersects Spring Creek. The Crawford Creek drainage is covered by map 82F/10.

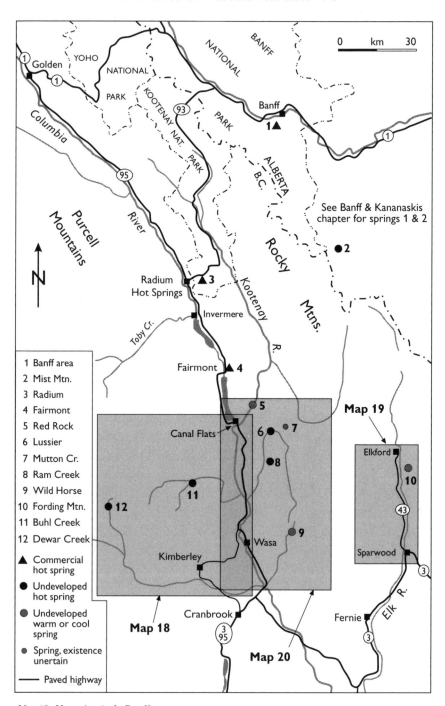

Map 17. Hot springs in the East Kootenays

CHAPTER 6

The East Kootenays

The heart of the East Kootenays is the broad, straight valley of the Columbia and Kootenay rivers. Lying between the Rocky Mountains on the east and the Purcell Mountains on the west, the area offers spectacular mountain scenery, skiing, hiking, and other outdoor activities. The area also features excellent hot springs, including two of the best known in British Columbia (Fairmont and Radium) and the second-hottest spring in Canada (Dewar Creek). Fairmont and Radium are fully developed resorts. Lussier and Ram Creek have pools built mainly by volunteers, and the others are largely in their natural states.

Highways 93 and 95 run the length of the East Kootenays. The valley has ample tourist facilities, particularly in the larger communities of Cranbrook, Kimberley, and Invermere and at the resorts built around Radium and Fairmont hot springs. If you wish to car-camp, there are numerous private campgrounds and some lovely provincial park campgrounds. The largest of these is at Wasa, just off Highway 95. If it's full, try Whiteswan Lake Provincial Park east of the settlement of Skookumchuck.

Except for Dewar Creek, which requires a long hike to reach, most of the springs in this chapter are short walks from roads. Some require long drives on logging roads, but most of the popular springs are fairly close to the main highways. If you are just passing through the area, it's easy to visit a couple of these springs. But if you are spending some time in the region hiking, skiing, or just relaxing, you might want to try them all.

Dewar Creek Hot Springs
Undeveloped

Maps 17 & 18 • Colour photo, page 200

Up to 82.2°C (180°F)

One of the finest hot springs in Canada, this undeveloped and unspoiled spot has a large volume of very hot water in a lovely, subalpine setting west of Kimberley. The springs have remained unspoiled because reaching them requires a long drive on logging roads followed by a long hike on a rough trail. The trip is best in late summer, when the trail has dried out, the bugs are gone, and the soaking and fall colours are at their best.

Getting There

If you are a strong hiker, you can visit Dewar Creek hot springs in a long day trip from Kimberley. It's more enjoyable to make a weekend out of it, though. Camp along the way or nearby and do some additional hiking in the area.

From the main traffic light and intersection in Kimberley, drive 5.7 km (3.5 mi.) south along Highway 95A to the St. Mary Road turnoff to the west. This junction is well marked, but if you miss it, continue to the settlement of Marysville and then backtrack for a kilometre to the paved turnoff. If you are coming from Cranbrook, take Highway 95A about 24 km (15 mi.) north to Marysville.

The pavement ends in 17.4 km (10.8 mi.) by St. Mary Lake. Use headlights and watch for logging trucks past here. In 12.8 km (7.9 mi.), just past the 39 km sign, go straight ahead at a major junction. After another 9.5 km (5.9 mi.), you cross a large bridge over White Creek; 0.5 km (0.3 mi.) past the bridge is an important Y junction. The St. Mary West Fork Forest Service road goes left, but you take the right fork. To this point the road is very good gravel, and the driving time from Highway 95A is a bit less than an hour.

From the Y junction, the route essentially follows the main road to its end near the head of Dewar Creek. When you are 11.6 km (7.2 mi.) past the St. Mary West Fork turnoff (0.3 km (0.2 mi.) past the yellow 12 km sign), go straight ahead, ignoring a road that branches sharply left and crosses Dewar Creek. In another 4 km (2.5 mi.), at the next Y junction, take the left (main) road, labelled "Dewar Creek road." There's yet another junction after another 6.6 km (4.1 mi.). The main road goes left and soon crosses Dewar Creek; don't take it, but instead take the slightly rougher right fork. Go left in 0.8 km (0.5 mi.) and after another 0.6 km

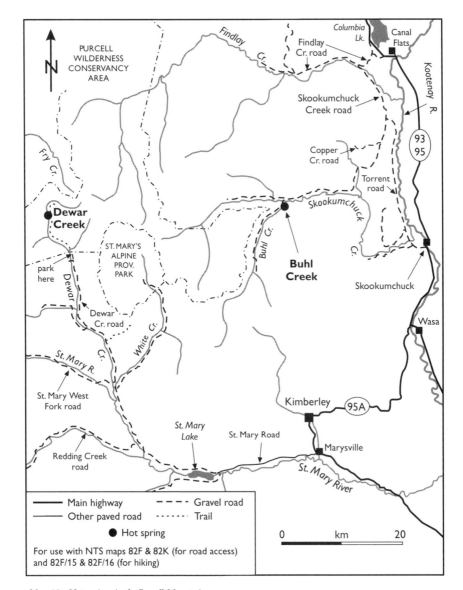

Map 18. Hot springs in the Purcell Mountains

(0.4 mi.) pull into a large grassy area on your left. Park here; it's also a good spot to camp. The 63.8 km (39.6 mi.) from Highway 95A will take about 1½ hours, and all but the last kilometre is on good gravel.

The hike from here to the hot springs is about 9 km (5.6 mi.) each way, with an elevation gain of about 180 m (600 ft.). The hike in will take an experienced hiker about two to three hours and somewhat less on the way out. It will take longer if you are out of shape, are not used to strenuous hiking, or lose the trail. Wear good hiking boots, because the trail can be rough and extremely muddy in places. In mid- to late summer, parts of the trail will be brilliant with wildflowers, but it is an enjoyable hike at any time of the year.

Pick up the trail in the parking lot at the Purcell Wilderness Conservancy information sign and self-registration box. Soon you cross a wooden bridge over Wesley Creek. The trail follows the east (right) side of Dewar Creek to where it forks abruptly, about halfway to the springs.

The left branch of the trail is used by parties on horseback. It crosses Dewar Creek and, farther upstream, crosses back to the east side. Hikers should follow the right (east) branch of the trail, which follows the creek bank for a bit and then climbs and follows the slope above before dropping down to rejoin the horse trail in a flat meadow. The trail here is a bit vague in places, and there are several variant paths. No matter which you take, you should rejoin the horse trail in about 25 minutes. Make a mental note of the route here to aid you on your return trip.

Ten minutes after rejoining the horse trail, you'll reach another fork. The upper branch climbs to several private cabins and then drops down to rejoin the shorter, lower trail. It's only another half-hour to the springs from here. The trail climbs steeply along the east bank of Dewar Creek and then levels out and breaks out into a large, open, slabby area just a few metres below the hot springs. If you are not stopping at the springs but are continuing up Dewar Creek, pick up the route at the top of the slabs.

The Springs

These springs are among the largest and most spectacular in British Columbia. Hot water issues from numerous vents for at least 120 m (400 ft.) along the east bank of Dewar Creek. It's very hot, reaching 82.2°C (180°F). The water is clear, with only a slight sulphur smell and a pleasant, light mineral taste. The main bathing pools are strung out along Dewar Creek, but the whole area is interesting and worth exploring.

At the slabby area where you first encounter the springs, hot water flows from several sources at the top of the slabs. It runs across the flat rocks and over steep cliffs to Dewar Creek some 20 m (65 ft.) below. The flat area, roughly 15 m by 50 m (50 ft. by 160 ft.), is coated with tufa. There is a shallow, one-person bathing pool on the slabs, but it is far too hot, except perhaps in a deluge or in winter.

Tufa-covered benches at Dewar Creek hot springs.

It's an easy scramble down to where hot water bubbles from the base of the cliffs. A couple of interesting small soaking pools have been constructed at the edge of Dewar Creek. When the water is high these are inaccessible and submerged, but at lower water they offer prime soaking. The cliffs above are coated with layers of hollow-sounding spring deposits, and the abundant brilliant green algae and red iron oxide stain add colour to the rocks here.

To reach the other main soaking pools, it's easiest to climb back to the flat area above the cliffs and follow a trail to a spot where people have camped above Dewar Creek. A little trail here drops down to the creek and leads to another open area of tufa slabs, meadows, and boulders above and beside the creek. Many small hot springs emerge from bedrock and gravel along the creek. The main bathing pools are in this area, all built of rocks with only a small amount of plastic sheet and pipe. They change considerably from year to year, and people have reported that in some years there have been no bathing pools at all.

Just upstream from the tufa slab are several rock pools at various heights above the creek. The upper of these is very hot, fed by a little spring that is too hot to keep your hand in. Gas and hot water bubble up from the bottom of this pool. Successively lower pools are supplied by outflow from this one; the preferred hangout is the one closest to Dewar Creek, which can be diverted to cool the pool. These pools each hold several people and have nice gravel bottoms. If you get overheated, you can always go for a quick dip in clear, cold Dewar Creek. All pools have large, smooth boulders nearby, ideal for changing and sunning.

Possibly the most interesting area is a few metres downstream, under the overhanging cliffs directly under the old campsite. Very hot water issues from numerous cracks in the rock here. If Dewar Creek is at the right level, often the best soaking is in a creekside pool beneath these cliffs.

Algae in shades of green, yellow, brown, blue-green, and orange live in the scalding water. Rust-coloured iron oxide and white calcium bicarbonate (baking soda) precipitate from the water and coat the rocks; together with the algae, these give a beautiful, variegated, and abstract look to this spot.

You may find light grey mountain goat fur snagged on the rocks beneath these cliffs; animals like the natural mineral licks supplied by the springs. Also look for patches of dirt on ledges beneath these cliffs; these are places where goats bed down. The rocks are distinctly warm here, and if I were a goat I would like to curl up here, warm and dry, on a bitter winter night. But other animals besides humans and goats seek out these springs. Once, on the slabby area above the cliffs, I found the remains of a goat (fur and some cracked bones) that were being fossilized in the spring deposits. Wolf sign was also being fossilized, a quiet and sober indicator, perhaps, of a memorable dinner enjoyed a few years ago.

About 40 m (130 ft.) upstream from this area, there is another small warm spring that collects in a mediocre, muddy, single-person soaker. Another 30 m (100 ft.) upstream are a few more warm sources percolating out of the rocks. There are a couple of lukewarm trickles on the far bank of Dewar Creek, but they are far too small and cool to be interesting.

Comments

People visit these springs at all times of the year. In spring, roads may not have been repaired, the trail may still be very muddy, and high water levels in Dewar Creek restrict soaking possibilities. In summer and fall, you follow a good hiking and horse trail to the springs. The flowers in the meadows are at their best in July, and in fall the autumn colours are lovely. Also by late summer and fall, Dewar Creek is low and the bathing pools, which often wash out or flood, have been rebuilt by visitors and

Hot water glistening on a tufa-coated hillside at Dewar Creek hot springs.

volunteers. Unfortunately, late September brings hunting season and all that it entails. The area is increasingly visited on skis in the winter, but you must know what you are doing: this is avalanche country.

Fortunately, these superb springs have always been too remote to attract serious interest by developers. Today they are in an ecological reserve within the Purcell Wilderness Conservancy, established in 1974. As such, the springs seem safe from any development. All motorized vehicles are prohibited in the conservancy.

The springs aren't marked on most maps. They are at UTM grid reference 347335 on NTS map 82F/15. Map 82F/16 is useful for the approach. The Cranbrook Forest District recreation map, free from Forest Service offices, is a good general map for the area and shows the main approach roads and campsites.

Camping and Hiking

If you are car-camping, you will find many suitable spots along the road. The parking area at the end of the road is also fine for camping.

The area around the springs is mostly rocky and uneven, not suited to comfortable camping. Nor should you camp right at the springs; not only is it against park regulations, but the area *is* an ecological reserve with extremely delicate ecosystems. If you are camping, continue up the trail for about 10 minutes past the hot springs to locally named Bugle Basin, where Dewar Creek turns east and opens out. There are abundant places to camp here, and the view down the valley is lovely. Bring a stove for cooking and leave the firewood alone. You can also find camping spots close to the creek along the trail on the hike in.

The entire area is popular with hikers and backpackers, and there are numerous possibilities for extended trips. Lovely St. Mary's Alpine Park, east of Dewar Creek, has 29 lakes and tarns surrounded by meadows and steep ridges. For detailed route information, consult the park brochure prepared by the Ministry of Lands, Parks and Housing and available in Wasa on Highway 95. The guidebook *Mountain Footsteps* by Janice Strong (Calgary: Rocky Mountain Books, 1994) and the older *Exploring the Purcell Wilderness* by Anne Edwards, Patrick Morrow, and Arthur Twomey (Vancouver: Douglas & McIntyre, 1978) give good introductions to the natural history and trails in the region.

Fording Mountain (Sulphur) Warm Springs

Undeveloped

Maps 17 & 19   24°–26°C (75°–79°F)

Reach these lukewarm, seldom-visited springs in the southeast corner of the province by a long drive on a maze of logging roads and an easy hike.

Getting There

The road system is complicated and currently changing. The Forest Service in Cranbrook (250-426-1700) should be able to give you the current road conditions and route.

From Cranbrook, follow Highway 3 east for 87 km (54 mi.) to Fernie and another 29 km (18 mi.) to Sparwood; take Highway 43 north towards Elkford. About halfway to Elkford there is a major turnoff on your right leading to a bridge over the Elk River. Cross the Elk River, turn left (north), and take another bridge across the Fording River. From here, it's 9.2 km (5.7 mi.) to the springs. The route generally follows the broad Elk River valley. The last few kilometres are not driveable, but the walk along the old road is easy. When the terrain opens out to show a broad, marshy area on the left side of the road and slightly below, you are just about there. The springs are about halfway along this open area.

The Springs

The springs are marked by a conspicuous elliptical pool with a small diving board. Warm water bubbles up from two sources in the bottom of the pool, and another spring is present at the second bend in the pond's outflow stream. The water has a very strong rotten-egg, sulphur smell, hence the local name Sulphur Springs. The dissolved mineral content is high, mainly sulphate, calcium, sodium, and bicarbonate. Because of the strong smell and cool water, the pool isn't used much by people, but it's very popular with the resident algae and sulphur-oxidizing bacteria, as well as the visiting elk, moose, and deer.

Maps and Comments

Take NTS map 82G/15 and the Cranbrook Forest Service road map to help with navigation on the roads. The springs are at UTM coordinates 508373 on map 82G/15, and the open marshy area is shown on this map west of Fording Mountain. There is good camping nearby.

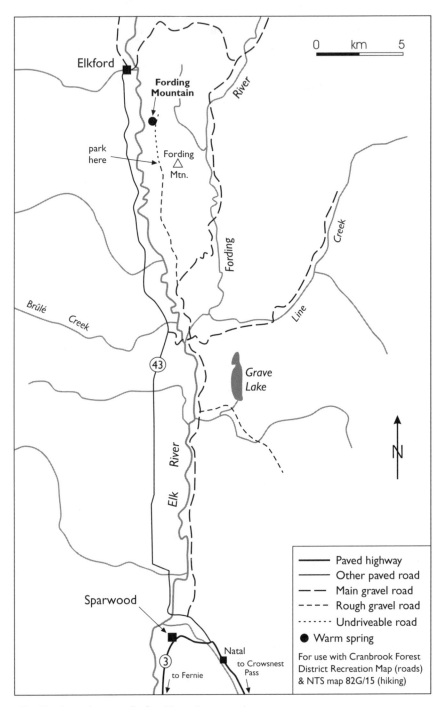

Map 19. Approach routes to Fording Mountain warm springs

Wild Horse Warm Springs

Undeveloped

Maps 17 & 20

12.5°, 28.5°C (55°, 83°F)

These undeveloped springs are reached by a long drive up a very rough, abandoned logging road. The volume of water is large, but the temperature is only lukewarm. A round trip from Fort Steele will take three to four hours, depending on the condition of the approach road. It is likely to be in the best shape from mid-summer to early fall. Whenever you go, you will probably have the area to yourself.

Getting There

Drive to Fort Steele, 17 km (10.5 mi.) north of Cranbrook on Highway 93/95. Turn east onto the Wardner-Fort Steele road (Norbury Lake Provincial Park turnoff). In 0.3 km (0.2 mi.) take the Wild Horse River Forest Service road, which angles left as the paved road heads downhill. After 7.3 km (4.5 mi.), stay right where the Lakit Lookout road branches left. The road, excellent to here, now becomes increasingly rough but is possible for most cars if you are an experienced back-road driver.

Drive another 10.9 km (6.8 mi.), then go left uphill; the East Wild Horse River road branches right and downhill. The road crosses to the east side of Wild Horse River after 3.0 km (1.9 mi.). In another 0.6 km (0.4 mi.), stay left at a Y junction. Cross two wooden bridges in quick succession in 4.7 km (2.9 mi.). The second bridge is over the river; there is a cabin above it. After 1.5 km (0.9 mi.), there is another Y junction. This point is about 28.3 km (17.6 mi.) and a little over an hour from the highway.

Park here or drive about 0.3 km (0.2 mi.) down the right-hand fork to an open camping area. If you look over the bank here, you can see the springs flowing into the creek from the far side about 100 m (330 ft.) downstream. There's no trail to the springs, but the bush isn't as bad as it looks; a five minute hike should put you there. Wild Horse River is easy to cross in late summer.

The Springs

Almost all the water flowing into Wild Horse River from the east bank is spring water. Warm water pours over a metre-high tufa bench into the river, and a large cold spring also flows into the river at the base of the tufa. This is a large spring, about equal to Lussier and Ram Creek springs

Wild Horse hot springs.

combined. The flow of warm and cold water together about equals that of Wild Horse River at low water.

The cold springs (12.5°C (55°F)) issue from various sources in the meadows and merge to form a single cool creek. The largest cold spring emerges from tufa and moss about 100 m (330 ft.) from the tufa bench. There is also a small cold spring on the west bank of the creek.

Warmer water flows from at least six vents on the tufa bench and for at least 50 m (160 ft.) above it. Maximum recorded temperature is a cool 28.5°C (83°F), and the water is clear, odourless, and tasteless. The main dissolved constituents are sulphate and calcium. At the top of the tufa bench, a waist-deep soaking pool that is about 2 m by 3 m (6 ft. by 10 ft.) has been dug. Warm water and gas bubble up from the slightly murky bottom. The water is too cool for an extended stay except perhaps on a hot summer day.

What little algae is present is bright green. A great deal of green moss grows on the tufa bench. Some of it has what looks like a dusting of frost; this moss is on its way towards being petrified and incorporated into the tufa bench. The water may only be warm, but the tufa bench continues to grow.

Comments

The springs are on Crown land at UTM grid reference 096188 on NTS map 82G/14. The provincial government map 82G/NW shows most of the access roads.

The Cranbrook Forest District recreation map shows roads continuing to the Lussier River road at the northwest corner of Top of the World Provincial Park, possibly tempting you with the thought of a warmer dip in Ram Creek or Lussier Hot Springs. Unfortunately, this road is impassable about a kilometre past the Wild Horse springs.

There are plenty of camping possibilities around here. The extensive logging gives a rather bleak feel to the area, although the forest is slowly growing back. Logging extended right down to Wild Horse River, and even the spring area was logged, a practice that probably wouldn't be tolerated today. The area is lush with fireweed, paintbrush, and many other flowers that make the area brilliant with colour in the summer.

There used to be other springs in the area. Tufa has been found downstream from the springs for about 1 km (0.6 mi.), and there may be tufa deposits above the road. All other springs now seem to have dried up.

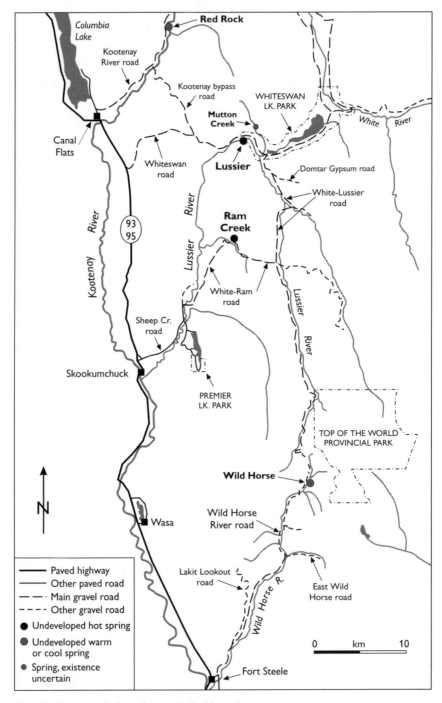

Map 20. Hot springs in the southwestern Rocky Mountains

Lussier (Whiteswan) Hot Springs

Partly developed

Maps 17, 20 & 21 • Colour photo, page 202. Also featured on the front cover 43.4°C (110°F)

These easily accessible, undeveloped springs are just inside Whiteswan Lake Provincial Park, a short drive east of Highway 93/95. They are popular with local folk, so you are unlikely to have them to yourself.

Getting There
A quick trip to Lussier need take little more than an hour return from the highway. A leisurely visit, which might include a picnic at Whiteswan Lake, will take half a day. You can easily visit Lussier and Ram Creek springs the same day; allow at least four hours for both.

From Highway 93/95   This is the easiest and most direct approach. If you are coming from the south, follow Highway 93/95 north for 24.1 km (15.0 mi.) from the gas station in Skookumchuck to the Whiteswan Lake Provincial Park turnoff. If you are coming from the north, this turnoff is 4.7 km (2.9 mi.) south of the Kootenay River bridge at Canal Flats.

From the turnoff, follow the excellent gravel Whiteswan Forest Service road. Watch for logging trucks and open-range cattle. For the last few kilometres of the road you get excellent views of narrow, spectacular Lussier Creek canyon. At 18.3 km (11.3 mi.) from the highway, a sign marks the entrance to Whiteswan Lake Provincial Park. Immediately after this is a parking area on your right, beside a small changing room/outhouse. Driving time from Highway 93/95 to Lussier is about 20 minutes.

From Ram Creek Hot Springs   The drive from Ram Creek to Lussier takes less than an hour in most cars. From Ram Creek springs, continue 5.9 km (3.6 mi.) up the narrow gravel road to a four-way junction. Turn left and follow the main road (excellent gravel) down the valley to the Whiteswan Lake Provincial Park notice board. The bleak look of this valley is a result of clearcut logging, strip mining for coal, and a 1985 forest fire. Turn left (west) on the main road; Lussier Hot Springs are 3.4 km (2.1 mi.) down the road and 25.6 km (15.9 mi.) from Ram Creek.

The Springs
If you walk up the road about 100 m (330 ft.) past the parking area, you can see the hot spring pools beside the creek below. To reach them, take

Soaking pools at Lussier Hot Springs, at the edge of the creek.

the covered wooden stairway leading down from the changing room/out-house and follow the moderately steep path down to the springs. It's just a couple of minutes' walk from the car.

Hot water wells up into a wooden box at the base of a retaining wall. The water has a moderate sulphur smell (nothing objectionable) and a maximum temperature of 43.4°C (110°F). The water is rich in dissolved minerals, particularly chloride and sodium, which give it a tangy mineral taste. The water flows into a rock-lined hot tub about 3 m (10 ft.) across and about a metre deep. Until a few years ago, there was a covered bath-house over one of the pools, but happily it's gone now and all the pools are open to the rain and stars.

Several rock pools, each big enough for several people to sit in, collect the outflow from the wooden pool; each is cooler than the one above. The upper pools are pleasant soaking temperatures; the lower are barely warmer than Lussier Creek. The creek itself is greenish with a slightly milky tint. On a hot day it is cool, not icy, and makes a good refresher after some time in the pools.

I enjoy these springs, and they are popular with families. They are good for small children (but keep them away from the creek). The grey of the limestone rocks and the slightly blue spring water complement each other and are soothing to the eyes. It's peaceful beside the creek, although the quiet may be broken by the roar of the occasional logging truck passing by above. The 19 steps on the walkway make this site unsuitable for wheelchairs.

Comments

Any time of the year is a good time to visit Lussier, but the pools are often a bit too cool during spring runoff. In winter, the road is sometimes closed because of snowstorms; check with the parks office in Wasa (250-422-3212) if you are unsure about road conditions.

The site tends to be very crowded on weekends. Try to get there early in the morning if you want the pools to yourself.

There is good camping in the park a few kilometres past the springs, with about one hundred campsites in six very scenic campgrounds. The campgrounds are open May through October; there is a fee. Outside the park there are numerous camping possibilities on the Lussier Forest Service road on the way to Top of the World Provincial Park and Ram Creek Hot Springs. Whiteswan and Alces lakes have good fishing, boat launch sites, and beaches for swimming. Power boats are prohibited on Alces Lake.

If you are not camping, Cranbrook, Kimberley, and Fairmont are your best bets for motels and restaurants. Fill up there or in Skookumchuck; there's no gas in Canal Flats.

Ram Creek Hot Springs

Undeveloped

Maps 17 & 20 · Colour photo, page 201

Up to 36.6°C (98°F)

Ram Creek Hot Springs are undeveloped and are a short drive east of Highway 93/95 in a small provincial government ecological reserve. They aren't as well known or popular as Lussier, and the water is warm, not hot. Because the springs are on the cool side, Ram is best in late summer when the water is at its warmest. The access roads are blocked by snow for much of the winter.

Getting There

Ram Creek isn't a big expedition; the trip is less than two hours return from Highway 93/95, four hours if you include Lussier via the back roads.

From Highway 93/95   If you are driving north on Highway 93/95, the turnoff onto Premier Lake Provincial Park (the Sheep Creek road) is about 0.5 km (0.3 mi.) north of the gas station at Skookumchuck. If you are coming from the north on 93/95, the Premier Lake turnoff is 28 km (17 mi.) south of the Kootenay River bridge at the town of Canal Flats and 23 km (14 mi.) south of the Whiteswan Lake Provincial Park turnoff.

Follow the paved Sheep Creek road. At 7.9 km (4.9 mi.) from the highway, continue straight ahead, ignoring the turnoff on the right to Premier Lake. At the next fork, in another 1.6 km (1 mi.), take the right (main) branch. Pavement ends in 0.8 km (0.5 mi.), where you turn right onto the White-Ram Forest Service road. Now follow the twisty main road. The hot spring is 21.1 km (13.1 mi.) from the highway, 0.4 km (0.2 mi.) past the yellow 11 km sign. There's good parking on the left. Driving time from the highway is about half an hour, and most cars should have no difficulty with the road.

From Lussier Hot Springs   This approach is suitable for all but very low-slung cars but is likely to be closed by snow in winter. Drive 3.4 km (2.1 mi.) east from Lussier Hot Springs to just before the park information sign and take the White-Lussier Forest Service road branching off on your right. Watch for big trucks and use headlights. The road follows the Lussier River valley, which was heavily logged in the past but has fine views of craggy peaks on either side. In 3.8 km (2.3 mi.) bear right; the left branch of the Y goes to Domtar Gypsum Mines. At a junction in

The hillside pool at Ram Creek Hot Springs.

another 4.8 km (3.0 mi.), don't go straight ahead but turn right on the main road, which crosses the creek on a wooden bridge. In 1.1 km (0.7 mi.), follow the small Top of the World Park sign and stay right on the main road. Follow the main road to a major crossroad in 6.3 km (3.9 mi.).

Take a right turn onto the White-Ram Forest Service road. (The branch straight ahead leads in about 16 km (10 mi.) to the parking lot at the entrance to Top of the World Provincial Park. This is a wilderness park with few facilities but over 40 km (25 mi.) of hiking trails.)

The road this far is excellent gravel. From here to the Ram Creek springs it is rougher but should be fine for all but very low vehicles. In about 5 km (3 mi.) you start to descend steeply into the Ram Creek valley. Ram Creek Hot Springs are about 5.8 km (3.6 mi.) from the Top of the World turnoff, where the road bends sharply left. There is good parking on the right. The 22 km (14 mi.) drive from Lussier will take about 45 minutes to an hour.

The Springs

From the parking area, walk about 75 m (250 ft.) up one of several trails to the main pools. Clear, odourless water issues from several sources beneath steep cliffs of limestone. The maximum recorded temperature is 36.6°C (98°F), and it seems to be hottest in late summer. The water has a low mineral content, mainly bicarbonate, sulphate, and calcium.

The main bathing pool is divided in two by a little stone wall. The larger and cooler pool is fed in part by overflow from the smaller pool and in part by a plastic pipe. The large pool is about 7 m (23 ft.) across and a metre deep. It is lined with limestone rocks, has a good, gravelly bottom, and comfortably holds a dozen bathers.

Many people find this pool too cool for an extended stay. The adjoining small pool is warmer and good for spending a lazy afternoon or evening. It holds about four bathers, has a clean gravel bottom, and is fed by hot water bubbling up from just above the pool. There are large rocks to sit on around this pool complex. Somebody has made a little wooden bench beside the pool, carved with such slogans as "Nudes or Prudes."

About 75 m (250 ft.) farther up the trail is another warm pool, which is small and has an unattractive, silty bottom. Some people do try it, though. Outflow from the main pools and from two other warm streams collects in several shallow pools just above the road. These are warm but filled with algae.

Comments

The path to the pools is steep and rough. With a couple of strong helpers, it might be possible to get a wheelchair to the springs. If you get that far, you will find a way to get into the pools.

The hillside setting avoids the closed-in feeling that some springs have. It is open and spacious on the south, and limestone cliffs dominate the hillside above. In summer, numerous species of wildflowers surround the springs, but the most abundant low plant near the pools is poison ivy: beware. Ram Creek Hot Springs lose something by not being right beside the main creek, but the easy access and general absence of plastic sheet and pipes make it a pleasant, low-key spot that grows on you with repeated visits.

Camping and Accommodation

Premier Lake Provincial Park has 55 tent and RV sites, open May through October; there is a camping fee in summer. This park also has excellent swimming, boating, and fishing, as well as an archaeological site. To reach the park, turn south 8.1 km (5.0 mi.) from the highway and continue 7 km (4 mi.) to the park. Whiteswan Lake Provincial Park near Lussier also has good camping. There are a few spots a switchback or so down the road from Ram Creek springs where you can camp; bring water.

If you prefer motels and restaurants, Fairmont and Kimberley have a reasonable selection. There is no gas in Canal Flats; the closest places to fill up are near Fairmont and at Skookumchuck.

Buhl Creek (Skookumchuck) Hot Springs   Undeveloped

Maps 17 & 18 • Colour photo, page 202   About 40°C (104°F)

These pleasantly warm, undeveloped springs are worth a visit in late summer if you don't mind a long drive up a logging road. The best time to visit is late summer, when the water is warmest and Skookumchuck Creek is at its lowest. At other times, the warmest pool is too cold and is flooded by the river. The area is frequented by hunters in fall, another reason to go in late summer.

Getting There
A round trip from Highway 93/95 will take about four hours. There are two ways to reach the Skookumchuck Forest Service road from Highway 93/95, depending on whether you are coming from the Canal Flats-Invermere area or from the Skookumchuck area.

From Canal Flats and North   If you are coming from Canal Flats, drive north on Highway 93/95 for 1.9 km (1.2 mi.) from the bridge over the Kootenay River at Canal Flats. Turn left onto Thunderhill Road and follow the main road across the tracks and up the hill to a junction at 4.4 km (2.7 mi.). If you are coming from Invermere or Fairmont, turn right onto the Findlay Creek (Blue Lake Forest Centre) road near the south end of Columbia Lake and drive 2.3 km (1.4 mi.) to join Thunderhill Road just before the 5 km sign. In 3.6 km (2.2 mi.), turn left onto the Skookumchuck Forest Service road. In another 9.9 km (6.1 mi.), shortly after the 17 km sign, you reach the Torrent road, where the alternate approach from Highway 93/95 meets this route.

Go straight ahead (ignoring the Torrent road). In 5.5 km (3.4 mi.) ignore the Copper Creek turnoff. Continue on for another 14.1 km (8.7 mi.) past the Bradford Creek turnoff; continue straight ahead along the north bank of Skookumchuck Creek. The road, good gravel to here, now becomes narrower and rougher.

Go past the Skookumchuck Creek recreation site (at the 43 km sign). In another 2.1 km (1.3 mi.), follow the main road across Skookumchuck Creek and then immediately make a sharp left at the 45 km sign. Go 0.2 km (0.1 mi.) along this old road to its end atop the old bridge abutment. You've arrived. The 45 km (28 mi.) drive from Canal Flats (50 km (31 mi.) from Skookumchuck) will take about an hour and 15 minutes. In wet weather the last 15 km (9.3 mi.) can be a challenge for cars: it can get very slippery.

From Skookumchuck on Highway 93/95   From Highway 93/95 just south of the bridge over the Kootenay River, turn west onto Farstad Way and drive past the Skookumchuck pulp mill. At 1.5 km (0.9 mi.) from the highway go right onto the Torrent road, and in another 1.0 km (0.6 mi.) go right (don't take the Tamarack Lake road). Follow the good gravel road for 23 km (14 mi.) to the intersection with the Skookumchuck Forest Service road; turn left and follow directions in the preceding section.

The Springs

As you drive in, you'll see a large, shallow pool on your right. This and the little ponds that drain into it are fed by tepid to cool springs and creeks. They are much favoured by green algae, frogs, insects, and snakes but don't tempt me.

The best springs are on the upstream side of the old bridge abutment. The best pool, algae-free and about 3 m (10 ft.) across by 50 cm (20 in.) deep, is right at river level (see colour photo, page 202). Warm water (about 40°C (104°F)) and gas bubble up from the clean gravel bottom. The water is clear and tasteless with just a hint of sulphur smell. It's an enjoyable pool for a quiet soak. Skookumchuck Creek is clear and very cool. There is a good swimming spot just downstream from the bridge abutments.

Comments

You can camp at the springs, at one of the Forest Service recreation sites in the area, or at any number of other spots along the way. If you need gas before you start out, you won't find it in Canal Flats.

Fairmont Hot Springs

Commercial resort

Maps 17 & 21 · Colour photo, page 203   31.5°–49°C (88.7°–120°F) at source

This is a hugely popular, modern resort on Highway 93 south of Radium Hot Springs. In addition to the commercial pools, some of the early bath-houses are still usable, making this one of the more interesting of the commercial springs described in this book.

The resort operates all year round, offering downhill skiing in the winter and hiking, golf, and other activities in the summer. Peak season (and prices) is from June through September. Summer weekends are especially crowded. November is the least busy month: golf season is about over and skiing hasn't yet started.

Getting There

The springs are close to the highway, so you can make your visit as long or as short as you wish. Driving time is about 3½ hours from Calgary, 9 hours from Vancouver, and about 4½ hours from Spokane, Washington. Fairmont is on Highway 93/95 between Canal Flats and Invermere, 112 km (70 mi.) north of Cranbrook, 33 km (20 mi.) south of the village of Radium Hot Springs. If you are coming from Calgary, follow Highway 1 to the Castle Mountain interchange, take Highway 93 to Radium, and then take 93/95 to Fairmont; total distance is about 300 km (185 mi.). The resort is well marked; turn east and drive 2 km (1.2 mi.) up the road to the parking lot.

The Springs

Hot spring water issues from two main areas. Water from the original bed of Fairmont Creek is piped to the swimming and soaking pools in the resort. The other group of springs (the "Indian Baths") is on a little knoll just north of the parking lot.

Water feeding the pools in the resort averages about 42°C (108°F). It's cooled with creek water as needed, chlorinated, and piped to the resort. All the publicly accessible pools are outdoors. Total area is about 930 m², making it the largest hot spring pool complex in Canada. The pool system has three sections. The largest is a huge swimming pool with lanes marked for swimmers and a temperature of about 30°C (86°F). There is a semi-detached diving pool at one end. A smaller section is the hottest (about 39°C (102°F)). It's too small for swimming but is good for soaking.

There is another pool reserved for those staying at the resort; it's kept at about 39°C (102°F). One visitor described the complex as "family-oriented, naturally heated swimming pools." The setting here is highly scenic, with large evergreen trees, flower gardens, and lush lawns. To the east the bare, craggy peaks of the Rocky Mountains are visible.

What really sets Fairmont apart from other commercial springs are the undeveloped *Historical Baths* (formerly called the *Indian Baths*). They are only about 100 m (330 ft.) from the resort but have a totally different character. From the wooden arch at the entrance to the parking lot, follow a trail for two minutes up and north to a small bathhouse on Emanation Hill, a bare tufa knoll. Alternatively, from the RV parking lot, go left along either of the two roads opposite the wooden washroom building.

The bathhouse has three individual bathing rooms, each with its own entrance. In each room, water is piped into a small cement bathtub and then flows out through a drain at the far end of the tub. Each room has a bench for changing and sitting, louvred windows, and a skylight. They are a bit dark, and temperature in the tubs can be anywhere from too hot to frigid. But they are free to all, are open 24 hours a day all year, and are a world apart from the huge, crowded pools below. You'll either love them or loathe them; I love them.

Hike a few metres up above the bathhouse to the flat tufa bench atop the knoll. Water issues from several sources on this bench and flows into a 1 m by 2 m (3 ft. by 6 ft.) pool dug out of the tufa. Two people can fit into this pool, or you can sit on the edge and soak your feet. There are several other shallow scoops in the tufa in this area, but nothing worth soaking in. Outflow from the bathhouse and the other springs coats the rocks with new tufa and orange, brown, green, and blue algae, giving the entire hill a colourful appearance.

The several springs on the hill are a bit hotter than those feeding the commercial pools; maximum recorded temperature is 49°C (120°F). The water is colourless, odourless, and tasteless. The high mineral content is mostly sulphate, bicarbonate, calcium, and magnesium. The water is weakly and harmlessly radioactive.

Another popular spot is reached by a trail leading downhill from the south end of the RV park. You'll find a little waterfall and pool formed by overflow from the main pools. It's a pleasant spot and you can soak for free.

The large swimming pools and landscaped grounds are popular with guests at Fairmont Hot Springs …

Facilities

The resort is fully accessible to wheelchairs, and the staff is trained in helping people with disabilities. The changing rooms are clean and well equipped, with hot showers, soap, and locking lockers. The snack bar, coffee shop, and gift shop are open to the public. The resort complex adjoining the public pools offers dining rooms, lounges, convention facilities, and rooms. Other motels and private campgrounds can be found in Fairmont and nearby Windermere and Invermere.

Rates, Hours, and Address

The pools are open year-round from 8:00 AM to 10:00 PM. Admission is $6.00 for adults and $4.00 for children between three and 12, GST included. For more information, contact:

Fairmont Hot Springs Resort
P.O. Box 10
Fairmont Hot Springs, BC V0B 1L0
250-345-6311
1-800-663-4979 (toll-free from Canada and United States)
Fax: 250-345-6616

History

In 1964, during construction of the first golf course at the resort, bulldozers unearthed numerous artifacts, now in the Windermere Museum, indicating that indigenous people had occupied this site for over 7000 years. The springs were on major trade and hunting routes and were used by both the Ktunaxa and Secwepemc for healing.

The first mention of the hot springs by white explorers was by Sir George Simpson in 1841. They were missed by the explorer David Thompson in 1807, but he did notice tufa in the vicinity. In 1885, the springs and surrounding land were granted by the Crown to John Galbraith; his wife, Sarah, named the place Fairmont, after her father's home in West Virginia. For many years, the Galbraith family made the springs freely available to all visitors. An early description of the springs was given by Susan Somerset in her 1890 book *Impressions of a Tenderfoot*:

> I started for the Hot Springs after tea. A climb over a steep trail of nearly a mile brought me to the first basin, the water of which is perfectly hot and very clear; it is eight or nine feet long, about two feet deep and four feet wide; the overflow leaves a curious rocky-looking deposit, and in the crevices of

... but the Indian Baths a couple of minutes away have few visitors.

the sandstone below quantities of maiden-hair fern grow. It is curious to see such delicate ferns growing here where the temperature is so low at night; but if one feels the ground, it proves quite warm, and must have, therefore, the same effect as a hot-bed.

On going a couple of hundred yards further and making a steep descent, I found myself by the side of a mountain stream. Another large basin had been formed here, and into it the clear water comes bubbling up boiling hot, looking like champagne, while by the side of it runs the icy cold water of the mountain stream. I felt much tempted to have a bathe, but just as I made up my mind to do so two miners appeared on the scene.

In 1923 the then-owner, Mr. William Heap Holland, from Manchester, England, diverted the hot springs in Fairmont Creek and built the first swimming pool on the site of the present pools. He also built a restaurant, a tent camp, and bungalows: the days of Fairmont as a resort centred on the hot springs had arrived. Around this time, Holland built the bathhouse on Emanation Hill; it survives unchanged today. He also built a special bath exclusively for the use of the native people and allowed them to use it free of charge.

During these years, Holland abandoned the name Fairmont in favour of Radium to emphasize the radioactive nature of the water, then in vogue as a cure-all. The post office retained the name Fairmont, however, and the ensuing confusion with Radium Hot Springs led Holland to abandon the name Radium in the late 1930s.

In 1957, the Holland family sold the resort to Earl and Lloyd Wilder and two other local businessmen, and it has remained in the Wilder family since then. The Wilder ownership has brought rapid expansion and development of the area. The first golf course was opened in 1965, and the ski hill began operation in 1969. The present pool and lodge were built from 1969 to 1972. Today Fairmont hosts roughly 500,000 visitors a year, making it the largest and most popular hot spring resort in British Columbia. *The Legacy of Fairmont Hot Springs* by Janet Wilder, published in 1989 and available at the resort, contains much information on the history of Fairmont.

Radium Hot Springs
Commercial pool

Maps 17 & 21 • Colour photo, page 204   35°–47.7°C (95°–118°F) at source

This popular, developed pool complex in Kootenay National Park is tucked under the mountains in a tight canyon right beside Highway 93. Peak season is from June through September. An hour is plenty for a quick visit, but children will want more time.

Getting There
The springs are on Highway 93, 3 km (2 mi.) east of the town of Radium Hot Springs. If you don't have a national park permit, you will have to buy a day pass for $5 at the entrance to Kootenay National Park, 1.3 km (0.8 mi.) west of the springs. From the park entrance, drive another kilometre through spectacular Sinclair Canyon to the aquacourt.

If you are coming from Calgary or Banff, follow Highway 1 to the Castle Mountain interchange and take Highway 93 to the hot springs, about 260 km (160 mi.) from Calgary. Driving time is about 3 hours from Calgary and about 1½ hours from Golden. Pull into the parking lot and walk through the underpass to the pool complex.

The Springs
There are two open-air pools, one hot and one cool. Hot water (up to 47.7°C (118°F)) emerges from four sources in the canyon of Sinclair Creek beneath the pools. At the source, the water is clear and odourless, with a low dissolved mineral content, mainly sulphate, bicarbonate, and calcium. The spring water is filtered and chlorinated. The springs are the most radioactive of any hot springs in Canada and are one of the most radioactive in North America. The radioactivity is too weak to be harmful, though.

The cool pool, a regular rectangular swimming pool, is 24 m (79 ft.) long and 1 to 3 m (3 ft. to 10 ft.) deep. Hot water is cooled with creek water to about 27°C (81°F), too cool for soaking but good for swimming laps.

The large hot pool is in a separate part of the complex from the cool pool. The water temperature is kept at a very relaxing 40°C (104°F). Depth is everywhere less than 1.5 m (5 ft.). At one end there is a gentle, sloping cement "beach" to lie on, and elsewhere there are sitting ledges in the pool. A round, concrete structure in the centre of the pool is a popular place to sit; the source of the springs is directly below this.

The hot pool fits curvaceously against the cliffs above, giving a wonderful sense of being *in* the canyon. It's all very nicely done, and sometimes you can see bighorn sheep on the ledges above the pools.

Facilities

Of all the commercial springs in Canada, Radium is most welcoming to people with disabilities. The pools and changing rooms are fully accessible to wheelchairs. A plastic wheelchair is available for use in the pools; just ask for it ahead of time. The staff are friendly and trained in helping people with disabilities. The changing rooms are clean and spacious, with baby-changing tables, hot showers, soap, and locking lockers ($0.25). Towels and swimsuits are available for rent. A massage clinic operates year-round, and a snack bar is open from May to October. The entrance lobby of the pool displays historic pictures and educational exhibits.

Accommodation and camping are available at a variety of privately operated motels across the road from the pools and in nearby Radium Hot Springs village.

The hot pool at Radium Hot Springs, where hot water wells up into the island in the middle of the pool.

The original log-cabin bathhouse at Radium, about 1925.

Rates, Hours, and Address

The pool operates year-round from 9:00 AM to 11:00 PM from late May to mid-October and from 12:00 PM to 9:00 PM the rest of the year. Hours are sometimes slightly curtailed in winter. Admission is $5.50 for adults and $5.00 for seniors and children between three and 17. Towels and suits are available for rent. For more information, contact:

Radium Hot Springs Pools
P.O. Box 40
Radium Hot Springs, BC V0A 1M0
250-347-9485
1-800-767-1611 (toll-free from Canada and United States)

History

Like the springs at Fairmont, these springs were used by the Ktunaxa people for centuries before the coming of Europeans in the 1840s. The first registered owner was an Englishman, Roland Stuart, who in 1890 purchased 65 ha (160 acres), including the springs, for $160. Little development occurred until 1911, when the first log-cabin bathhouse was built and interest was kindled in building a road from Banff to Windermere that would pass right by the springs. Construction difficulties were severe, however, and progress on the road was slow.

In 1919, the B.C. government ceded the land in the region to the federal government for use as Kootenay Dominion Park, in return for federal completion of the road. The highway, the first through the Canadian Rockies, was finally completed in 1923, the same year the government expropriated the springs and surrounding land from Roland Stuart. The pools have been operated by Parks Canada ever since.

By 1927, a new and larger bathhouse and pool had been constructed to serve the increasing numbers of visitors. The facilities were destroyed by fire in 1948, and new buildings and pools were opened in 1950. These facilities are essentially those that operate today, although there were extensive renovations in the mid-1960s.

Today up to 3000 people a day, 400,000 a year, visit the hot springs. More renovations are planned in the next few years.

OTHER SPRINGS IN THE EAST KOOTENAYS

No other hot springs are confirmed from this region. Provincial government map 82K/SE marks a hot spring near where Delphine Creek flows into Toby Creek, southwest of Invermere, but this and nearby springs are cold soda springs. There is also a rumour of a hot spring up Jumbo Creek, a large tributary of Toby Creek. Maps 82K/8 and 82K/7 would be useful for tracking these down.

The *Geothermal Resources of British Columbia* map (see References) shows a spring called Mutton Creek but gives no precise location, temperature, or other details. The only Mutton Creek in the region is 2 km (1 mi.) northeast of Lussier Hot Springs. Possibly this name is a pseudonym for Lussier or an old name for Ram Creek, but it might also be a separate spring. The topographic map of the area is 82J/4. There is an old trail up the east side of Mutton Creek; a hike up this trail might turn up something.

Red Rock Cool Springs

Undeveloped

Maps 17, 20 & 21

About 20°C (68°F)

The best feature of these springs is the beautiful setting beside the Kootenay River. From Highway 93/95, turn into Canal Flats immediately north of the bridge over the Kootenay River (about 4.7 km (2.9 mi.) north of the Whiteswan turnoff to Lussier Hot Springs). Follow the main road for 1.3 km (0.8 mi.) and turn right onto an excellent gravel road across from McGrath Avenue, opposite the firehall. Almost immediately, turn left onto the Kootenay River Forest Service road. Use headlights and beware of logging trucks. At 9.4 km (5.8 mi.) from the firehall, stay left; the right branch crosses the Kootenay River. In 5.1 km (3.1 mi.), the road passes close to the river under a large, reddish cliff.

The springs issue from the sand and gravel river bank just beneath the road. There are no permanent bathing pools, partly because the water is too cool and partly because the Kootenay River would wash them away every spring and fall. The water contains much dissolved gas, and at low river levels the bubbles make the surface of the water look like freshly poured ginger ale. The temperature is about 20°C (68°F); the water is colourless, odourless, and tasteless. The depth is about 50 cm (20 in.), and the water contains a small amount of green algae. The water forms a small creek that flows directly into the Kootenay River. At high water this spring is completely flooded by the Kootenay River.

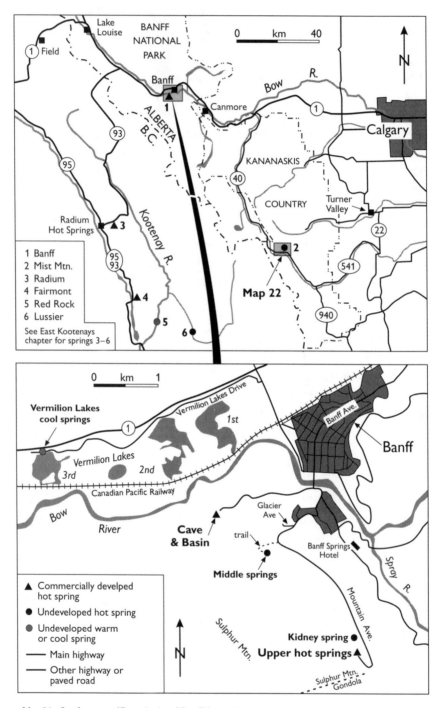

Map 21. Southwestern Alberta (top) and Banff (bottom)

CHAPTER 7

Banff and Kananaskis

The springs described in this chapter are in two areas on the east side of the Rocky Mountains west and southwest of Calgary. The hot springs near the town of Banff led to the creation of Banff National Park, Canada's first national park, and they are among the best known in Canada. In contrast, the Mist Mountain warm springs in Kananaskis Country are among the most obscure in Canada.

Banff is one of the most popular tourist destinations in Canada, certainly the most popular in the Canadian Rockies. For many visitors to Canada, the town of Banff is one of the "must-see" spots. The scenery is spectacular. The possibilities for hiking, skiing, and other outdoor activities in the surrounding park are equally spectacular, although only a small fraction of the visitors take advantage of them.

The town of Banff is about a 1½ hour drive from Calgary, Radium Hot Springs, and Golden, depending on weather and road conditions. There are many motels, hotels, bed-and-breakfasts, and campgrounds in and around Banff, but from June through September these fill up quickly. You might try Canmore just east of the park boundary. For information about accommodation and activities in and around Banff townsite, contact:

Banff Visitor Centre
224 Banff Avenue,
Banff, AB T0L 0C0
403-762-1550

The hot springs at Banff are south and southwest of town on the flanks of Sulphur Mountain. They are: the Upper hot springs (a commercially developed pool), the Cave and Basin hot springs (developed, but there is no longer any swimming), and the Kidney and Middle warm springs (undeveloped). You can easily visit all of them in an afternoon. There is also a cool spring beside one of the Vermilion Lakes west of town. Upper hot springs and Cave and Basin are open year-round, and the Middle and Kidney springs are just short walks from the road.

Kananaskis Country is the term used for the Rocky Mountains and foothills southwest of Calgary. The area has excellent hiking, camping, swimming, and fishing and is far less crowded than Banff National Park. For information on camping, accommodation, and recreational activities, contact:

Kananaskis Village Centre
403-591-7555

or stop at the Tourism Information Centre on Highway 4, 6 km (4 mi.) south of Highway 1 (phone 403-678-5277).

Much has been written about the history, both natural and human, of the Banff area. Ben Gadd's *Handbook of the Canadian Rockies* (see References) is an excellent introduction to the natural history of the area. For detailed descriptions of the springs around Banff, R.O. van Everingen's *Thermal and Mineral Springs in the Southern Rocky Mountains of Canada* (see References) has no equal.

Cave and Basin Hot Springs

Commercial display

Map 21

28°–35°C (82°–95°F)

These, the first hot springs developed at Banff, are in many ways the most interesting, even though the swimming pool that was open to the public for many years is now closed. The historical and natural history exhibits are excellent and are open all year round. To get there, drive through Banff townsite and across the Bow River on Banff Avenue. Turn right at the traffic light just past the river and follow the paved road 1.3 km (0.8 mi.) to the parking lot.

The Springs

There are four springs here. The main attractions, the Cave and Basin springs, are in the building. Two smaller springs are visible on the Discovery Trail above the Cave and Basin.

You reach the *Cave spring* through a tunnel about 9 m (30 ft.) long leading from the lobby of the building past the cashier. The cave is roughly circular, about 12 m (40 ft.) across and 6 m (20 ft.) high. Although it is artificially lit, a bit of daylight filters through a hole in the roof. This hole was the only means of access until the tunnel was blasted through in 1887.

Most of the interior of the cave is filled with a circular pool. People haven't been allowed into the pool for many years, but it's interesting to look at. Spring water bubbles up from the bottom of the pool and also flows in from a little stream at the back of the cave. Maximum water temperature is about 31°C (88°F), and the water has a strong sulphur odour. The mineral content is moderately high, mostly sulphate, calcium, bicarbonate, and magnesium. Originally the ceiling of the cave was decorated with a rich collection of stalactites formed by minerals deposited from the springs, but these were long ago snapped off by souvenir hunters.

The *Basin spring* is at the west end of the aquacourt; you can get an excellent view of it from the observation deck above. This was the original bathing pool at Banff, but swimming has been prohibited since 1971 because the water couldn't be properly chlorinated. It's too bad, because the pool looks inviting. The water is warm, blue, and clear, with water and gas bubbling from the bottom. The pool, about 8 m by 12 m (25 ft. by 40 ft.), is partly walled with cement, but the steep rock wall at the back is largely

The Basin spring, in probably the late 1920s.

unchanged since the earliest photos were taken in the 1890s. The water is warmer than that of the Cave spring, reaching about 35°C (95°F). The mineral constituents are similar to those of the cave water, but concentrations are about double.

The building also hosts various exhibits and displays, including one on the origin of the springs, a small gift shop, and a little coffee shop. Outside the building, the large concrete pool of the aquacourt, now empty of people, was once fed by water from the Cave and Basin springs. The supply was supplemented as needed by water from two small springs (the Pool springs) on the slopes above the building. A small fountain in the middle of the pool breaks up the empty expanse of concrete.

The Discovery Trail, a good wooden boardwalk reached by stairs just outside the building entrance, takes you to the *Pool springs*. The walk takes about 15 minutes return and is well worth the time. There are informative signs along the way telling much about the human history and natural history of the springs and the uses of the spring water. At one point you can look down through the hole at the top of the cave, through which people used to lower themselves into the pool. Today the hole is covered with wire mesh, but you can still see people below. The warm (29° to

32°C (84° to 90°F)) spring at the end of the boardwalk is notable for its beautiful purple algae.

The Marsh Trail is another short walk well worth the effort. The boardwalk starts below the aquacourt and loops across the swampy area between the hot springs and the Bow River. This walk features tropical fish, of all things. Outflow from all the Cave and Basin springs mixes with swamp water here and keeps the water warm (for Banff) all year round. Over the years people have introduced various species of fish, including guppies, into the marsh. Today, the mosquitofish and sailfin molly, native to the Gulf of Mexico region, and jewelfish, native to Africa, are present year-round. You can often see these fish from the viewing platform, and the interpretive signs give more details on the plant and animal life here. There's a bird blind at the end of the trail; it's a good place to sit and watch waterfowl. Park naturalists offer free, informative tours of Discovery and Marsh trails several times a day.

Exhibits inside the building are fully wheelchair accessible, and the Discovery and Marsh trails are largely wheelchair accessible.

The Basin spring today. The bathhouse and bathers are gone, but the pool itself hasn't changed much since the 1920s.

Rates, Hours, and Address

The facility is open daily from 9:00 AM to 6:00 PM from June through Labour Day. Hours are somewhat shorter in the winter. Admission to the building, cave, basin, and exhibits is worth the modest admission fee. The Discovery and Marsh trails are free. For information, contact:

Cave and Basin National Historic Site
311 Cave Avenue
P.O. Box 900
Banff, AB T0L 0C0
403-762-1556
Fax: 403-762-1565

Comments

In 1996, biologists began serious study of the life in the springs. They are particularly interested in an inconspicuous little snail, the Banff Springs Snail (*Physella johnsoni*) that is found nowhere else in the world. Unlike the tropical fish seen on the Marsh Trail, the snails are native to the springs. They seem to cling to algae mats at the water's edge and probably feed on the algae.

The snails were first recognized as a distinct species in 1926, when they lived in nine of the spring sources at Banff. Today, they are found only in one of the Middle springs and four of the springs at the Cave and Basin site. This snail is the most at-risk wildlife species in Banff National Park, and is classified as "threatened."

The threat comes, of course, from human activity. Illegal swimming and bathing create waves, breaking up the algae mats that the snails need to survive. Partly for this reason, all springs at the Cave and Basin, and the Middle Springs, are closed to bathing and even hand-dipping. Parks Canada is vigorously prosecuting those who disobey the closures, and early in 1999, the courts handed stiff fines to a group of trespassers.

History

Native people certainly used these springs long before Europeans arrived. Each group had its own name for them. For example, the Blackfoot name for the site of Banff townsite is Nato-oh-sis-koom, meaning "holy springs."

(Banff was named by Lord Strathcona, one of the chief promoters of the Canadian Pacific Railway, after his birthplace, Banff, Scotland.)

Europeans first became aware of the springs in 1859. They didn't attract much attention until 1883, when several men involved in construction of the Canadian Pacific Railway "discovered" the Basin spring and climbed down into it. They built a small cabin by the spring and used it through the winter of 1883–1884.

In 1885, one of the workmen, Frank McCabe, applied for title to the springs on behalf of himself and several others. Much legal wrangling ensued over conflicting claims and over who actually had found the springs first. The Deputy Minister of the Department of the Interior, A.M. Burgess (for whom the world-famous Burgess Shale is named), was in favour of keeping the springs out of private hands. In November 1885, the same month that the CPR was completed, Ottawa set aside the Banff springs and surrounding land as a park reserve.

Following legal surveys and payment of compensation to those claiming rights to the springs, Banff National Park was formally created in 1887. This was Canada's first national park and only the third in the world (after Yellowstone in Wyoming, founded in 1872 to protect its hot springs and geysers, and Royal National Park in Australia, established a few years later). Thus, one of the largest park systems in the world sprang from bickering over ownership of the Cave and Basin hot springs.

In 1887, the government built bathhouses at the Cave and Basin pools; these were renovated and expanded in 1903. The present swimming pool opened in 1914. At that time it was the largest swimming pool in Canada. For many years bathing was allowed in both the Cave and Basin pools, but by 1976 these were closed and only the swimming pool remained open.

In 1993 the swimming pool was closed, partly because the foundations and concrete of the pool were deteriorating, partly because attendance and revenues were decreasing, and partly because Parks Canada policy shifted its emphasis from recreation to preservation and education.

Upper Hot Springs

Commercial pool

Map 21 · Colour photo, page 205

29°–47.3°C (84°–117°F) at source

This commercially developed pool on the slopes of Sulphur Mountain is probably the most popular hot spring in the Canadian Rockies. The spring is the warmest at Banff, and the pool is open daily all year round.

Drive through Banff townsite and across the Bow River on Banff Avenue. Turn left at the traffic light just across the river and follow the signs and paved road (Mountain Avenue) 3.6 km (2.2 mi.) to the parking lot just below the pool complex.

The Springs and Facilities

The source of the spring water is enclosed in a small structure just above the pool building. The water is piped to the building, where it is chlorinated and filtered before going to the swimming pool. At its source, the water has a mild sulphur smell and a much higher content of dissolved sulphate, calcium, bicarbonate, and magnesium than the Cave and Basin springs. Temperature fluctuates greatly throughout the year. Maximum temperature (about 41°C (106°F)) is in late fall and winter. The water is coolest (about 33°C (91°F)) during spring runoff. Maximum and minimum recorded temperatures are 47.3°C (117°F) and about 29°C (84°F), respectively. When the temperature is very low, the water is heated slightly before going to the pool. Runoff from the spring flows over a little brick wall beside the driveway and has formed an extensive orange tufa bench between the driveway and Mountain Avenue.

The pool is outdoors in a spectacular forest setting looking down the Bow Valley and across to Mt. Rundle, which dominates the view above Banff. The pool is irregularly shaped; water is an eye-pleasing blue and averages about 40°C (104°F). The pool is drained and cleaned every night and fills in about seven hours, in time for the next day's crowd.

The pool and facilities are accessible to wheelchairs. Change rooms are clean and have warm showers with soap, blow dryers, and locking lockers ($0.25). For those who would rather watch than swim, there are nice benches and pleasant sitting areas above the pool, where you can look down into the pool. The building has a small exhibit of historic photos, a gift shop, and a small restaurant. A spa features a steam room, massage, hot plunge baths, and aromatherapy sweat wraps.

Upper hot springs at Banff with a view across the Spray River to Mt. Rundle.

Rates and Hours

From mid-June to mid-September pool hours are 9:00 AM to 11:00 PM. The rest of the year, the hours are from 10:00 AM to 11:00 PM on Friday and Saturday and 10:00 AM to 10:00 PM from Sunday through Thursday. Admission is $7.00 for adults, $6.00 for children and seniors. Rates are lower in the winter season. Towels and suits are available for rent. A visit to the spa costs $30. For more information, phone:

> 1-800-767-1611 (toll-free from Canada and United States) or
> 403-762-1515
> Fax: 403-760-1347

History

The springs were first seen by Europeans in 1881, and the first log shack bathhouse was built in 1886. By 1900, the water was used by several establishments. Water was piped to a privately owned bathhouse and hotel near the site of the present pool building. Water also went down the hillside to Banff Springs Hotel, which opened in 1888, and to Dr. Brett's sanatorium, near the bridge across the Bow River. In general, the Upper springs were thought to have greater curative powers than the other springs, probably because of their higher temperature and mineral content, but the Cave and Basin springs were favoured for recreational bathing.

In 1905, a new government bathhouse was opened where the Rimrock Hotel stands today, after fire had destroyed the previous one. The present facilities were built in 1932 to accommodate the growing number of visitors, and the interior was renovated in 1961. In 1995 and 1996, facilities were extensively renovated. In 1992, about 330,000 people used the facilities, down from over 400,000 in 1985. Whether this decline will continue remains to be seen, but the spring continues to be one of Banff's best known and most popular attractions.

Kidney Spring

Undeveloped

Map 21

Up to 39°C (102°F)

This small, undeveloped spring is a short walk below the Upper springs. From the parking lot for the Upper springs, walk down Mountain Avenue about 50 m (160 ft.) past the Rimrock Hotel to a No Parking sign on the left (uphill) side of the road. There is a steep dirt bank of eroded tufa deposits behind the sign. Just right of this bank, follow a faint trail and old pipes up to an open meadow immediately below the spring. The source is about 30 m (100 ft.) above the road and a walk of just a couple of minutes from the Upper springs parking lot.

The warm water flows from a tufa bank into a cement cistern. The cistern is just the right size for one person. It's seldom used, but if it isn't full of algae, it offers highly satisfying soaking. Chemically, the water is similar to that of the Upper springs, but the rate of flow is much smaller. It has a moderate sulphur smell and hosts stringy colonies of white algae and a few patches of yellow, sulphur-loving bacteria. The cistern and old pipes visible near the road date from before 1927, when the water was piped to a swimming pool at the Banff Springs Hotel.

The small pool, a perfect size for one person, at the Kidney spring.

Middle Springs

Undeveloped

Map 21

35°C (95°F)

These warm springs on the hillside between the Cave and Basin and Upper springs are undeveloped and are largely in their natural state. Although they are marked on many of the tourist maps, they are now off-limit to the public, for reasons discussed below. Access to the springs was formerly by a short trail that took off from Mountain Avenue about 0.5 km (0.3 mi) past Glacier Drive.

The main spring flows out of a low cave at the base of a horseshoe-shaped tufa cliff. Another spring, somewhat cooler, flows from the ground just outside the cave. The entrance is on the left side. The cave, in a large tufa deposit, is about 4 m by 3 m (13 ft. by 10 ft.) and up to 3 m (10 ft.) high (mostly less). There is a pool in it; warm water and gas bubble up from the bottom of the pool.

The Middle springs are cooler than the other main Banff springs: maximum temperature is about 35°C (95°). Mineral content of the water is similar to that of the Upper and Kidney springs. The water has a strong sulphur smell and mineral taste. The spring water forms a little warm stream outside the cave that runs over a flat tufa bench covered with lush vegetation. The algae and bacteria growth is quite spectacular here, with white and brilliant green predominating. During the winter, the spring is popular with deer.

At one time, water from these springs was piped to the Banff Springs Hotel. Since then, these springs have been largely ignored, visited only by a few people who wanted a quiet and free soak. In the early 1990s, though, the springs became a popular party spot, and the resulting vandalism, deposits of trash, and water contamination led Parks Canada to close the springs to bathing in August 1995. The "threatened" status of the Banff Springs Snail, which lives in the warmest of the Middle springs, gave another and more compelling reason to keep the springs closed to bathing. Since November 1997, the springs and the approach trail have been part of the Middle Springs Wildlife Corridor. This corridor, a band of forest above Mountain Avenue, was established to allow large mammals to get from one side of the Bow Valley to the other and to safely bypass the town of Banff. Some people may think that closing the area to the public is unjustified, but, to me, preservation of biodiversity and species habitat far outweigh the mediocre soaking that is lost.

Vermilion Lakes Cool Springs

Undeveloped

Map 21

19.7°C (67°F)

These springs are right beside the road on the shore of Third Vermilion Lake. They are too small and cool to bathe in but are included for the curious.

From Banff, head out of town along Mt. Norquay Road. Just before reaching Highway 1, turn left along Vermilion Lakes Drive. Follow this paved road for 4 km (2.5 mi.) to a small float and a sign marking Third Vermilion Lake. Just past the sign and float, lukewarm water issues from under the road on the north (highway) side. The water follows the road for a few metres before flowing through a culvert into the lake. The water is tasteless, has a mild sulphur smell, and reaches a temperature of close to 20°C (68°F). White, green, and brown algae are abundant here. The best thing about this spot is the great view across the lake to Mt. Rundle and Sulphur Mountain.

Mist Mountain Hot Spring

Undeveloped

Maps 17, 21 & 22

33°C (91°F)

A seldom-visited spring that is a bit cool for extended soaking, Mist Mountain hot spring sits high on the side of Mist Mountain in Kananaskis Country southeast of Banff. It's for experienced back-country hikers only, because the approach is long and there is no trail. The area is raked by avalanches from late fall to early spring, so do this trip in summer or early fall. Good weather is essential.

Getting There

A visit to this spring will take a full day from Calgary or Banff. Round-trip hiking time from the road is about six hours. The Kananaskis Trail (Highway 40) leaves Highway 1 about 50 km (31 mi.) east of Banff and 70 km (43 mi.) west of Calgary. Drive south on the paved highway to Highwood Pass, about 74 km (46 mi.) from Highway 1. About 17 km (10.5 mi.) beyond the pass, you will reach the clearly marked Mist Creek recreation site. Make a U-turn here and park beside the road 0.8 km (0.5 mi.) back along the highway.

Look for an old road in the trees east of the highway. Hike a short distance along it to a junction; go right and follow the road uphill to its end. Climb steeply through bush and timber to treeline at the base of a steep, grassy slope (slippery when wet). Continue up to the crest of the ridge, locally known as Eagle Ridge. Follow the ridge crest northwest for about 1.5 km (0.9 mi.) to its summit and then drop west down a steep, grassy slope to the col between Eagle Ridge and Mist Mountain.

From the col, you can see the spring across the valley that drains the southeast side of Mist Mountain. Look for a creek that comes from brown rocks above timberline and just below a big cliff. The spring is at the head of the creek at about the same elevation as the col, roughly 2470 m (8100 ft.). To reach the spring from the col, contour west over scree, rock, and meadows.

The Spring

The spring is at the top of a long, narrow scree gully. Warm water flows from the rocks at a rate of about 50 litres a minute into a pool about a metre across. There are no tufa deposits, but the water contains abundant orange and brown algae that coat the surrounding rocks.

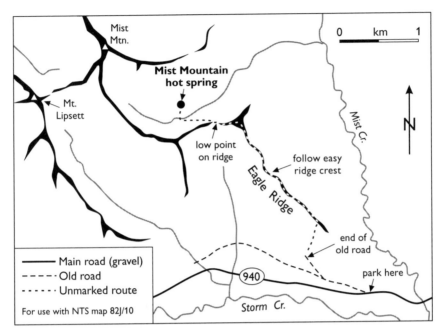

Map 22. The approach route to Mist Mountain hot spring

Comments

Take good hiking boots and NTS map 82J/10 on this trip. The spring is at UTM grid reference 492012 on this map. A pair of binoculars is handy for spotting the spring from the top of Eagle Ridge and the col. The walk along Eagle Ridge is easy and gives excellent views of the Highwood valley and surrounding mountains. Mist Mountain, one of the highest peaks in the region, dominates the view to the northwest like a giant obelisk. Gillean Daffern's guidebook, *Kananaskis Country Trail Guide* (Calgary: Rocky Mountain Books, 1985), has good descriptions of the Eagle Ridge hike and other excursions in the area. The 1996 edition of the guide omits this hike.

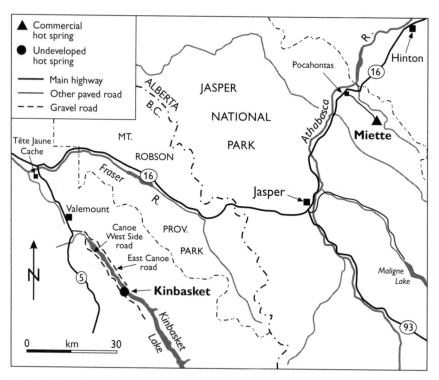

Map 23. Hot springs near Jasper and Valemount

CHAPTER 8

Jasper and Valemount

The two springs described in this chapter are not far off Highway 16, the Yellowhead Highway. Miette is a popular, commercially developed hot spring in Jasper National Park, on the east side of the Rocky Mountains. The other, Kinbasket, is an undeveloped, usually flooded spring near Valemount in British Columbia, west of the Rockies.

Valemount is on Highway 5 about 20 km (12 mi.) south of Tête Jaune Cache just south of Highway 16. It's about 320 km (200 mi.) north of Kamloops, 275 km (170 mi.) east of Prince George, and 700 km (435 mi.) from Vancouver. Jasper, Alberta, is 100 km (60 mi.) east of Valemount on Highway 16. It's about 290 very scenic kilometres (180 mi.) to Banff, 360 km (225 mi.) to Edmonton, and about 800 km (500 mi.) to Vancouver.

The main towns near the springs, Jasper and Valemount, are about an hour's drive apart. Jasper, centre of the largest of Canada's Rocky Mountain parks, is similar to Banff in that it depends largely on tourism, skiing, and Parks Canada administration. Jasper, however, is a prettier, more spacious town than Banff and always seems less crowded. Valemount is a utilitarian town that offers boating, fishing, mountaineering, hiking, excellent bird-watching, and many other outdoor activities.

Miette Hotsprings

Commercial pool

Map 23 · Colour photo, page 206   46°–55°C (115°–131°F) at source

Miette is the only hot spring in Jasper National Park and the hottest in Canada's Rocky Mountain parks. Because it's accessible by car it is popular with tourists. The development is tastefully done, and the setting in the eastern part of the Rocky Mountains is spectacular. The spring is a bit off the main tourist track, keeping the crowds down and giving it a low-key feel compared with Banff.

The spring is open seven days a week from about May 20 into early October. The dates vary slightly from year to year, depending on weather and snow; check with the park administration if you are visiting near the beginning or end of the season. July and August are the most crowded months. In September, most tourists have gone and the weather is often fine.

Getting There

A visit to Miette makes a nice afternoon outing from Jasper. You can reach Pocahontas, Alberta, on Highway 16 by driving 46 km (28 mi.) east from Jasper or 33 km (20 mi.) west from Hinton. The hot springs are 17 km (10.6 mi.) south of Highway 16 along a good paved road. Be sure to stop at the viewpoint overlooking the Fiddle River and the limestone walls of Ashlar Ridge. Driving time to the springs is about an hour from Jasper and about 45 minutes from Hinton.

The Springs

Three hot springs issue from along the bank of Sulphur Creek and are piped to the soaking pools. The bathing facilities are housed in a utilitarian building above a large parking lot. There are two swimming pools, both about 10 m by 20 m (30 ft. by 60 ft.) and both kept around 40°C (104°F). One of the pools has a depth of 1 m (3 ft.) everywhere; the other varies from 1 m to 1.5 m (3 ft. to 5 ft.) deep. The water is chlorinated and filtered. Both pools contain benches to sit on. These pools are not designed for those wishing to swim laps, but they are very popular with families.

After your soak, don't miss the short walk to the source of the hot springs. From the upstream end of the parking and picnic area, follow a wide, paved trail that goes down to and across Sulphur Creek and continues upstream along the ravine. In a couple of hundred metres, you

Hot Springs Cove, where hot water mixes with the ocean to produce the perfect soaking temperature, on the west coast of Vancouver Island, page 72

A hot waterfall fringed by lush ferns and moss at the main hot spring at Sloquet hot springs, in the Lower Mainland of B.C., page 53

The soaking pools at Sloquet hot springs, with Sloquet Creek rushing past, in the Lower Mainland of B.C., page 53

The rustic hot tubs at Clear Creek hot springs, near Harrison Lake, in the Lower Mainland of B.C., page 62

The hotel and hot pool at Harrison Hot Springs Hotel, in the Lower Mainland of B.C., page 58

The large outdoor swimming pool at Harrison Hot Springs Hotel, page 58

Scenic hot springs, on a steep hillside far above the highway, in northwestern Washington, page 90

The main pool at Ainsworth Hot Springs, with a view over Kootenay Lake, in the West Kootenays, page 109

Twilight at Halcyon Hot Springs, on Upper Arrow Lake, in the West Kootenays, page 130

The large circular pool at Nakusp Hot Springs, including a small, very hot section on the right, in the West Kootenays, page 117

Brilliant, multi-coloured algae and tufa deposits at Dewar Creek hot springs, in the East Kootenays, page 142

Ram Creek Hot Springs, in the southwestern Rocky Mountains, in the East Kootenays,
page 158

Lussier Hot Springs, in Whiteswan Lake Provincial Park, in the East Kootenays, page 155

One of the pools at Buhl Creek hot springs, in the East Kootenays, page 162

One of several large pools at Fairmont Hot Springs Resort, in the East Kootenays, page 164

The hot pool at Radium Hot Springs, by the cliffs of Sinclair Canyon, in Kootenay National Park, page 169

The pool at Upper hot springs, on the slope of Sulphur Mountain above the town of Banff, in Banff National Park, page 182

Miette Hotsprings and limestone crags of the Rocky Mountains, in Jasper National Park, page 192

One of the beachside pools on Hotspring Island, in Gwaii Haanas National Park Reserve, on the Queen Charlotte Islands, page 236

Liard Hot Springs, on the Alaska Highway, in northeastern B.C., page 246

Atlin warm springs, in northwestern B.C., page 260

The hot pools at McArthur hot springs, in the Yukon Territory, page 267

Lukewarm ponds on giant tufa mounds at Rabbitkettle Hotsprings, in Nahanni National Park, in the Northwest Territories, page 272

reach the remains of the old aquacourt. All that is left are some decaying concrete walls and a flat area, grassy and treed, that was once the main pool. One of the three springs (temperature about 46° to 49°C (115° to 120°F)) is situated beneath the aquacourt. Water is piped from there to the present-day pools. There is another spring on the west side of the creek upstream from the aquacourt; it's largely hidden underground now and piped to the pools. To see the third and hottest spring, continue up the trail on a wooden boardwalk to where it crosses the creek. Total walking time from the parking lot is an easy 10 minutes. Above the creek, you can see hot water issuing from cracks in the bedrock. It flows into an open cement basin from where it is piped to the pools. The water reaches about 55°C (131°F) and has a strong sulphur smell and taste. It's rich in dissolved minerals, mainly sulphate, calcium, and bicarbonate.

Facilities
The building and changing facilities are accessible by wheelchair, and one of the bathing pools has a wheelchair ramp leading down into it. The changing rooms are clean. Both men's and women's have cubicles for changing, hot and cold showers, sinks with mirrors, soap, and locking lockers. Visitors with disabilities may park close to the entrance to the building.

A café serves cappuccino and light lunches, and there is a restaurant at the motel just before the parking lot. Or you can dine *al fresco* at one of the picnic tables in the trees by the parking lot. Bighorn sheep, deer, squirrels, and assorted birds are regular visitors to the picnic area.

Self-guided interpretive displays and walks will give you a better understanding of the history, natural and otherwise, of the hot springs and surrounding area. Several moderately strenuous hikes start at the hot springs. Check the posted maps for details. If you plan to take an extended hike, NTS map 83F/4 covers the area and shows the locations of the hot springs.

Rates, Hours, and Address
The pools are open from about mid-May through Thanksgiving. Hours are from 8:30 AM to 10:30 PM from mid-June to Labour Day and from 10:30 AM to 9:00 PM the rest of the season. Admission to the pools is $5.50 for adults, $5.00 for children and seniors. Towels and bathing suits are available for rent. For information, contact:

Jasper National Park
P.O. Box 2579
Jasper, AB T0E 1E0
403-866-3939
1-800-767-1611 (toll-free from Canada and United States)

There is some commercial accommodation near the springs and at Pocahontas. Jasper has many motels, but they fill up quickly in the summer. Hinton, outside the park, is less attractive but often has vacancies long after Jasper is full. There are many campsites in the park; check with any tourist information booth for information on availability. For help finding accommodation, try:

Parks Canada Information Centre in Jasper: 403-852-6176
Jasper Tourism and Commerce in Jasper: 403-852-3858

History

In contrast to the springs in Banff National Park, little is known of the early history and use of Miette Hotsprings. It seems certain, however, that they were known to early fur traders, given the intense exploration of the region by members of the Hudson's Bay and Northwest companies in the 19th century.

The coal-mining and construction town of Pocahontas sprang up in 1909, and proposals to build a sanatorium at the hot springs were soon made to the superintendent of parks. Lack of road access deterred any large-scale development, but a small stream of people made their way up the horse trail from Pocahontas to the squalid and primitive facilities at the springs. The trip was not for the unfit: several people died along the trail from the unaccustomed exercise.

In 1932, a road from Pocahontas to the springs was opened to the public at certain times. The old, now-ruined, aquacourt was built from 1936 to 1938, and the road was upgraded. The new facilities were a vast improvement over the previous log pools and canvas tents. During the war years, use was restricted to those with a doctor's certificate, but full public access resumed in 1945.

In 1984, the aquacourt was permanently closed because of unstable slopes above, rotting concrete, and aging equipment, and the present facilities were opened in 1986. Today Miette sees about 100,000 visitors a year, far fewer than the more famous Banff springs. It remains a quiet, friendly spot.

The pools at Miette Hot Springs.

Kinbasket Lake (Canoe River) Hot Springs Undeveloped, flooded

Map 23   44°–60°C (111°–140°F)

These undeveloped springs in the Rocky Mountain Trench south of Vale-mount were, unfortunately, a casualty of the Mica Dam hydroelectric project. They are covered by Kinbasket Lake for all but a brief period each year.

Since 1973, when the Mica Dam was built, these springs have been under many metres of lake water for most of the year. They are accessible for a few weeks when the lake is at its lowest level, usually in late winter and early spring before spring runoff causes the lake to rise towards its maximum.

Getting There

This trip is an easy afternoon outing from Valemount. Drive 3.7 km (2.3 mi.) south from Valemount on Highway 5 to the Cedarside Road turnoff (just after the small Kinbasket Lake signs on Highway 5). Turn left (east) onto Cedarside and follow the paved road as it turns sharply left again and parallels the highway for a short distance before turning right. Continue on the pavement to an intersection just past the railway tracks (2.0 km (1.2 mi.) from Highway 5). Go straight through the intersection and follow the wide gravel road for 5.1 km (3.1 mi.) and turn sharply right onto the Canoe West Side Forest Service road. This is an active logging road, so watch for logging trucks and use your headlights. Distances given by the kilometre signs beside the road begin at this junction. The drive down the west side road gives good views of Kinbasket Lake and the Rocky Mountains beyond.

The springs are at the lake shore (or beneath the lake) below the 26 km marker, about a 45 minute drive from Highway 5. There's a good pullout and parking by a small creek about 100 m (330 ft.) past the marker. There is no trail to the lake shore. The best approach is to walk south along the logging road for another 100 m (330 ft.) and then head down into the overgrown logging slash. It's about a 20 minute bushwhack to the shore; walk back north along the shore to the springs.

For a longer but more attractive approach, you can walk several kilometres along the shore to the springs. Just after the 22 km marker on the logging road, take a side road on the left that drops steeply to a log dump on the lake. Hike south along the lake shore for about 3 km (2 mi.) until you find the springs. The walk is easy (gravel and boulders), but there is one creek to cross.

If you have a boat, another possibility is to drive 22 km (13 mi.) down the East Canoe Forest Service road to Canoe Reach Marina, which has a concrete boat ramp. Kinbasket Lake has many deadheads and is subject to strong, sudden winds.

The Springs

Before flooding, this spring was reportedly a four-star soak. When I visited the area, the springs were under many metres of lake water. Three sources are reported close together, with water temperatures ranging from 44° to 60°C (111° to 140°F) and a fairly substantial combined flow rate of about 150 litres per minute. Water is reputedly tasteless, with a slight sulphur smell.

Comments

These springs are on Crown land (and water). The logging roads, although public, are heavily used by logging companies. The B.C. Forest Service recreation map for the Robson Valley Forest District (free from Forest Service offices or the Information Centre in Valemount) shows the logging roads and Forest Service campsites in the area. Valemount has abundant motels and restaurants and is a good base for exploring the area.

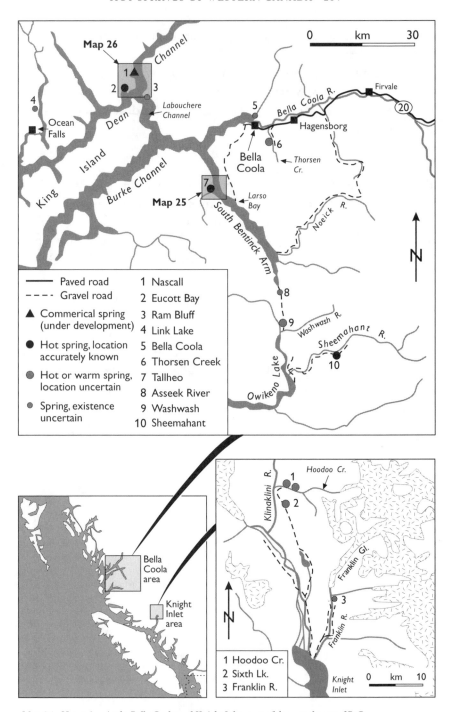

Map 24. Hot springs in the Bella Coola and Knight Inlet areas of the central coast of B.C.

CHAPTER 9

Central Coast

This chapter describes a group of undeveloped hot springs near Bella Coola and Ocean Falls and gives what little information I have about springs near the head of Knight Inlet. More effort is needed to reach these springs than most others in the southern part of the province. You can't drive to any of them, and for most you need boat or plane transport. Several require substantial hiking to reach. You can enjoy the springs on the shoreline at any time of the year; the others should be visited in the summer, when the logging camps are operating and snow is gone from the logging roads.

If you don't have your own boat, it will be expensive to reach most springs near Bella Coola. Fishing charters are available in Bella Coola, but you might find it cheaper to ask around on the dock and see if anyone is going your way and is willing to give you a ride there and back. Alternatively, Wilderness Airlines in Bella Coola runs scheduled and charter service to various points in the area and may be willing to drop you near the spring of your choice; phone 604-276-2635 for rates and information. Vancouver Island Helicopters in Bella Coola is another, more expensive possibility for charter flights; phone 250-982-2425 for information.

Knight Inlet Hot Springs

Undeveloped

Map 24

58°C (?) (136°F)

Several hot springs have been reported in the region near the head of Knight Inlet. They have eluded most searchers, including me, largely because of the difficult access. You can reach the main logging camp at the head of Knight Inlet by scheduled or charter air service from Campbell River on Vancouver Island; phone CoVal Air (250-287-8371) or Western Straits (250-923-8143) in Campbell River for rates and schedules.

The main logging camp is on the east side of the Klinaklini River, about 3 km (2 mi.) from the dock at the head of Knight Inlet. The main logging road follows the east side of the Klinaklini River valley and passes a series of lakes, of which the third and largest is Devereux Lake. There is a hot spring on the east side of Canyon Lake, locally known as Sixth Lake, about 27 km (17 mi.) from tidewater. From near the south end of Canyon Lake, take a side road that runs along the east side of the lake. The springs flow into Canyon Lake near its southeast end. A large flow of hot water (58°C (136°F)) seeps from the ground at various places, collects into a small stream, and flows into Canyon Lake near its southeast end. These springs are reportedly not very good for soaking.

Better springs are reportedly present on Hoodoo Creek, about 4 km (2.5 mi.) farther up the road from Canyon Lake. They are about 1.5 and 6.5 km (0.9 and 4.0 mi.) up the north side of Hoodoo Creek and are visible from the bank of the creek.

Another spring has been reported up the Franklin River, but I don't know anybody who has seen it. If you feel adventurous and are thoroughly experienced in wilderness travel, you may want to hunt for it. From the dock at the head of the inlet, take the road east to the Franklin River valley. The road follows the river about 4 km (2.5 mi.) up the valley to a bridge, which, at last report, could still be crossed on foot or mountain bike. Continue up the deteriorating road on the east side of the river to its end, roughly 16 km (10 mi.) from tidewater. The spring is rumoured to be about halfway between the road end and the toe of the Franklin Glacier. Good luck!

The loggers at the Klinaklini camp will be able to give you more detailed instructions for getting to some of these springs. Take NTS maps 92N/4 and 92N/5.

Sheemahant Hot Springs

Undeveloped

Map 24

Hot

This little-known gem is the southernmost of a cluster of springs centred on Bella Coola. It's hard to reach but worth the effort. The spring is at UTM grid reference 710377 on NTS map 92M/15, but you don't need the maps to find it.

From Bella Coola, take a scheduled or charter air flight to the logging camp near the mouth of the Sheemahant River on Owikeno Lake. A good gravel main line logging road runs north from the camp. About 2 km (1 mi.) along the road, turn right onto the Sheemahant River road. In about another 2 km (1 mi.) the road crosses to the south side of the Sheemahant River, and in another 8 km (5 mi.) you will reach the springs. You can't miss them, because the bathhouse is right beside the road, at a point where the road follows a steep hillside just above the river.

Hot water issues from cracks in bedrock about 15 m (50 ft.) up a steep hill above the road, cascades down the cliffs, and forms a small, hot creek. Some of this water is piped down the hill into an old boiler, which serves as a holding tank where the water can cool down before being piped to the little bathhouse. The water is too hot to keep your hand in and has a very slight odour and very little taste.

Loggers constructed the bathhouse and tub and continue to maintain them. The bathhouse is a wooden shed, with steps and a boardwalk leading to it. It's surrounded by mosquito netting, a nice touch that is much appreciated in mosquito season. The cement tub, which is about 1.5 m by 2 m (5 ft. by 7 ft.), has a drain for cleaning. There is little algae at this spring, and the loggers keep the tub and area very clean.

Tallheo (Hot Springs Creek) Hot Springs

Undeveloped

Maps 24 & 25

32°–69°C (90°–156°F)

These springs on the shore of South Bentinck Arm are probably the most popular springs in the Bella Coola area. You can reach them by boat or plane. One approach that has become popular in recent years is from Larso Bay. From the end of the pavement, about 0.5 km (0.3 mi.) past the marina in Bella Coola, follow the logging road for 38 km (23.6 mi.) to Larso Bay on South Bentinck Arm across from the springs. This is about a 1½ hour drive from town on an active logging road; check with Interfor in Bella Coola to find when it is open to the public. There is a camp-ground and boat launch at Larso Bay. The hot springs are 6 km (4 mi.) across the inlet. Chart 3730 and NTS map 93D/2 cover the area.

Hot water bubbles and seeps from the ground from Hot Springs Creek north along the shoreline for at least 500 m (1600 ft.). One cluster of springs is about 200 m (650 ft.) north of the creek; water temperatures reach about 46°C (115°F), and there are a few unattractive, algae-filled bathing ponds. The best and largest springs are farther north, where the hottest water (up to 69°C (156°F)) and gas issue from cracks in the bed-rock. The water is clear, odourless, and tasteless, with a moderately low content of dissolved minerals, mainly sulphate, sodium, chloride, bicar-bonate, and silica. The main soaking pool, constructed of concrete and rocks, is tucked into a little rocky hollow about 2 m (6 ft.) above the high-tide line. It is about 2 m by 3 m (6 ft. by 10 ft.) across, about a metre deep, and a perfect temperature for soaking. Cedar boughs and salal hang over your head as you relax and enjoy the view over the inlet. There is a good little campsite just north of the springs, behind a big spruce tree.

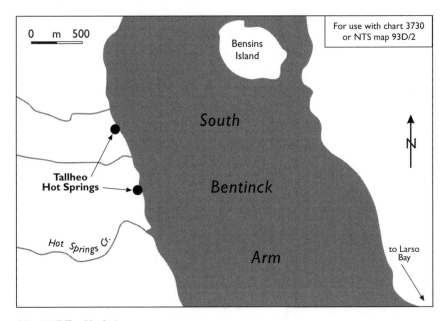

Map 25. Tallheo Hot Springs

Thorsen Creek Hot Springs
Undeveloped

Map 24   Hot?

There is a spring up Thorsen Creek, which flows north into the Bella Coola River near the airport, and with new logging in the area it should be fairly easy to reach. Take the logging road up the east side of Thorsen Creek until you are opposite the largest tributary coming in from the west. This point is about 5 km (3 mi.) from the highway. Cross Thorsen Creek wherever you can. The spring is a short distance up the tributary and is reportedly hot enough for soaking. Try this spring in late fall or early spring when the water level in Thorsen Creek is low; take NTS map 93D/7.

Nascall Hot Springs
Under development

Maps 24 & 26   27.3°, 43.8°C (81°, 111°F)

These well-known springs are on private land and are currently being commercially developed. Until recently they were one of the better free soaks on the coast. Access is by boat or plane.

The hotter of the two springs is about 2 m (6 ft.) above the high-tide line. The water is odourless and tasteless, with a low content of dissolved minerals (mainly silica, bicarbonate, sodium, and sulphate). There is a smaller and cooler spring about 30 m (100 ft.) behind the main source.

As this book went to press, construction was underway on new facilities, scheduled to open in summer, 1997. Plans call for a new bathhouse and a 20-room lodge with a lounge and bar. The facilities are mainly aimed at clients of fishing charter outfits, but the public will be allowed to use the springs for a nominal fee.

Eucott Bay Hot Springs
Formerly partly developed

Map 24 & 26   37°–55°C (99°–131°F)

These springs are among the largest and best known on the coast. The springs are popular with boaters because Eucott Bay offers good anchorage and shelter for small craft. You can reach the springs by boat or plane. Chart 3729 and NTS map 93D/6 cover the area.

The main spring (55°C) percolates from beneath large blocks and boulders on the east side of the bay, about 3 m (10 ft.) above the high-tide line and about 30 m (100 ft.) from the shore. It forms a small stream that runs down to the mud flats. The water has a weak sulphur smell and a very strong mineral taste. The taste isn't surprising, considering that the dissolved mineral content is one of the higher of Canadian springs. Chloride, sodium, calcium, and sulphate are the main minerals. Years ago there was a raft with a floating bathhouse just offshore and a wooden bathhouse on land. Today a pipe carries water into a crude cement-and-stone bathtub, about 2 m (6 ft.) across. Algae is often abundant, detracting from the quality of the soaking for many people. In summer, horseflies love this spot, also detracting from the soaking experience. Fall, winter, and spring are your best bets for an insect-free bath.

There are several other small springs and pools along the shores of Eucott Bay. The largest are on the southwest side; water up to 41°C seeps from several spots about a metre above high tide. The soaking pools here are several shallow, body-sized scoops in the mud.

Between 1909 and 1981, the springs were a favourite spot of residents of Ocean Falls, a former pulp mill town situated about 20 km (12 mi.) to the west. In its heyday, the town had over 3000 residents and there were even a few permanent residents at Eucott Bay, where they scraped together beer money by fishing for crabs and doing a bit of logging. One enterprising fellow even thought of making money from the rather peculiar clay found just below high tide near the main springs: he tried to market it as hot spring mud for mud baths and beauty packs.

The pulp mill that was the life of the town closed in 1981. Today fewer than a hundred people remain at Ocean Falls. Eucott has only a few pilings and some ancient, ruined bathtubs as mute evidence of past development. The extensive and recent logging slash that fringes much of the bay clearly indicates the main modern use of the area.

OTHER SPRINGS IN THE BELLA COOLA AREA

Only one of the following springs is definitely known to exist; the others fall into the category of rumours and old, unconfirmed reports.

An old report mentions a warm spring at the head of South Bentinck Arm (Map 24) near the mouth of the Asseek River, but nobody I've talked to has been able to find it or heard of anybody who has visited it.

There is a warm or hot spring somewhere near the Washwash River

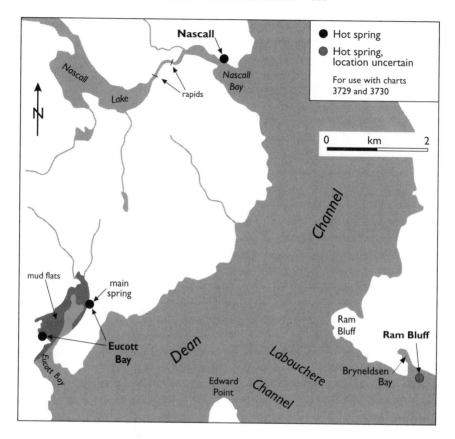

Map 26. Hot springs in the Dean Channel area of the central coast of B.C.

(Map 24), easily accessible by logging road from the head of South Bentinck Arm. The loggers have built some crude bathing facilities, but apparently the soaking is mediocre.

A 1925 report mentioned a warm spring in the tidal flats near Bella Coola (Map 24), but because the information was secondhand, it may not be correct. Nobody I've talked to in Bella Coola has heard of it.

Another spring allegedly exists on the west side of Link Lake, north of Ocean Falls (Map 24). It was reported by a fisheries officer, but nothing else is known about it.

There is a report of a warm spring in Bryneldsen Bay near Ram Bluff on Labouchere Channel (Maps 24 and 26). Several people have scouted the shoreline looking for springs without success. A tugboat operator told me, however, that there are several unusually warm spots in the inlet, suggesting that there might be an underwater hot spring nearby.

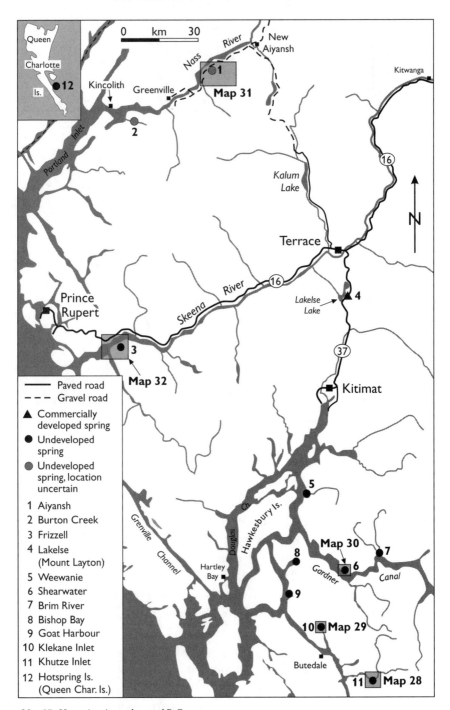

Map 27. Hot springs in north coastal B.C.

CHAPTER 10

North Coast and Queen Charlotte Islands

This chapter describes an assortment of springs in the north coast region of British Columbia, most on or near tidewater. The spectacular fiords and inlets south of Kitimat contain some good springs, which are popular with residents of Kitimat and Kemano. Just south of Terrace, Lakelse (Mount Layton) Hot Springs are possibly the hottest in Canada and have recently been redeveloped as a commercial resort. Several seldom-visited springs have been reported along the lower reaches of the Skeena and Nass rivers. Finally, one of the best springs in Canada is found in the Queen Charlotte Islands. Any time of the year is good for a visit to springs along the shoreline and Mount Layton. The others are best visited in summer and fall. With few exceptions, these springs are accessible only by boat or plane. Charter boats are available in Kitimat and Prince Rupert; inquire locally for information and rates.

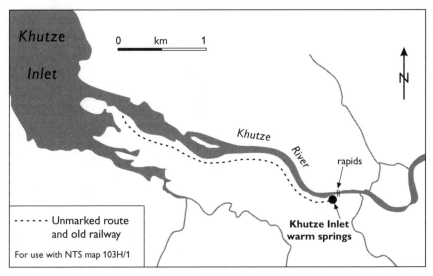

Map 28. Khutze Inlet warm springs

Khutze Inlet Warm Springs

Maps 27 & 28

Undeveloped

23°C (73°F)

From the head of Khutze Inlet, hike up the south side of the Khutze River to the first rapids on the river, about 3 km (2 mi.) from tidewater. The source of the springs is in river gravel a few metres south of the bank. The water is lukewarm and has no sulphur smell. The content of dissolved minerals, mostly sulphate and sodium, is low.

Be prepared for bushy travel to this spring. The trip is probably best when the Khutze River is low (early spring and fall), since the springs might be flooded at high water. Map 103H/1 shows the location of the rapids but not the springs, which are at UTM grid reference 409815. In the 1920s, when there was considerable interest in some gold properties farther up the river, miners built a railway up the valley. You can still see traces of it as you hike up the valley.

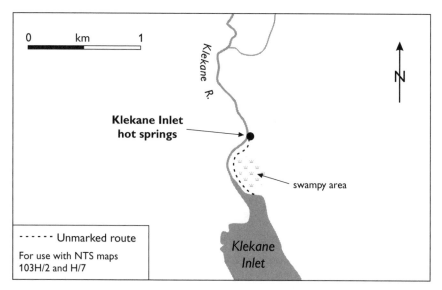

Map 29. Klekane Inlet hot springs

Klekane Inlet Hot Springs

Undeveloped

Maps 27 & 29

Up to 56°C (133°F)

Several small springs are present in the thick bush beyond the tidal flats at the head of Klekane Inlet. Hike up the east side of Klekane River for about 400 m (1300 ft.). The springs are hard to find, but with some searching you should find two small springs flowing from bedrock about 15 m (50 ft.) above creek level. Several other vents issue into the creek itself. Hottest water is about 56°C and is tasteless, with just a hint of sulphur smell. There is allegedly another spring on the mud flats on the west side of Klekane River. Early spring is probably the best time to visit: the water in the river is low, and the underbrush hasn't developed summer luxuriance. In the fall the area is infested with grizzly bears in search of salmon. The relevant marine chart is 3739. The area is right on the boundary of NTS maps 103H/2 and 103H/7.

These springs aren't much visited these days, but years ago they were popular. From 1919 into the 1960s, there was a busy, active cannery at Butedale, about 10 km (6 mi.) away, and the springs were frequented by residents of the village. Some people even built a cabin near the springs, and you might find the ruins as you search for the springs.

Goat Harbour Hot Spring   Undeveloped

Map 27   44°C (111°F)

This spring is a seep from a fracture in bedrock on the shoreline at high-tide level near Kid Point at the entrance to Goat Harbour, about 20 km (12 mi.) south of Bishop Bay. The water is hot, but there are no soaking possibilities since the source is on steep rocks right at the high-tide line. Chart 3740 and NTS map 103H/7 cover the area.

Bishop Bay Hot Springs   Partly developed

Map 27   Up to 44°C (111°F)

These excellent hot springs are the most popular on the north coast shoreline. They are at the head of Bishop Bay, off Ursula Channel. Tie up at the good, recently renovated dock and follow the short path to the bathhouse. If you prefer to anchor, the best anchorage is towards the waterfall on the south side of the bay.

The bathhouse at Bishop Bay Hot Springs.

The main source of the hot water is a crack in the bedrock a few metres above the high-tide mark. The water is odourless and tasteless, with a low content of dissolved minerals. There is a much smaller, cooler vent a few metres from the main source. Water flows into a small, covered bathhouse that holds a concrete-block pool about 3 m (10 ft.) across and about a metre deep. Overflow water feeds a small tub outside the bathhouse. Not far from the bathhouse is a small campground, a covered picnic table, and outhouses.

The site is now a recreation reserve maintained by the B.C. Forest Service and has been proposed as a park. In recent years, this spring has become very popular, too popular in the eyes of many local residents. During fishing season it is not uncommon to find several dozen boats tied up at the dock and anchored in the bay. The marine chart for the area is 3742.

Shearwater (Europa Bay) Hot Springs

Partly developed

Maps 27 & 30

42°–45°C (108°–113°F)

These hot springs are on the north shore of the western part of Gardner Canal in a small bay, locally called Europa Bay, about halfway between Europa and Shearwater points. They are popular with people from Kemano and Kitimat, and some people consider them the best springs on the north coast. There is an old logging camp on the east side of the bay; only one building remains standing. The springs are several hundred metres west of the large creek flowing into the head of the bay. Marine chart 3745 covers the area.

Three springs bubble from a horizontal fracture in small bedrock cliffs, about 2 m (6 ft.) above high tide. The middle spring has the hottest water and greatest flow. The dissolved mineral content is moderately high, mostly sulphate, sodium, and bicarbonate. The water has a slight sulphur smell. A bathing pool about 4 m by 5 m (13 ft. by 16 ft.) has been blasted out of the bedrock, and a sturdy shed has been built over the pool. A plaque bolted to the nearby bedrock gives the names of the forestry crew that built the pool. There is another, smaller vent about 15 m (50 ft.) west along the shoreline of the pool, and several seeps can be found just below high-tide line just east of the main bathing pool.

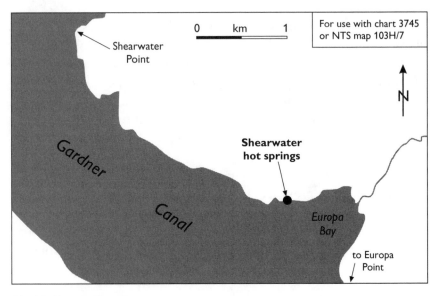

For use with chart 3745
or NTS map 103H/7

0   km   1

N

Shearwater
Point

Shearwater
hot springs

Gardner
Canal

Europa
Bay

to Europa
Point

Map 30. Shearwater hot springs

Brim River Hot Springs
Map 27

Undeveloped
Above 38°C (100°F)

These springs are about 200 m (650 ft.) up the Brim River from the head of Owyacumish Bay off the north side of Gardner Canal. The river is tidal as far as the springs, and at high tide you can take a small boat up the river to the springs. At other times, you will have a short, bushy walk from a fallen-down cabin on the mud flats to the springs.

Water and gas bubble up into a little stream on the east bank of Brim River. The hottest recorded temperature is 38°C (100°F), but local residents report that it is much hotter. There are no permanent soaking pools. Bring a shovel to make your own in the sand and mud; the tide and river will wash them away before the next visitors arrive. Marine chart 3745 and NTS map 103H/9 might be useful.

Weewanie Hot Springs
Map 27

Partly developed
Up to 47.6°C (118°F)

This popular spot is on the east side of Devastation Channel about 35 km (22 mi.) south of Kitimat. You will have no trouble finding it; it's in a small bay and the bathhouse is visible from the water. There's no dock here, but you can tie up to one of the buoys and row ashore.

The main spring is on a steep slope about 20 m (65 ft.) above the high-tide line. Hot water and gas bubble from a crack in the bedrock. The water is odourless and tasteless and has a moderate content of dissolved minerals, mainly sulphate, sodium, and silica. During periods of heavy rain, the temperature in this spring is noticeably lower than in dry periods. Water is piped down to a small cement-block bathhouse on the shore. It has a low ceiling and feels a bit like a bunker. But once you ease into the bathtub, the water is great.

The B.C. Forest Service and the Kitimat Yacht Club maintain this site. The springs are popular with boaters and fishers from Kitimat and can be very crowded on weekends in fishing season. Tenting is possible on the shore near the springs. There are picnic tables, an outhouse, and fire rings. The area is covered by marine chart 3743.

Lakelse (Mount Layton) Hot Springs

Commercial resort

Maps 27 & 34

45°–86°C (113°–187°F) at source

These well-known springs are on the highway between Terrace and Kitimat. Known for many years as Lakelse Hot Springs, they have recently been redeveloped into a year-round resort under the name Mount Layton. There is a large supply of hot water here, and one of the several springs has the hottest spring water in Canada.

The resort is on Highway 37, 23 km (14 mi.) (15 minutes) south of Terrace and 38 km (23 mi.) (20 minutes) north of Kitimat on an excellent paved highway. The resort is well marked, and you can't miss the pools and water slides, which seem oddly incongruous here, on the west side of the highway.

The Springs

The hot springs complex is in the valley bottom east of Lakelse Lake. This is low, partly marshy country that slopes gently down to the lake. Hot water issues from numerous sources in a 30 ha (75 acre) area on both sides of the highway. Water from many of these springs is pumped to the hotel and pool complex, where it is filtered and treated with ozone. The hottest and greatest flow (86°C (187°F)), near the present pool, is the hottest spring known in Canada. The water is colourless, odourless, and tasteless. The dissolved mineral content, mainly sulphate, sodium, and chloride, is moderately high. The water is claimed to be high in lithium, but the analyses are contradictory.

Other springs with temperatures reaching about 84°C (183°F) are present on the east side of the highway. Some have been diverted to the resort, and others have been submerged in recent years by ponds built by the busy colony of beavers that lives in the swamps. But one is still in its natural state. It's not fit for soaking, but if you must visit it, look for an old road taking off from the east side of the highway at the 38 km sign. Walk east, then south along the road for 0.5 km (0.3 mi). Look for a large boulder about 10 m (30 ft.) west of the road; you will know it's the right boulder if there is another equally large one about 5 m (15 ft.) east of the road. The road at this point is straight and runs southeast-northwest. Crash through the thick bush to the large boulder, and go another few metres west to a little stream. Follow this downstream (north) for about 15 m (50 ft.) to the main seeps, which are strung out along the stream for about 50 m (160 feet). The water is too hot for soaking and the pools are filled with rust-coloured algae and slime. Bears are abundant in the area.

Rates, Hours, and Address

The pools are open year-round. Hours are 10:00 AM to 10:00 PM during the summer, but are curtailed somewhat during the winter. There is one large pool held at 30°C (86°F), and a smaller hot pool at 41°C (106°F). The Turtle Pool, a shallow pool kept at 32°C, contains various brightly coloured fixtures for play and is popular with young children. These fixtures were originally used at Expo 86 in Vancouver, where they formed the Aqua-H2O attraction. Five water slides grace the landscape, including two small ones for children.

The main pool deck and pools are wheelchair accessible. The changing rooms are clean, and the showers have plenty of hot water. Locking lockers are $0.25, and towels can be rented. There is a coffee shop, dining room (open evenings, except Monday), and bar. The dining room features vegetables grown on the property in a large, hydroponic greenhouse heated with hot spring water. The hotel, an integral part of the pool complex, has 22 rooms.

Admission fees are for a two hour visit. Seniors and children between three and 12 are $2.50; children under two are free. Rates for all others are $6.75 for use of the pools and all water slides, and $4.50 for the pools and kiddie slides. On Wednesdays there is a special two-for-one rate. Hotel guests have free use of the pools, but the water slides are an extra $5 a day. For more information, contact:

Mount Layton Hot Springs Resort Ltd.
P.O. Box 550
Terrace, BC V8G 4B5
1-800-663-3862
250-798-2214
Fax: 250-798-2478

History

Before European contact, Haisla and Tsimshian people made therapeutic use of these springs, since they were near a well-travelled trail through the valley. In 1904 and 1905, sections of this trail were rebuilt as a wagon road to supply construction of a railway that was intended to run from Kitimat to northern British Columbia, but it was never built. During this flurry of activity, however, the land from the lake shore to the hot springs was acquired by Bruce Johnstone. Despite the failure of the railway project, Johnstone built a hotel at the springs in 1910. By advertising widely

Mount Layton Hot Springs Resort at Lakelse Hot Springs.

in the United States, he managed to make his Lakelse Hot Spring a viable business. In 1929, Johnstone and his partners built a second hotel and a bathhouse on the lakefront. Water was piped from the springs to large enamel bathtubs in the bathhouse.

Disaster struck in 1936. Business, which because of the Depression was not great, was killed by floods that cut the Terrace area off from the rest of the province for the entire summer. The original hotel burned down, and creditors called in Johnstone's mortgage.

The springs lay dormant until 1958, when local businessman Ray Skoglund bought the property. He developed a large and popular commercial operation that included a hotel, campgrounds, and a boat canal. After Skoglund sold the property in 1969, the new owners let upkeep slide, and the facilities deteriorated. In 1978, the facilities were destroyed by a flood. The following year the resort closed and ownership reverted to the province. Local residents continued to enjoy many of the natural pools, as they had for years, despite the muddiness of the pools.

In the late 1980s, the land was acquired from the government by Bert and Marlene Orleans, who developed the property under the present name of Mount Layton Resort. Many of the springs that had remained in their natural states under previous owners were capped and the water pumped to the pool complex, permanently damaging the delicate and poorly studied ecology of the spring system.

Aiyansh Hot Springs
Undeveloped

Maps 27, 31 & 34   30°–60°C (?) (86°–140°F)

These springs are south of the Nass River between the Nisga'a villages of Laxgalts'ap (Greenville) and Gitwinksihlkw (Canyon City). From downtown Terrace, take Highway 16 west for about 1 km (0.6 mi.) and then turn north onto Kalum Lake Drive, which leads to the Nass valley. The road is paved for the first 64 km (40 mi.) and then is good gravel. Shortly after the pavement ends, you enter Nisga'a Memorial Lava Bed Provincial Park. This park contains some of the youngest (about 250 years old) lava flows in Canada, and you will probably want to stop at one of the pullouts and have a close look at the lava beds.

About 95 km (60 mi.) from Highway 16 you reach a major junction. Take the left (west) fork and drive down the lava beds and the Nass valley.

In 7.0 km (4.3 mi.) you pass the turnoff to the village of Gitwinksihlkw. In another 10.6 km (6.6 mi.) you pass the 18 km signpost. Continue for another 2.0 km (1.2 mi.) to the 20 km signpost, where the road is very close to the river. Park here. Driving time from Terrace is about 2 hours.

Walk west down the road for 225 m (750 ft.) to a "Slow" sign on the south side of the road. Keep walking; in about 20 m (65 ft.) you should find the trail taking off into the bush on the south side of the road. The trail is flat at first, then climbs a few steps and stays on a sidehill before dropping to the springs, about a 5 to 10 minute walk from the road.

The soaking pool is about 4 m (13 ft.) across and is fed by two pipes, one with very hot, sulphurous water and the other with cool water. There is a covered sitting area beside the pool and a nearby outhouse. The pools are just a couple of metres above the extensive beaver swamps that flood much of the area to the west, and parts of the trail (and possibly the pools) may be flooded at high water.

These springs were little visited until 1997, when people from Gitwinksihlkw built the trail and the pool. This is a sacred site of the Nisga'a Nation and should be treated with respect and care. The springs are in the heart of land covered by the Nisga'a treaty, and when the treaty is implemented, access privileges will be set by the Nisga'a Nation.

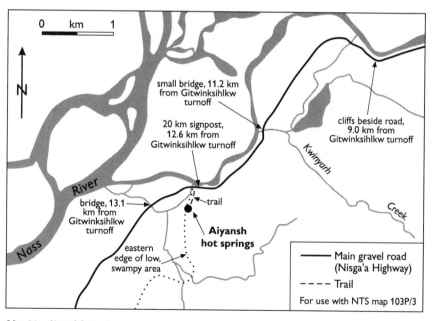

Map 31. Aiyansh hot springs

Burton Creek Hot Springs
Undeveloped

Maps 27 & 34
45°C (113°F)

These seldom-visited springs are across the mouth of the Nass River from the Nisga'a valley of Kincolith (Git-Gincolx). Kincolith can be reached by regularly scheduled plane service out of Prince Rupert. A road that will connect Kincolith with the other villages in the Nass valley and with Terrace is scheduled to be built in the next few years. You need a boat to reach the mouth of Burton Creek from Kincolith; you might be able to get one of the locals to run you across Nass Bay to the mouth of the creek. Don't forget to arrange for a return trip. Sand bars, mud flats, tide rips, and silty water can make crossing Nass Bay treacherous.

From tidewater, follow a rough trail up the north side of Burton Creek for about 1.5 km (0.9 mi.) and 45 minutes to a small tributary. This side creek is the first tributary from the north that is marked on NTS map 103I/13. The small spring bubbles from the gravel bed of the side creek. Water temperature is about 45°C (113°F); the moderately high dissolved mineral content consists mostly of sulphate, bicarbonate, and sodium. There is a knee-deep pool about 2 m by 4 m (6 ft. by 13 ft.) with a nice, sandy bottom. Soaking is excellent.

Frizzell Hotsprings
Formerly partly developed, now undeveloped

Maps 27, 32 & 34
38°–46°C (100°–115°F)

These springs are on the south side of the Skeena River, across from Highway 16 east of Prince Rupert. The only access is by boat at high tide. The approach is for experienced boaters only, because the Skeena is big and muddy and can be very rough, particularly in the late afternoon, when tides, winds, and currents fight one another.

The springs are on privately owned Lot 6449, about 2 km (1.2 mi.) northeast of Hotspring Point. They are about 30 m (100 ft.) above the high-tide line in a little gully just west of a small creek. They are not obvious from the water; look for a bit of a clearing that holds the remains of an ancient bathhouse.

Hot water issues from three closely spaced vents with temperatures of 38°, 40.5°, and 46°C (100°, 105°, and 115°F) and forms a small stream that runs down to the mud flats of the Skeena River. There is one small soaking pool. The water is odourless and slightly gassy, with a moderately low content of dissolved minerals, mainly sulphate and calcium.

Frizzell is another of those once-popular, partly developed springs that has fallen into disuse. In the early years of this century Port Essington, at the junction of the Skeena and Ecstall rivers, was a thriving cannery town. The springs, just 8 km (5 mi.) upriver, were popular with the Japanese fishermen who made up a large proportion of the population of Port Essington. In the 1920s, the springs were bought by George Frizzell, a well-known butcher and businessman in Port Essington and Prince Rupert. He built a bathhouse and planned further development, but Port Essington was already beginning its long, slow decline into oblivion. By 1930, the bathhouse was abandoned, and since then only casual use has been made of the springs.

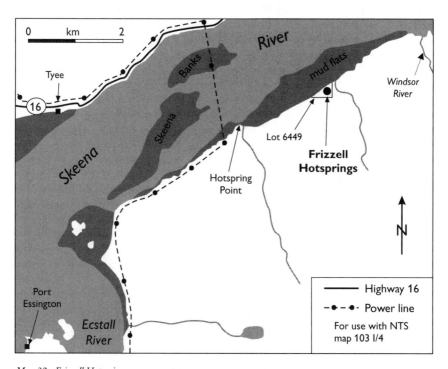

Map 32. Frizzell Hotsprings

Hotspring Island   Partly developed

Maps 27 & 33   •   Colour photo, page 206   52°–76.6°C (126°–170°F)

The Queen Charlotte Islands (Gwaii Haanas) have just one known hot spring, Hotspring Island, but it is one of the best springs anywhere.

The Queen Charlotte Islands are accessible by plane, ferry, or your own boat. The town of Sandspit on Moresby Island is served by daily flights (Canadian Airlines International). Queen Charlotte City and Skidegate on Graham Island are served by a ferry that makes three trips a week between Prince Rupert and Skidegate. Call B.C. Ferries at 604-669-1211 for reservations, current schedules, and rates.

Hotspring Island is a small island off the east coast of Moresby Island in Gwaii Haanas National Park Reserve and Historic Site. The park is administered jointly by the Canadian Parks Service and the Haida Nation. This is a wilderness park; there are no facilities of any kind. You need a permit ($15) to visit many of the sites in the park, including Hotspring Island. Permits can be obtained in Skidegate or on Hotspring Island. For further information, contact:

Canadian Parks Service
P.O. Box 37
Queen Charlotte, BC V0T 1S0
250-559-8818

or

Haida Gwaii Watchmen
P.O. Box 609,
Skidegate, BC V0T 1S0
250-559-8225

Getting There

Boat and plane are the only means of access to Hotspring Island. Helicopters are not allowed to land on the island. Charter companies operate out of the towns of Queen Charlotte and Sandspit. A one-way charter in a small floatplane to Hotspring Island will cost at least $200; charter boat rates begin around $100. You can obtain a current list of plane and boat charter companies from:

Queen Charlotte Travel Infocentre
P.O. Box 337
Queen Charlotte, BC V0T 1S0
250-559-4742
Fax: 250-559-8188

Kayakers sometimes arrange for truck transport from Sandspit to Moresby Camp and then kayak 100 km (60 mi.) to the springs. The journey, mostly in fairly sheltered water, is spectacular, but it is only for well equipped parties of experienced ocean kayakers. Chart 3308 covers the immediate area of Hotspring Island.

Most people put ashore in front of the buildings on the south side of the island. On calm days, you can put ashore on a beach on the west side. Floatplanes and many boats use the shallow, sheltered water between Hotspring Island and House Island. A good trail leads across Hotspring Island to the springs. Camping isn't permitted on the island. There is an excellent (but exposed) campsite for small parties at Ramsay Point on Ramsay Island, and camping is also available on nearby House Island. A bit farther away, there is good camping on the southeast corner of Faraday Island, on the remains of an old homestead.

When you arrive, you must check in with the caretakers in the cabins just east of the springs. You will have to buy a permit before using the springs. You can also buy a "passport," listing the various Haida sites in the park. If you get it stamped at the sites you visit, you will have a nice souvenir of your visit.

The Springs

There are at least a dozen springs and seeps on the south side of Hotspring Island, on the beach, and up to 10 m (30 ft.) above it. You are required to take a bath before using the other pools. The bathhouse is just above the beach and is filled with hot spring water. From the bathhouse, walk down to the beach and west along it to a bluff and then scramble up the trail to an excellent soaking pool on top of the bluff. You can also reach this pool by a trail that leads up and west from the bathhouse. This pool is the best and most popular soaking pool at Hotspring. It was dug out of tufa, reinforced with a bit of concrete-and-stone retaining wall, and

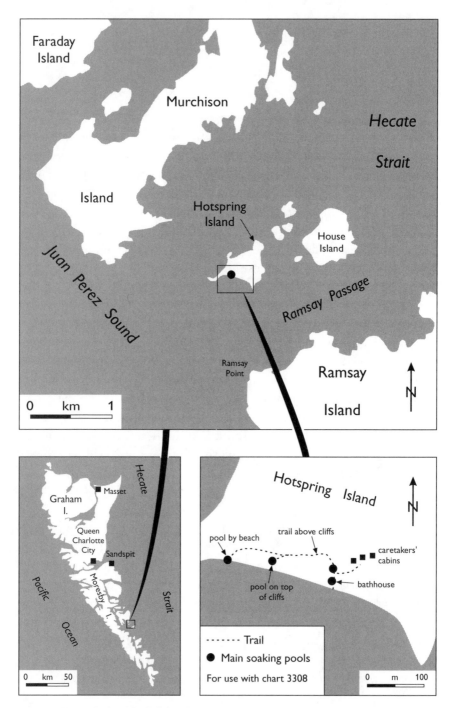

Map 33. Queen Charlotte Islands (bottom left), Hotspring Island (top), and the area around the springs (bottom right)

is fed by 70°C (158°F) water. The pool is about 2 m by 4 m (6 ft. by 13 ft.) and roughly a metre deep and holds a large family at one time. The view over the water and across Juan Perez Sound is stunning; there is nothing else in North America that can compare with the beauty of this spot. If you are very lucky, you may see some whales passing by as you soak.

When you have had enough, spend some time exploring the beach, and then try some of the other pools. One is about 100 m (330 ft.) west of the bluff pool, right on the beach. It's scooped out of dirt and isn't as nice or as popular. Yet another is a few metres above the bathhouse. It isn't used much but boasts the hottest water on the island. The water is clear, with a very faint odour and a strong mineral taste. The high mineral content is mainly chloride, sodium, calcium, and sulphate.

History

The Haida know the site as Gandla K'in ("hot water island") and used the pools for healing and spiritual purposes. Fur trader Joseph Ingraham was the first European to see the springs, in 1791. He called the area Smoke Bay because of the steam rising from the springs. The present name of Hotspring Island was bestowed by the great Canadian geologist George Mercer Dawson, who visited the spot in 1878. Early in the 20th century a log cabin was built near the springs. The springs became popular with everyone travelling up and down the east coast of Moresby Island: fishermen, prospectors, loggers, and people who came to just relax for a few days. Today the springs are again under the care of the Haida people, as they have been for millennia.

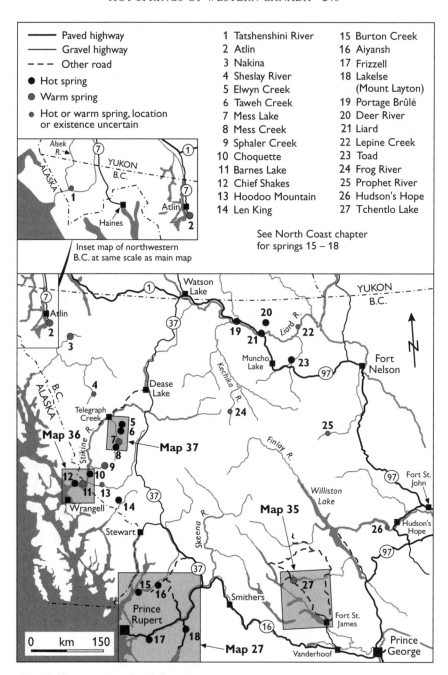

Paved highway
Gravel highway
– – – Other road
● Hot spring
● Warm spring
● Hot or warm spring, location
or existence uncertain

1 Tatshenshini River
2 Atlin
3 Nakina
4 Sheslay River
5 Elwyn Creek
6 Taweh Creek
7 Mess Lake
8 Mess Creek
9 Sphaler Creek
10 Choquette
11 Barnes Lake
12 Chief Shakes
13 Hoodoo Mountain
14 Len King

15 Burton Creek
16 Aiyansh
17 Frizzell
18 Lakelse
(Mount Layton)
19 Portage Brûlé
20 Deer River
21 Liard
22 Lepine Creek
23 Toad
24 Frog River
25 Prophet River
26 Hudson's Hope
27 Tchentlo Lake

See North Coast chapter
for springs 15 – 18

Inset map of northwestern
B.C. at same scale as main map

Map 34. Hot springs in northern B.C.

CHAPTER 11

Northern British Columbia

The vast northern half of British Columbia contains few hot springs compared with the southern half of the province. There may be some geological reasons for this discrepancy, but probably more important is the sparse population of northern B.C. The region has relatively few roads and, in general, hasn't been as well explored as farther south. Some of the springs are excellent, though, and Liard is one of the largest and most interesting in Canada. This chapter describes the 21 springs reported from northern B.C. and two in southeastern Alaska, just outside the province.

The springs at Liard, Tchentlo Lake, and Atlin are easy to reach by car. The others are for experienced, well equipped wilderness travellers only. They require long backpack trips, kayak expeditions, or plane or helicopter trips. Liard has been semi-developed as a provincial park; the other springs are mainly undeveloped except for crude soaking pools.

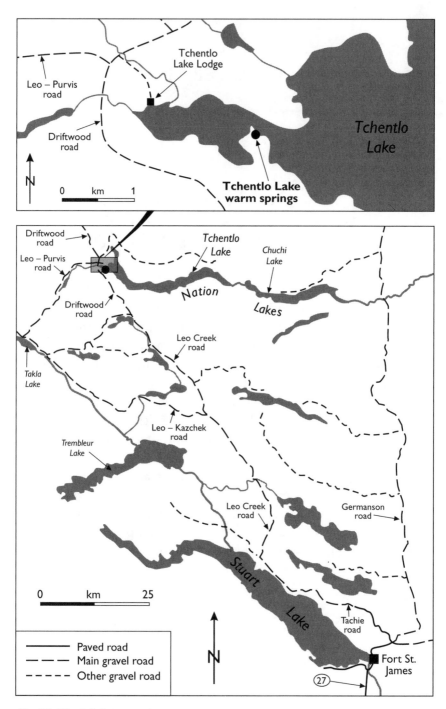

Map 35. Tchentlo Lake warm springs

Tchentlo Lake Warm Springs

Undeveloped

Maps 34 & 35   Up to 24°C (75°F)

These springs are on the shore of Tchentlo Lake, the westernmost of the chain of lakes in north-central British Columbia known as the Nation Lakes. The springs are a bit cool, but the fairly easy access and beautiful setting make them worth a visit.

Vanderhoof is on Highway 16 about 100 km (60 mi.) west of Prince George. Just west of Vanderhoof, follow Highway 27 north for 54 km (33 mi.) to Fort St. James, your last chance for gas and food. From the shopping centre drive through town and, just after crossing the railway tracks, turn left onto a paved road 5.7 km (3.5 mi.) from the shopping centre. The pavement ends in another 16.1 km (10.0 mi.); in another 25.1 km (15.6 mi.), turn right onto the Leo Creek Forest Service road.

From here, follow signs leading to Tchentlo Lake Lodge. Just after the yellow 38 km marker on the Leo Creek road, go straight ahead, ignoring the turnoff left to the Leo-Kazchek Forest Service road. Just after the 68 km marker, bear right onto the Driftwood Forest Service road. In another 14.8 km (9.2 mi.), the Leo-Purvis road branches left; ignore it and turn right onto the Tchentlo Lake Lodge road in another few hundred metres. The lodge is right on the lake very near the west end of an elongate bay. The 133 km (83 mi.) drive from Fort St. James takes about two hours, and the road is in excellent condition during the summer.

To reach the springs, you'll need a boat. You can rent a boat or canoe at the lodge for $10 per hour. There is a $3 charge if you bring your own boat and wish to use the boat ramp at the lodge. The springs are on a small bare point that is visible from the lodge about a kilometre away on the south side of the bay.

There are three springs filling three pools, all on the east side of the point facing the open lake. The highest is the coolest and muddiest and is little used. The middle pool is the warmest (24°C (75°F)). It's about 3 m by 1 m (10 ft. by 3 ft.) and about 50 cm (20 in.) deep. The lowest pool, about 2.5 m (8 ft.) in diameter, is a couple of degrees cooler than the middle one but has the highest rate of flow. All three pools have gas bubbling up into them and comfortable, somewhat muddy bottoms. The water has a strong soda taste but no odour.

The point is devoid of trees and is composed largely of old tufa mounds. The springs are a bit cool for extended soaking, except perhaps on a hot summer day, but the setting is lovely. The point is covered with grass, wild mint, and many wildflowers, particularly yellow mimulus. The spot is not good for camping, but there is an excellent Forest Service campsite just across the inlet at its narrowest spot. There are also several good Forest Service campsites along the logging road from Fort St. James.

For information about rates and availability of boats at Tchentlo Lake Lodge, contact:

Tchentlo Lake Lodge
P.O. Box 1658
Vanderhoof, BC V0J 3A0
Radiophone: H425357 (Mt. Dixon channel)

The meadows at Tchentlo Lake warm springs, where soaking pools (not clearly visible in photo) have been dug. Tchentlo Lake Lodge, on the far lakeshore, can be seen near the right edge of the photo.

Alaska Highway Region

Several hot and warm springs occur in the northeast corner of British Columbia along the general line of the Alaska Highway between Dawson Creek and the Yukon border. These springs are in the eastern part of the northern Rocky Mountains and, as such, are cousins to the better known Banff and Miette springs. The best known of these, Liard Hot Springs, is in a provincial park and has been partly developed into a popular roadside stop. The other springs are undeveloped and seldom visited.

The Alaska Highway (Highway 97) extends northwest from Dawson Creek for 1022 km (635 mi.) to Watson Lake and continues from there to Whitehorse and on to Fairbanks, Alaska. The road is paved except for a short stretch north of Liard Hot Springs.

Prophet River Hot Springs   Undeveloped
Map 34

These springs are reported to be at 57°39′N, 124°01′W, on the south side of the Prophet River, about 56 km (35 mi.) from the Alaska Highway. The location of the springs is marked by tufa deposits.

Toad Hot Springs   Undeveloped
Map 34   Hot

These springs are on the north bank of the Toad River a couple of hundred metres upstream from its junction with the Racing River. River boats and experienced kayakers can reach the springs from the settlement of Toad River on the Alaska Highway. Another possible approach is by a rough road that leaves the Alaska Highway at Toad River and passes very near the springs. There are about 15 pools, some big enough to hold five people. The water is hot, with a strong sulphur smell. There is an ancient burial ground on a hill near the springs. Take NTS map 94K/14.

Liard Hot Springs

Partly developed

Maps 34 & 38 • Colour photo, page 207

Up to 54°C (129°F)

These excellent springs are the main attraction of Liard River Hotsprings Provincial Park. The park is at kilometre 800 on the Alaska Highway about 320 km (200 mi.) northwest of Fort Nelson, British Columbia, and 230 km (143 mi.) southeast of Watson Lake in the Yukon. The park is on the north side of the highway; the entrance is well marked. The park and springs are open year-round. There is no fee for day use, but there is a camping fee ($12 per vehicle) except in winter.

The park hides many hot and warm springs and pools, most small. The two hottest and largest have been developed for bathing. From the parking lot, pick up a brochure and map and then follow a good boardwalk for about 600 m (2000 ft.) and 10 minutes to the first of the two main pools. This, the *Alpha pool*, is fed by several bubbling springs with temperatures up to 54°C (129°F). The pool is large, about 5 m (16 ft.) wide and 20 m (65 ft.) long, with a gravel bottom and underwater benches. Stairs descend into the pool from the wooden deck above the pool, and change rooms are nearby. Water temperature decreases from the source to

Mist rising from the Alpha pool, the most popular soaking pool at Liard Hot Springs.

a pleasant 42°C (108°F) at the outlet stream; there will be a spot that's just to your liking. This pool is popular with children.

The boardwalk continues from the Alpha pool to the Hanging Gardens viewpoint above the pool. Here, a warm stream precipitates tufa, forming a series of terraces and small pools. Encouraged by the warm water, the vegetation here is very lush.

From the Alpha pool, a trail leads up the slope for about 300 m (1000 ft.) (five minutes) to the second main pool, the *Beta pool*. This pool, bigger than Alpha, is largely in its natural state. From changing rooms, wooden steps descend into the pool. The water isn't as hot as Alpha (about 43°C (109°F)) and tends to be pea-soup murky and muddy. Don't let that put you off, because it's less crowded than Alpha and it's a good temperature for an extended soak. With a depth of about 6 m (20 ft.), it's too deep for unsupervised children. Lush foliage, alive with butterflies in the summer, surrounds the pool and gives it an exotic touch.

The hot spring water has a conspicuous sulphur odour. It is moderately high in dissolved minerals, particularly sulphate and calcium. The combined flow of the individual sources is about 2400 litres per second, one of the largest in British Columbia. White algae is common in many of the hot streams and vents.

The large volume of hot water raises the average air temperature by about 2°C (4°F) and has created a special microclimate. At least a dozen species of plants that are well outside their normal range exist here because of this special climate. About 14 species of orchids grow here, and look for small, sticky, carnivorous sundew plants in the bogs. Some plants, including cow parsnip and ostrich ferns, reach giant size, giving the area a bit of a tropical feel. The Hanging Gardens and the warm marshes along the boardwalk to the Alpha pool are excellent places to study the unique plant communities.

The warm marshes are home to a thriving population of lake chub. These fish, about 5 cm to 10 cm (2 in. to 4 in.) long, are conspicuous from the boardwalk and also in the little pools of the Hanging Gardens. They are the only fish found in the marshes and are not known elsewhere in the region. Wildlife is abundant here. Visitors commonly see moose and deer browsing on the dense vegetation in the marshes. Bears, both black and grizzly, are common; for your safety, please follow the posted precautions regarding these bears. Over one hundred species of birds have been sighted in the park.

These springs were used for centuries by the Kaska, who lived in the Liard River valley, and were well known to 19th century fur traders. In the 1920s, the springs became known as Tropical Valley or "steam heated valley," and for many years newspapers carried stories of this valley with banana trees, monkeys, and parrots. The story was not firmly debunked until 1935, and even today people are occasionally surprised not to find monkeys in the trees by the Hanging Gardens. During construction of the Alaska Highway in 1942, a construction camp was located nearby, and road workers built the first boardwalk to what they called Theresa hot springs (now the Alpha pool). In 1957, this special area was set aside as a provincial park to preserve and protect its unique natural features.

During summer weekdays, you can learn more about the history, natural and human, of the park. Naturalists offer interpretive walks and evening talks and slide presentations. A schedule is posted on the bulletin board.

The park has 53 campsites with picnic tables, firepits, and firewood. It's a popular and beautiful campground, clean and well maintained. In summer it fills up quickly, so try to arrive before noon to be sure of a spot. There is a restaurant across the highway from the campsite. Lower Liard River Lodge, about 1 km (0.6 mi.) west along the highway, has a motel, gas station, and restaurant; phone 250-776-7341 for rates and details. For more information about the park, contact:

B.C. Parks District Office
#250, 10003 - 110 Avenue
Fort St. John, BC V1J 6M7
250-787-3407

Deer River Hot Springs
Undeveloped

Maps 34 & 38
Up to 42°C (?) (108°F)

These springs are a long walk from the Alaska Highway; hence, they are seldom visited despite being large and hot. They are for experienced and well equipped wilderness travellers only.

From the highway bridge across the Liard River at Liard Hot Springs, follow a trail upstream along the north bank of the Liard to the mouth of the Deer River, about 16 km (10 mi.) from the highway. Follow the Deer River for 13 km (8 mi.) upstream to the springs, which are on the west side of the river. The trail up the Liard is in poor condition, and some people have become lost trying to follow it. Take NTS maps 94N/12 and 92M/9.

Numerous springs, pools, and tufa deposits are present here. The springs may have the largest total volume of all the springs in Canada. The largest spring reportedly fills a blue pool about 30 m (100 ft.) across and 6 m (20 ft.) deep. The water is colourless and tasteless, with a marked sulphur smell. The highest temperature is either 32°C or 42°C (90° or 108°F), depending on which report you believe. Chemically, the water is probably similar to the other springs in the Liard area.

Portage Brûlé Hot Springs   Undeveloped

Maps 34 & 38   20°–48°C (68°–118°F)

Portage Brûlé hot springs are situated on the north bank of the Liard River about 3 km (2 mi.) downstream from the mouth of the Coal River. The Alaska Highway crosses the Coal River about 65 km (40 mi.) north-west of Liard Hot Springs. Access is on foot from the highway, but approach details are unknown. NTS map 92M/10 will be helpful.

About eight seeps issue from bedrock along about 250 m (820 ft.) of river bank between the Liard River and a clay bank above. Many of the springs have formed small tufa terraces and mounds. Several have small pools, but I don't know if these are suitable for soaking.

Temperatures range from 20° to 48°C (68° to 118°F), with most springs being about 35°C (95°F). The water is colourless and odourless and is moderately high in dissolved solids, mainly bicarbonate, calcium, sulphate, chloride, and magnesium. Gas bubbles from some springs. Much of the tufa is red, orange, or brown, providing a strong contrast with the abundant green and red algae.

Lower Stikine and Unuk Rivers Region

Several hot springs exist in the rugged Coast Mountains along the lower Stikine River, and another is reported in the equally rugged Unuk River region. These springs are difficult to reach and are best left to experienced, well equipped boaters and wilderness travellers. Choquette, Barnes Lake, and Chief Shakes springs can be approached by boat, but helicopter is the best access to the others. Barnes Lake and Chief Shakes are just inside southeast Alaska, but the approach route is the same as for Choquette hot springs and those interested in Choquette will want to visit Chief Shakes.

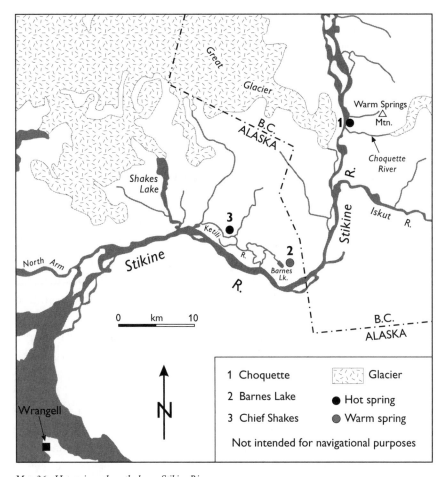

Map 36. Hot springs along the lower Stikine River

Sphaler Creek Warm Springs

Map 34

Undeveloped

Warm

These springs are near the head of Sphaler Creek, a large tributary of the Stikine River not far from the Alaska-B.C. border. They are not worth a visit unless you have a scientific interest in hot springs. The springs are at UTM grid reference 640231 on NTS map 104G/3, about 10.5 km (6.5 mi.) downstream from Round Lake. The best approach is by a long, expensive helicopter trip from Dease Lake or Stewart, which you probably won't want to take unless somebody else is paying the bill.

Sphaler Creek is roaring, silty, and very large. In most parts of the country it would be called a river, but in western British Columbia it's just another creek fed by glaciers draining the Coast Mountains. From the air you can see the tufa deposits at the springs. There are three or four small sources strung out for about 20 m (65 ft.) along the north bank of the creek a few metres above the high water mark. The water is depositing calcareous tufa, which is coated with bright green algae. Water is tepid to warm, with a moderate sulphur smell. It's too cool for soaking, but it doesn't really matter since there is nowhere to build soaking pools.

Choquette (Fowler, Stikine River) Hot Springs

Maps 34 & 36

Undeveloped, flooded

50°–60°C (?) (122°–140°F)

These are the northern of three springs on the lower Stikine River, not far from the Canada-U.S. border, and the only one of the three that is in Canada. Flooding by beavers has decreased the use of the springs, and most boaters bypass them in favour of Chief Shakes farther downriver.

Access is by boat up or down the Stikine, which is navigable from tidewater to Telegraph Creek. During the gold rush days and well into the 20th century, sternwheelers made regular trips from Wrangell, Alaska, upriver to Telegraph Creek. Near the border there was a customshouse, which was staffed during times of heavy traffic. The last sternwheeler trip up the Stikine was made in 1916, but propeller-driven vessels continued to make trips up and down the river for many more years. The last important commercial transport on the Stikine was during World War II, when much material used in building the Alaska Highway was shipped via the river.

Today the river sees much less traffic. The trip from Telegraph Creek to Wrangell is occasionally made by parties of experienced kayakers, rafters, and canoeists, who generally allow about six to eight days for the 200 km (125 mi.) trip. It is a spectacular trip, going from dry, semi-arid country at Telegraph Creek through the U-shaped valleys of the Coast Mountains, where glaciers extend almost to river level, and finishing in the islands and inlets of southeast Alaska. Small motorboats can also make the trip up the river from Wrangell. The river is swift and dangerous for both kayak and motorboat; it's for experienced boaters only.

Choquette hot springs are on the east side of the Stikine River opposite the Great Glacier at UTM grid reference 320018 on NTS map 104B/13. A free map of the lower Stikine River, produced by the B.C. Forest Service, shows the hot springs, campgrounds, and other features. The springs are about 23 km (15 mi.) from the border and about 1 km (0.6 mi.) north of the Choquette River. Reach the springs from the Stikine by taking a kayak or shallow-draft boat up a small slough; its mouth is almost directly opposite an old cabin. This cabin is the site of an old homestead run by a man named Fowler, hence the old name Fowler hot springs. Another name (the official one) is Stikine River Hot Springs.

Over 15 springs issue from cracks in the bedrock walls at the edge of the flat valley bottom. Today most of these are in large beaver ponds that drain into the slough. At least four outlets remain above pond level, spread out over 60 m (200 ft.) along the cliffs. The temperatures of these springs range from 50° to 60°C (122° to 140°F), though higher temperatures (up to 66°C (151°F)) were reported in the past. The water is odourless and tasteless, with a low mineral content (mainly chloride, sulphate, sodium, and silica).

The beaver ponds have a temperature of about 25°C (77°F), and some visitors use them for swimming. Gas bubbles and upwelling of water in the southern part of the main pond indicate the presence of the submerged springs.

Barnes Lake (Paradise) Warm Springs
Undeveloped
Maps 34 & 36
Up to 27°C (81°F)

These springs are on the north side of the Stikine River, about 2 km (1 mi.) west of the Canada-U.S. boundary at 56°40.8′N and 131°52.9′W, on the Bradfield Canal C-6 U.S. Geological Survey map. They are seldom visited and are not recommended because they are merely warm and are hard to find.

If you have a kayak or very shallow draft boat, turn up the Ketili River, a side slough north of the Stikine River, about 8 km (5 mi.) downstream from the international boundary. Bear right about 200 m (650 ft.) from the Stikine and paddle upstream, following an intricate series of channels to Barnes Lake (best done at high water). From the east end of Barnes Lake, walk east-northeast through thick bush (lots of devil's club) for about 500 m (1600 ft.) to the springs. They are hard to find, and the heavy bush and odourless water do not make the search any easier. The two springs are on either side of a small creek that flows through a narrow bedrock valley.

The main spring flows into a shallow pool about 3 m (10 ft.) across near the base of a conspicuous knob on the west side of the creek. Water from the main spring reaches 26°C (79°F) and is low in dissolved mineral content, mainly chloride and sulphate. The second spring, about 200 m (650 ft.) upstream, is a 27°C (81°F) seep emerging from mud at the base of a cliff.

Chief Shakes Hot Springs
Partly developed
Maps 34 & 36
Up to 52°C (126°F)

These popular springs are the best of the three that are accessible from the lower Stikine River. The water is hot, the surroundings are lovely, and if you are kayaking, the springs are easy to find. A visit to this spot makes a pleasant stop near the end of a kayak trip down the Stikine. They are a popular day trip from Wrangell and Petersburg. The facilities and site are maintained by the U.S. Forest Service.

The springs are at 56°43.0′N, 132°00.3′W, just north of the Ketili River. They are marked on U.S. Geological Survey Petersburg C-1 map. If you are kayaking down the Stikine, the Bradfield Canal C-6 map is also useful.

If you are coming up the Stikine, head north up the Ketili River and turn right (upstream) along the Ketili shortly past some old cabins. About 3 km (2 mi.) from the Stikine River and just after a small island, turn north up a narrow, slow-moving slough to a landing and some wooden steps.

If you are coming down the Stikine from Canada, turn north at the east end of the Ketili River, about 8 km (5 mi.) downstream from the international boundary. Follow the slow, meandering main channel downstream for about 10 km (6 mi.). Shortly after a small, rusty slough enters from the right and just before an island, turn right (north) and paddle about 200 m (650 ft.) up a narrow, slow-moving estuary to the landing and wooden steps. From here, a short walk along a trail brings you to the springs.

The first pool you reach is a cedar tub, about 2 m (6 ft.) across, in a very attractive little bathhouse surrounded by large Sitka spruce and hemlock. The water is a good bathing temperature. A few metres farther along the trail you reach an outdoor pool on the edge of a large, gently sloping meadow. This is a lovely spot to camp, especially in late summer when the mosquitoes have gone. There are some small change rooms, tent sites,

The hot tub at Chief Shakes Hot Springs, a popular stop for kayakers.

and fire pits; and the pool is close at hand and very alluring. The tub is fed by two hoses, one hot and the other cold, so you can adjust the temperature to your liking. The facilities were badly damaged by flood waters late in 1994 but have since been repaired.

The main spring issues from the base of a cliff about 100 m (330 ft.) beyond the tubs and is piped down-slope to the tubs. Several other springs exist in the area south of the bathhouse, flowing from near the base of some cliffs. Most of these are smaller and cooler than the main spring. The water is odourless, with very little algae and a low mineral content (mainly sulphate, sodium, and silica).

Len King Hot Springs Undeveloped

Map 34 40°C (?) (104°F)

A small hot spring is known to exist on the south bank of King Creek (also known as Len King Creek), about 6.5 km (4.0 mi.) upstream of its junction with the Unuk River. It's for die-hard experienced bush travellers only. There are no roads or trails up the creek; helicopter is your easiest means of access. NTS map 104B/7 shows King Creek. The water temperature is reported to be about 40°C (104°F); the water has a high sulphate content, so you might be able to smell it from nearby.

MOUNT EDZIZA PROVINCIAL PARK

Four springs, three active and one recently deceased, are known on the west side of Mount Edziza Provincial Park and the surrounding Mount Edziza Recreation Area. The park was established in 1972 to preserve the spectacular, geologically young volcanic wilderness centred on Mt. Edziza (elevation 2690 m (8825 ft.)). Like Mt. Meager in southern British Columbia and Mt. Baker in northern Washington, Mt. Edziza is a recent volcano, with hot spring activity presumably related to the volcanic activity.

The park and surrounding recreation area are wilderness, with no facilities of any kind and no road access. Your options are to charter a floatplane or helicopter from Dease Lake, arrange for horses out of Telegraph Creek or Dease Lake, or, if you are experienced in wilderness travel, settle

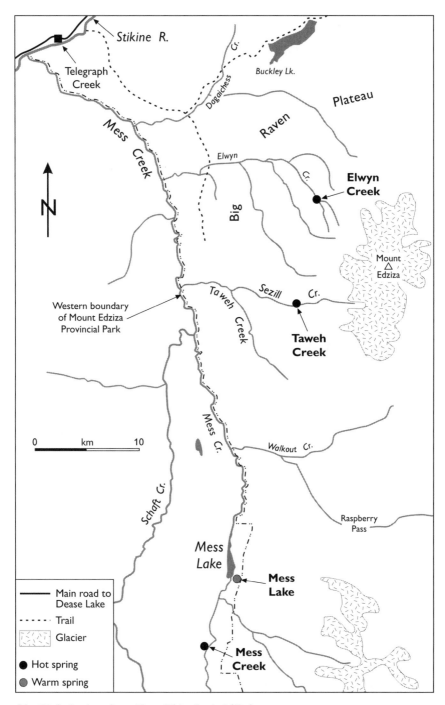

Map 37. Springs in and near Mount Edziza Provincial Park

in for a long backpacking trip. B.C. Parks in Smithers (250-847-7320) can provide more information about the park and a list of local guides and outfitters.

Mount Edziza Park is stunningly beautiful. The hot springs are a very minor feature of the landscape and aren't worth a separate trip. But if you are planning a holiday in the park, you will find that a visit to the springs is worth the effort of getting there. The scenery and varicoloured tufa deposits, among the most interesting in the province, are the main attractions of the springs. The soaking isn't bad either, but use the existing pools and avoid any temptation to "improve" them or build new ones.

Mess Creek Hot Springs
Maps 34 & 37

Undeveloped

42.5°C (108.5°F)

The southern of the four sets of springs in the Mt. Edziza area is just outside the park and recreation area. The springs are on the west side of Mess Creek, about 7 km (4 mi.) south of Mess Lake at UTM grid 850620; NTS map 104G/7 covers the area. Two vents are located at the base of a small limestone cliff at the edge of a swampy area about 50 m (160 ft.) from the creek bank. The water forms a pool about 20 m by 10 m (65 ft. by 30 ft.) across and about a metre deep. Dissolved mineral content, mostly bicarbonate, chloride, sodium, sulphate, and calcium, is moderately high. Tufa is actively replacing the moss along one side of the pool. The water has a strong sulphur smell, and algae tends to accumulate in the pond.

Mess Lake Warm Springs
Maps 34 & 37

Undeveloped

13°C (55°F)

Extensive tufa deposits cover a large area near the southeast end of Mess Lake, just outside the park and recreation area. The area is centred on UTM grid 880690; NTS map 104G/7 covers the area. The main vent is near the east side of the tufa benches and about 80 m (260 ft.) above the lake. In 1965, a strong flow of warm water issued from one of the vents, but during the 1970s, the flow diminished. By August 1983, the vent and nearby pools were almost dry, with only a trickle of tepid water issuing from the tufa mounds. Obviously, it's not the water that's the attraction here but rather the tufa deposits. Covering more than 120 ha (300 acres), they are some of the most extensive and interesting in British Columbia.

Tufa mounds and buildups mark the most recent vents. Some of these are concentric, ring-shaped mounds and pipes that were probably formed by minerals being deposited from geysers.

These springs and tufa deposits are probably the products of a volcanic eruption that took place about 1400 years ago a couple of kilometres east of the spring. The cooling lava is thought to have supplied the heat for the springs, and as the lava cooled over time, so did the springs.

Taweh Creek Hot Springs   Undeveloped

Maps 34 & 37   20°–46°C (68°–115°F)

Tufa deposits, small warm pools, and about eight hot and warm springs line both banks of upper Sezill Creek for a distance of about 700 m (2300 ft.). The most extensive tufa deposits and one of the two hottest vents (46°C (115°F)) are on the north bank of the creek within a couple of metres of the creek. The most interesting feature here is a natural Jacuzzi consisting of a tufa mound topped by a small pool fed by a jet of 43°C (109°F) carbonated water. Another 46°C (115°F) vent is present on the south side of Sezill Creek about 100 m (330 ft.) downstream from the Jacuzzi. The white, grey, brown, and orange tufa is a spectacular sight, particularly when the surrounding meadows are in full bloom. The water in all these springs is odourless, high in dissolved minerals (mainly bicarbonate, sodium, calcium, and silica), and has a pronounced soda-mineral taste.

The area is covered by NTS map 104G/10; the springs are between UTM grids 938947 and 954948 about 7 km (4 mi.) up Sezill Creek from its junction with Taweh Creek. Sezill Creek is unnamed on the topographic map, but is the first large tributary of Taweh Creek. Sezill means "it is hot" in the Tahltan language. The name was given not by Tahltan people but by geologist Jack Souther, who studied the region in the 1960s and 1970s.

Elwyn Creek Hot Springs

Undeveloped

Maps 34 & 37   19.5°–36°C (67°–99°F)

About 10 small hot and warm springs are present along a 500 m (1600 ft.) stretch of the headwaters of Elwyn Creek. They are between 1350 m and 1450 m (4440 ft. and 4720 ft.) in elevation and are centred at UTM grid 973049 (see NTS map 104G/15). The area is above timberline, and the springs are easy to find. Extensive tufa deposits host a series of warm ponds on the southwest side of Elwyn Creek; a few warm springs are present on the other side of the creek.

The water is clear and odourless with a slight mineral taste. It is high in dissolved minerals, especially bicarbonate, sodium, and calcium. The hottest water (36°C (99°F)) comes from a small vent midway between the creek and the easternmost pool.

This is a lovely, meadowed area on the northwest flank of Mt. Edziza. The pools are a bit cool for soaking, but there is good camping here. The spot is a good base for exploring the moonlike volcanic landforms and cinder cones on Big Raven Plateau on the north and west flanks of Mt. Edziza.

ATLIN AREA

The Atlin area in the northwest corner of British Columbia is reached from Jake's Corner on the Alaska Highway by an excellent gravel road (Highway 7). This is an old, historic mining area that many people believe is the most beautiful and mysterious part of the province. The hot springs here are not among the province's finest but are worth checking out if you are in the area.

Atlin Warm Springs

Undeveloped

Maps 34 & 38 · Colour photo, page 207   9°, 29°C (48°, 84°F)

There are three springs near Warm Bay, about 20 minutes south of Atlin on Warm Springs Road, an excellent gravel road. The most popular spring, locally called "the warm springs," is the closest to Atlin. The source of the spring is on the east side of the road. Warm water (29°C (84°F)) bubbles up into a soaking pool dug out of the mud and gravel. The pool, about 1 m (3 ft.) deep and 5 m (16 ft.) across, is too cool for many adults but is very popular with children. The outflow from the pool forms a little stream that parallels the road for a few metres before flowing through a culvert where the road is closest to Warm Bay. The spring is in a very pretty setting in a natural meadow (see colour photo, p. 207). There are good campsites with fire pits, and it's a popular spot with families and campers. The land is privately owned, but people are welcome to use the springs.

The second spring, locally called "the grotto," is situated about 2.8 km (1.1 mi.) farther south on Warm Springs Road. The spring is marked by a pullout with picnic tables, an outhouse, and a garbage can. The site is maintained by the B.C. Forest Service. The source is easily visible on the east side of the road. Cool water (9°C (48°F)) issues from a small limestone cave. There are no soaking pools here (too cool); the water forms a little creek that runs down to Atlin Lake. There are rumours of some warm seeps somewhere along this creek.

The third spring is on private land and is not open to the public. It's on the south shore of Warm Bay, about a quarter of the way from the head of the bay to the point. Warm water (29°C (84°F)) bubbles out of the ground about 150 m (500 ft.) from the shoreline and flows down to the bay. Water from the spring has been used to heat greenhouses on the old homestead.

Atlin warm springs.

Water in all the springs has a mild sulphur smell, and small amounts of gas bubble up in all three springs. Dissolved mineral content, mainly calcium and bicarbonate, is low. Rates of flow are quite large; the grotto has the largest of the three. Algae and watercress like the water and tend to build up in the pool and outflow creeks. The "warm spring" is actively depositing tufa in and near the outflow creek.

Nakina Warm Springs   Undeveloped

Map 34   Warm

There is a warm spring just above the large canyon on the Nakina River. The spring is on the south side of the river, about 50 m (160 ft.) upstream from Hurricane Creek. Helicopters offer your best access, and you can land nearby. I don't know if there is any soaking potential. The NTS maps for the area are 104N/1 and 104N/2.

OTHER SPRINGS IN NORTHERN BRITISH COLUMBIA

Other hot springs have been reported in northern British Columbia. Most are plotted on the *Geothermal Resources of British Columbia* map (see References). No other information is available; the springs may be cold or may not even exist.

Hoodoo Mountain   Existence uncertain

Map 34

The geothermal map shows a spring on the Iskut River about 35 km (22 mi.) upstream from its mouth. It's a plausible location, because nearby Hoodoo Mountain is a relatively young volcanic centre, somewhat similar to Mt. Edziza.

Sheslay River   Existence uncertain

Map 34

Jim McDonald's book mentions a spring on the east side of the Sheslay River about 16 km (10 mi.) north of the old town of Sheslay. It's supposed to be at 58°22′N, 131°52′W on NTS map 104J/5. Like Hoodoo Mountain, this is an area of recent volcanic activity, lending credence to the rumour of a spring.

Tatshenshini River
Map 34

Existence uncertain

The geothermal map shows a spring at 59°30′N, 137°40′W on the north side of the Tatshenshini River, just upstream from its junction with the Alsek River.

Frog River
Map 34

Location uncertain

22°C (72°F)

According to the geothermal map, there is a warm spring in the vast wilderness near the headwaters of the Frog River, at 58°02′N, 127°19′W on NTS map 94L/3.

Lepine Creek
Maps 34 & 38

Location uncertain

The geothermal map shows a small warm spring at 59°27′N, 124°49′W in the far northeast corner of British Columbia. It's supposed to be on the bank of Lepine Creek about 1.5 km (1 mi.) upstream from its confluence with the Liard River. NTS map 94N/7 covers the area.

Hudson's Hope
Map 34

Existence uncertain

The geothermal map shows a spring at 55°59′N, 122°00′W, just west of the town of Hudson's Hope. The spring is reported to be large and hot, but no details are available.

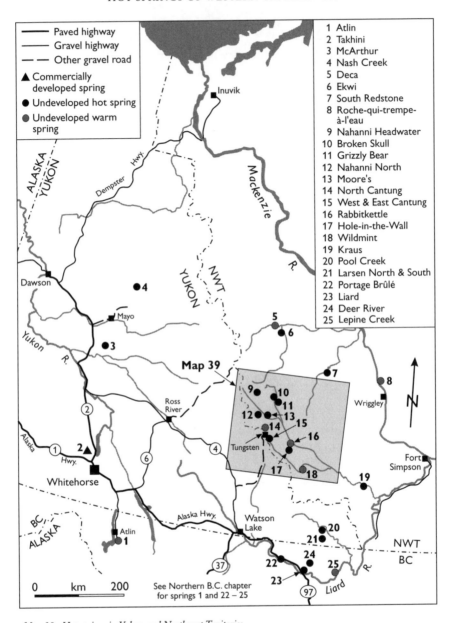

Map 38. Hot springs in Yukon and Northwest Territories

CHAPTER 12

Yukon and
Northwest Territories

The immense, sparsely populated part of Canada north of 60°N has 22 known hot and warm springs, including some of the largest and most spectacular in Canada. Many smaller springs no doubt remain to be discovered. Takhini Hot Springs is a developed resort on the road near Whitehorse; the other springs are difficult to reach and require advance planning and experience in wilderness travel. Helicopters give easy but expensive access to the springs, and a few are accessible by boat. Some of these springs are so remote that they probably see fewer than one visit a year.

The most comprehensive source of information for these springs is a 1976 Geological Survey of Canada report, *Data on Geothermal Areas, Cordilleran Yukon, Northwest Territories, and Adjacent British Columbia, Canada* (see References).

Western Yukon Territory

Takhini Hot Springs

Commercial pool

Map 38

47°C (117°F) at source

This is the only commercially developed spring in northern Canada. It's close to Whitehorse and is popular all year round with local residents and tourists.

From Whitehorse, drive about 12 km (7 mi.) north on the Alaska Highway and then turn right onto the Klondike Road (Highway 2). In 5.9 km (3.6 mi.), turn left onto Hotsprings Road (well signposted) and drive 10 km (6 mi.) to the parking lot at the springs.

Hot water flows from a single source. The water is clear and slightly gassy, has a very faint sulphur odour, and is moderately high in dissolved minerals, mostly sulphate and calcium. It is lightly chlorinated, mixed with cold water as needed, and then piped to the large soaking pool, which is maintained at about 36°C (97°F). The pool is drained, cleaned, and refilled every day. The mushroom-shaped pool has a semi-circular cap adjoining a long, narrow stem. The pool, large enough to accommodate 170 bathers, is about 1½ m (5 ft.) deep and has benches for sitting and relaxing. Outflow from the pool forms a little creek.

The pool is outdoors: in winter you can watch the stars, crisp and clear in -40°C air, while you stay cozy in the pool. Changing rooms are clean and well equipped, and contain hot showers and saunas. An enclosed walkway leads from the changing rooms to the pools. Also on the site are a restaurant and a campground for RVs and tents. Guided trail rides are available in the summer, and there are kilometres of trails for hiking, riding, and cross-country skiing.

From March through September the pool is open every day from 8:00 AM to 10:00 PM. The rest of the year it is open from 10:00 AM to 10:00 PM. All-day passes, which include use of the saunas, are $4 for adults, $3.50 for students and seniors, and $3 for children, plus GST. For more information, contact:

Takhini Hot Springs
R.R. No. 2, Site 19, Comp. 4
Whitehorse, YT Y1A 5X2
867-633-2706

Takhini Hot Springs, near Whitehorse, the only commercially developed springs in northern Canada.

These springs have been used for centuries. During construction of the Alaska Highway in the 1940s, the U.S. Army used the spring water for heating greenhouses. In 1977, when the current owners bought the property, the facilities were very run-down. The owners built a new pool and buildings, which opened in 1979. According to the operators, about 80,000 people visit the springs annually.

McArthur Hot Springs

Undeveloped

Map 38 · Colour photo, page 208

54.5°C (130°F)

These springs are in the McArthur Game Preserve 37 km (23 mi.) east of the Klondike Road (Highway 2) at the 500 km signpost. The springs are near the headwaters of Hotspring Creek, at 63°04′N, 135°42′W. NTS map 105M/4 covers the area. The usual approach is by a 20 minute helicopter trip from Mayo. Despite the costly access, these springs are regularly visited in the summer by helicopter parties, perhaps at least once a week. The soaking is delightful and the setting is spectacular.

The main vent area is a clearing in dense forest about 30 m by 50 m (100 ft. by 160 ft.) on the southeast bank of the creek. There are three large springs and several seeps in this area. Several shallow soaking pools with sharp, stony bottoms have been built out of rocks, each big enough for several people. Pick a pool that is cool enough for you.

The water has a maximum temperature of 54.5°C (130°F). It is clear, has a very slight sulphur odour, and has one of the lowest concentrations of dissolved minerals of any hot spring in Canada. There is no tufa in the area, but the cobbles in the outflow area are coated with white sinter.

There is a smaller spring area on the northwest side of Hotspring Creek about 200 m (650 ft.) upstream from the main source area. Green and brown algae grow in the pools and the outflow streams. Abundant wildflowers, wild mint, and parsley cover the meadows around the springs; it's a lush oasis in the midst of thick bush and barren rubble slopes.

Nash Creek Hot Springs

Undeveloped

Map 38   Hot

These remote springs are about 80 km (50 mi.) northeast of Mayo. They are on Nash Creek, about 12 km (7 mi.) upstream from where it flows into Wind River at 64°33.1′N, 134°42.5′W. Map 106D/10 covers the area, but the springs aren't shown. Approach is by helicopter from Mayo, a long packhorse trip (summer), or snowmobile (winter) from the community of Elsa just west of Mayo. There is a small, private airstrip at the springs.

The springs form a small, hot stream on the south bank of Nash Creek, at the lower end of the airstrip. A wooden deck spans the creek. A soaking tub, large enough for six people, has been built beneath the centre of the deck. The water is clear and odourless, and the temperature is just right for an extended soak. Abundant bright green algae grows in the stream.

Near the springs are a small changing shack and a building holding a small sauna. These and several nearby cabins were built by local guides and outfitters. Land status is uncertain, since the guides and native peoples living in the region both claim ownership of the springs.

Southeastern Yukon Territory

Three hot springs are known in La Biche River map area (94C) in the southeast corner of Yukon Territory. Soaking quality is unknown, but Larsen South appears to have the greatest potential. The easiest access is by helicopter from Watson Lake, about 180 km (110 mi.) west of the springs.

Larsen North Hot Springs
Undeveloped

Map 38
53°C (127°F)

These, the largest springs in this area, are situated at 60°11.45′N, 125°30.8′W. They flow from a gravel bar in the middle of a large tributary of Larsen Creek. During much of the summer, the gravel bar is covered by the creek, making this a late-summer expedition.

The water is clear and odourless and is low in dissolved minerals. Red and green algae live in the water, and tufa coats cobbles in the gravel bar.

Larsen South Hot Springs
Undeveloped

Map 38
43°C (109°F)

These springs are on the south bank of Larsen Creek at 60°11.9′N, 125°31.5′W. They are on an S-bend about one kilometre upstream from the junction with the Larsen North creek. The springs are near the downstream end of a tufa deposit about 40 m (130 ft.) in diameter.

Spring water flows into a pool about 7 m (23 ft.) across and 3 m (10 ft.) deep. The water is colourless and odourless and has a low concentration of dissolved minerals. Gas bubbles up from the bottom of the pool, and a small amount of green algae floats on top.

Pool Creek Hot Springs
Undeveloped

Map 38
54.5°C (130°F)

These springs are the hottest and smallest of the three in La Biche River map area. They are on the south side of the Beaver River, just downstream from the mouth of Pool Creek, at 60°22.9′N, 125°34.2′W.

Hot water flows from the base of a steep bank into a small pool on the terrace just above the Beaver River. The water is clear and odourless and is low in dissolved minerals. The pool has a partial crust of porous tufa and is covered by green algae.

Nahanni National Park

Nahanni National Park was established in 1971 to protect the incredible canyons (up to 1000 m (3300 ft.) deep), mountains, waterfalls, and hot springs along the South Nahanni River in the southwest corner of the Northwest Territories. The hot springs, although only moderately hot, are among the largest and most spectacular in Canada. Although remote, the park is becoming increasingly popular with adventurous wilderness travellers, especially kayakers and canoeists.

The area has been designated a United Nations World Heritage Site, one of 10 in Canada. This designation, together with the park status, should help preserve the region and its spectacular springs and tufa deposits.

The easiest way to see the park is on one of the many guided rafting or canoe trips. For park information and a list of companies offering trips into the park, contact:

Nahanni National Park Reserve
PO Box 348
Fort Simpson, NT X0E 0N0
867-695-3151
Fax: 867-695-2446

If you are an experienced wilderness river traveller, you can explore the park on your own. The book *Nahanni: the River Guide* by Peter Jowett (see References) is an excellent source of information on planning and enjoying your trip.

Kraus (Clausen Creek) Hotsprings   Undeveloped

Map 38   35°–36.6°C (95°–98°F)

These springs issue from sand and gravel on the south bank of South Nahanni River just downstream from the first canyon and upstream from Clausen Creek. NTS maps 95F/1 and 95F/8 cover the area. The springs take their name from Gus and Mary Kraus, who lived there intermittently between 1940 and 1971.

The main source of hot water is at the base of a rock wall and about 300 m (1000 ft.) from the river. The main attraction for bathers is a pool about 9 m (30 ft.) across formed by water bubbling up into river sand and

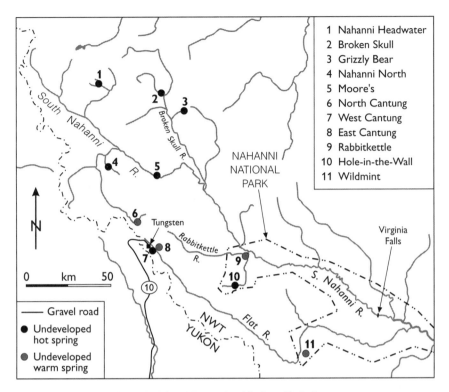

1 Nahanni Headwater
2 Broken Skull
3 Grizzly Bear
4 Nahanni North
5 Moore's
6 North Cantung
7 West Cantung
8 East Cantung
9 Rabbitkettle
10 Hole-in-the-Wall
11 Wildmint

NAHANNI
NATIONAL
PARK

Virginia
Falls

Tungsten

0   km   50

—— Gravel road
● Undeveloped
   hot spring
● Undeveloped
   warm spring

Map 39. Hot springs in the South Nahanni River region, Northwest Territories

silt. The water (36.6°C (98°F)) has a strong sulphur smell and is high in dissolved minerals, mainly chloride and sulphate. Some exotic plants, relics of the Kraus's garden, grow here, protected from the cold environment by heat from the springs.

Wildmint Hotsprings
Undeveloped

Maps 38 & 39   Up to 29°C (84°F)

These springs are about 11.3 km (7.0 mi.) east-northeast of Seaplane Lake, in Flat River (95E) map area at 61°26′N and 126°35′W. The springs are on the south side of a creek flowing west into the Flat River, about 2 km (1 mi.) upstream from the Flat River. Access is by helicopter or by kayak from Seaplane Lake, which is reached by floatplane.

There are three large pools, each dammed by curving walls of tufa. The upper, hottest pool (29°C (84°F)) is about 75 m (250 ft.) long and 3 m (10 ft.) deep. Gas bubbles up from the bottom of the pool. The middle pool is the largest (175 m (575 ft.) long, 15 to 40 m (50 to 130 ft.) wide, and about 2 m (6 ft.) deep); the lowest pool is the smallest and coolest. All three pools support a rich growth of vegetation, including wild mint, and algae. The water is colourless and odourless and has a low dissolved mineral content (mainly bicarbonate and calcium).

Rabbitkettle Hotsprings   Undeveloped

Maps 38 & 39 · Colour photo, page 208   21°C (70°F)

The name is a bit misleading; these springs are lukewarm, not hot. However, the tufa deposits are the largest and most magnificent in Canada. The springs are on the south bank of the Rabbitkettle River about 2 km (1 mi.) upstream from its junction with the South Nahanni River and about 5 km (3 mi.) from the warden station on Rabbitkettle Lake. They are at 61°56′N and 127°10′W in the Flat River (95E) map area. A story, possibly apocryphal, tells how the native people used to catch rabbits near the springs and cook them in the warm pools, hence the name Rabbitkettle.

The tufa deposits are extremely fragile and quickly break down under human feet. For this reason, those wishing to visit the springs must be accompanied by one of the park wardens stationed at Rabbitkettle Lake, who run guided tours twice a day during the summer. Visitors and guides climb the hill barefoot to minimize damage to the delicate tufa deposits.

The main attraction of these springs is an incredible flat-topped mound of tufa about 60 m (200 ft.) in diameter and 27 m (90 ft.) high. The tufa mound consists of individual terraces up to 4 m (13 ft.) high that give the impression of a giant white-and-yellow layer cake.

For such large tufa deposits, the rate of flow is very small, less than 2 litres a second. The main spring issues from the centre of the tufa mound. The water forms a pool about 4 m (13 ft.) across and perhaps 10 m (33 ft.) deep. The water is odourless and has a low dissolved mineral content, mainly bicarbonate and calcium. Bubbles rise from the bottom of the pool.

Hole-in-the-Wall Hot Springs

Maps 38 & 39

These springs are immediately west of Hole-in-the-Wall Lake on the north side of the creek. They are at 61°47′N, 127°17′W in Flat River (95E) map area. Approach is easy from Hole-in-the-Wall Lake, which is accessible by floatplane.

There are two spring areas roughly equal in volume about 300 m (1000 ft.) apart. The eastern area has two sources, both 47°C (117°F); the single source in the western area is 40°C (104°F). The water is odourless and very low in dissolved minerals. No tufa is present at these springs.

TUNGSTEN AREA

The small mining settlement of Tungsten, just east of the border between Yukon and Northwest Territories, was home to Canada's largest tungsten mine from 1960 to 1986. It is also home to a nice little hot spring, the only one even occasionally accessible by road in the Northwest Territories. From Watson Lake by the Alaska Highway, follow the Campbell Highway north to km 108. Take the Nahanni Range Road 200 km (125 mi.) east and north to its end at Tungsten.

The condition of the road varies from season to season and it may not be driveable in some years. Phone the Yukon Department of Highways (867-667-5322) for road information, or ask around in Watson Lake before starting out. Tungsten is a company town, currently largely unoccupied because the mine is shut down. There is a private airstrip at the townsite. Contact the owner of the town and mine, Canada Tungsten Mines (phone 867-777-2345), for access information and permission to use the airstrip or to visit the town and springs.

West Cantung Hot Springs

Maps 38 & 39

Partly developed

41°C (106°F)

These springs are about 2 km (1 mi.) southeast of Tungsten, about 300 m (1000 ft.) south of the Flat River and 300 m (1000 ft.) southeast of the airstrip. Access is by road from the town.

Hot water flows from several sources at the base of a slope. During construction of the airstrip, sand and gravel was dumped over the vents and a large bathing pool dug into this fill. Other sources slightly north have been covered with small bathhouses. These springs were popular with residents of Tungsten.

East Cantung Warm Springs

Maps 38 & 39

Undeveloped

29°C (84°F)

Small seeps of warm water issue from beneath boulders on the northeast side of the Flat River. They are at the base of a slope about 300 m (1000 ft.) from the river and about 200 m (650 ft.) downstream from the West Cantung hot springs. The springs are accessible by road from Tungsten.

The water is warm, has a faint sulphur odour, and supports a growth of green, yellow, and white algae.

North Cantung Warm Springs

Maps 38 & 39

Undeveloped

12°–32°C (54°–90°F)

This area of small warm springs is on the south side of Zenchuk Creek, about 20 km (12 mi.) northwest of Tungsten. They are situated at 62°6.9'N, 128°24.3'W in Little Nahanni River (105I) map area. Access along old roads from Tungsten appears feasible.

Several small springs seep from the ground over an area about 200 m (650 ft.) in diameter. Temperatures range from 12° to 32°C (54° to 90°F). The water is odourless and very low in dissolved minerals. Orange algae grows in the water, and white sinter has been deposited on boulders nearby, making the springs easy to spot from the air.

Upper Reaches of South Nahanni River

Several hot springs, including the hottest in northern Canada, occur in the mountainous country near the headwaters of the South Nahanni and Broken Skull rivers. These springs are far from civilization, and the few visitors usually fly in by helicopter.

Moore's Hotspring

Undeveloped

Maps 38 & 39   About 40°C (104°F)

These springs are described by Peter Jowett in *Nahanni: the River Guide* (see References). They are on the north bank of South Nahanni River about 2.5 km (1.5 mi.) east of the largest of the Island Lakes at 62°21'N, 128°9'W in Little Nahanni River (105I) map area. The source of the spring is about 100 m from the river; access is by a little side channel off the main river. Hot water with a strong sulphur odour bubbles up into a large, lush meadow. The water is sulphurous and very hot, but where it mixes with the river it's cool enough for soaking. The springs are named for John and Joanne Moore, who lived in a cabin about a kilometre upstream for a year in 1978. Joanne Moore's book *Nahanni Trailhead: a Year in the Northern Wilderness* (Ottawa, Deneau and Greenberg, 1980) describes their adventures in the area.

Nahanni North Hot Springs

Undeveloped

Maps 38 & 39   56°, 58°C (133°, 136°F)

These springs are on the northeast side of Lened Creek about 4 km (2 mi.) southeast of Drill Lake in the Selwyn Mountains. They are at about 62°22'N and 128°40'W; map 105I/7 covers the area. The springs issue from boulders about 400 m (1300 ft.) east of Lened Creek in an area devoid of trees and should be easy to spot from the air.

Two springs and several seeps are present in a zone about 60 m (200 ft.) wide. The water is clear and has a pronounced sulphur smell; maximum temperature is 58°C (136°F). The water is low in dissolved minerals and supports a colourful display of algae in the outflow streams. Some small tufa mounds are present nearby.

Nahanni Headwater Hot Springs

Undeveloped

Maps 38 & 39

Up to 64°C (147°F)

These seldom-visited springs, the hottest in the Northwest Territories, are in a remote part of Little Nahanni River map area (105I) at about 62°49′N and 128°50′W. They percolate from steep boulder slopes at an elevation of about 1370 m (4500 ft.), well above the creek below. The springs are visible from the air. There are two main springs about 20 m (65 ft.) apart and another source about 400 m (1300 ft.) farther south.

The water has a maximum temperature of 64°C (147°F) and is low in dissolved minerals. It has a faint sulphur odour. Varicoloured algae grows in the outflow streams.

Broken Skull Hot Springs

Undeveloped

Maps 38 & 39

38°, 45°C (100°, 113°F)

These springs are at about 62°45′N and 128°8′W in Little Nahanni River map area (105I) on the west bank of a tributary of the Broken Skull River.

The two springs issue from the base of a slope. The cooler spring (38°C (100°F)) bubbles into a large pool enclosed by tufa. The hotter source (45°C (113°F)) issues from the base of the tufa. The water is clear, odourless, and low in dissolved minerals. There are other tufa terraces nearby.

Grizzly Bear Hot Springs

Undeveloped

Maps 38 & 39

44.5°C (112°F)

These springs are on the south bank of a creek about 3.5 km (2 mi.) west of the southwest corner of Grizzly Bear Lake. They are in Glacier Lake (95L) map area at about 62°40′N and 127°55′W.

Four pools, each flowing into the one below, are about 15 m (50 ft.) above the level of the creek. Water bubbling into the top pool at about 44.5°C (112°F) is clear, odourless, and low in dissolved minerals. There is much tufa in the vicinity.

NORTHERN MACKENZIE MOUNTAINS

Several widely separated springs occur in the drainages of the Keele and Redstone rivers in the northern Mackenzie mountains. All are remote from civilization. When these springs are visited, which is rarely, access is usually by helicopter.

Ekwi Hot Springs
Undeveloped

Map 38   32°–46°C (90°–115°F)

This group of springs is in the Mt. Eduni (106A) map area at about 64°03′N and 128°15′W. They are on the Godlin River just upstream from its junction with the Ekwi River.

The largest and hottest (46°C (115°F)) spring flows directly into the river from the base of the steep, cliffy river bank. The spring is depositing small, salty stalactites on the overhanging cliff between the spring source and river. Two other springs issue from the top of the river bank; these are smaller and cooler (40° and 32°C (104° and 90°F)) than the main spring. All three springs are colourless and odourless.

The dissolved mineral content is the highest of all of Canada's hot springs. Most of this material is chloride and sodium, accounting for the salty taste of the stalactites and the water. The salinity is about 16,000 parts per million (1.6 percent), or about half that of sea water.

Deca Warm Springs
Undeveloped

Map 38   Up to 22°C (72°F)

These springs are on the north side of the Twitya River about 3 km (2 mi.) west of the mouth of Deca Creek. About 1 km (0.6 mi.) north of the river is a large tufa mound about 300 m by 200 m (1000 ft. by 650 ft.). The spring is adjacent to the uphill side of this mound. They are at about 64°10′N and 128°25′W in the Mt. Eduni (106A) map area.

The water bubbles into a pool about 6 m (20 ft.) across and roughly 1 m (3 ft.) deep. Water is clear, odourless, and low in dissolved minerals, mainly sulphate, chloride, and sodium. Tiny shrimp-like crustaceans live in the water.

Another cluster of springs lies about a kilometre west of these. They have large tufa mounds but are cooler (11° to 16°C (52° to 61°F)) than the main, eastern springs.

South Redstone Hot Springs

Undeveloped

Map 38

20°–54°C (68°–129°F)

This large spring system is about a kilometre south of the South Red-stone River at about 63°24′N and 125°52′W in Dahadinni River (95K) map area.

There are two main source areas. The northern and larger has numerous springs and tufa deposits in an area about 300 m by 200 m (100 ft. by 650 ft.). The hottest spring flows over part of a large, steep-sided tufa mound and forms a series of terraces. There is a shallow pool about 6 m by 9 m (20 ft. by 30 ft.) covered with brilliant green, yellow, and orange algae. The water has a slight odour and is low in dissolved minerals. Half a dozen other springs are present in this area.

Water in the southern spring area is cooler (50°C (122°F)), and the flow is smaller than at the northern system. The springs are about 1.5 km (1 mi.) south of the main system and are marked by extensive tufa deposits.

MACKENZIE RIVER VALLEY

Roche-qui-trempe-à-l'eau Warm Springs

Undeveloped

Map 38

21°–31°C (70°–88°F)

Several small warm springs extend along the east bank of the Mackenzie River near the tiny settlement of Wrigley. Reach Wrigley by following the Mackenzie Highway north from Fort Simpson or by boating down the Mackenzie River.

The springs are at the base of a prominent hill, Roche-qui-trempe-à-l'eau, about 3.5 km (2 mi.) north of Wrigley. The water issues from cracks in the bedrock over a distance of about 400 m (1300 ft.). Temperature is reported to range from 21° to 31°C (70° to 88°F). The largest flow issues from a talus slope near river level and collects to form a small creek just north of the main rock outcropping. A moderately strong sulphur odour might help you find the springs. The waters have about 12,000 parts per million dissolved solids, mostly sodium, chloride, and sulphate.

Appendix
Springs Listed by Temperature

This list gives all springs for which water temperatures have been measured, in order of decreasing temperature. Temperatures (in degrees Celsius) are the hottest measured at the source, regardless of whether the spring has been flooded by beavers or is cooled or heated for use in commercial pools. Question marks indicate that the temperature may not be accurate. Only those cool springs described in this book are listed.

Hot Springs (above 32°C)

86	Lakelse (Mount Layton) Hot Springs
82.2	Dewar Creek hot springs
76.6	Hotspring Island
69	Tallheo Hot Springs
68	Sloquet hot springs
68	Harrison Hot Springs
65	Gamma hot springs
64	Nahanni headwater hot springs
60.5	Halfway River hot springs
60	Pebble Creek hot springs
60	Kinbasket Lake hot springs
60(?)	Aiyansh hot springs
60(?)	Choquette hot springs
59	Meager Creek hot springs
58(?)	Knight Inlet hot springs
58	Nahanni north hot springs
57	Pitt River hot springs
56	Sol Duc Hot Springs
56	Klekane Inlet hot springs
55	Miette Hotsprings
55	Eucott Bay Hot Springs
54.5	Nakusp Hot Springs
54.5	Pool Creek hot springs
54.5	McArthur hot springs
54	Skookumchuck hot springs
54	Alpha pool (Liard Hot Springs)
54	South Redstone hot springs
53(?)	Scenic hot springs
53	Larsen north hot springs
52	Olympic Hot Springs
52	Chief Shakes Hot Springs
51.5	August Jacob's hot spring
51	Hot Springs Cove
51	Halcyon Hot Springs
50	St. Leon Hot Springs
49	Octopus Creek hot springs
49	Fairmont Hot Springs
48	Portage Brûlé hot springs
47.7	Radium Hot Springs
47.6	Weewanie Hot Springs

47.5	Ainsworth Hot Springs
47.3	Upper hot springs (Banff)
47	Takhini Hot Springs
47	Hole-in-the-Wall hot springs
46	Taweh Creek hot springs
46	Ekwi hot springs
46	Frizzell Hotsprings
45	Placid hot springs
45	Shearwater hot springs
45	Burton Creek hot springs
45	Broken Skull hot springs
44.5	Grizzly Bear hot springs
44	Baker Hot Spring
44	Goat Harbour hot spring
44	Bishop Bay Hot Springs
43.8	Nascall Hot Springs
43.4	Lussier Hot Springs
43	Clear Creek hot springs
43	Beta pool (Liard Hot Springs)

43	Larsen south hot springs
42.5	Mess Creek hot springs
42(?)	Deer River hot springs
41	West Cantung hot springs
40	Riondel hot spring
40(?)	Buhl Creek hot springs
40(?)	Len King hot springs
40	Moore's hotspring
39	Kidney spring (Banff)
38(?)	Brim River hot springs
37(?)	Sulphur hot springs
36.6	Ram Creek Hot Springs
36.6	Kraus Hotsprings
36	Elwyn Creek hot springs
35	No Good warm springs
35(?)	Kennedy Hot Spring
35	Wilson Lake warm springs
35	Cave & Basin hot springs (Banff)
35	Middle springs (Banff)
33	Mist Mountain hot spring

Warm Springs (32°C or less but above 20°C)

32	North Cantung warm springs
31.5	Crawford Creek warm springs
31	Roche-qui-trempe-à-l'eau warm springs
29	Turbid warm springs
29	Angel warm springs
29	Atlin warm springs
29	Wildmint Hotsprings
29	East Cantung warm springs
28.5	Wild Horse warm springs
28	Upper Halfway River warm springs

27	Shovelnose warm springs
27	Canyon Hot Springs
27	Barnes Lake warm springs
26	Fording Mountain warm springs
25	Ahousat warm springs
25	Mate Islands Warm Seep
25	Taylor warm spring
24	Tchentlo Lake warm springs
23	Khutze Inlet warm springs
22	Frog River
22	Deca warm springs
21	Rabbitkettle Hotsprings

Cool Springs (20°C and cooler)

20(?)	Red Rock cool springs	13	Mess Lake warm springs
19.7	Vermilion Lakes (Banff)		

Springs without Good Temperature Estimates

Springs in this list definitely exist, but I have no reliable temperature estimates. For some the name of the spring gives some indication of the probable temperature of the water. The springs are listed in the order in which they appear in the text.

Fry Creek hot (?) springs	Toad Hot Springs
Sheemahant hot springs	Sphaler Creek warm springs
Thorsen Creek hot springs	Nakina warm springs
Washwash River hot (?) springs	Lepine Creek
Prophet River hot springs	Nash Creek hot springs

Springs Rumoured to Exist

Other springs have been mentioned in various reports and books, but I have no temperature or reliable location data for them. Some probably exist. Some may have existed in the past but have since dried up. Others may only be rumours, passed on from report to report and may never have existed. The springs are listed in the order in which they are mentioned in the text.

Glacier Creek	Bella Coola
Fair Harbour	Link Lake
Kennedy River	Ram Bluff
Pipestem Inlet	Hoodoo Mountain
Snowshoe Rabbit	Sheslay River
Fosthall	Tatshenshini River
Mutton Creek	Hudson's Hope
Asseek River	

References

The written record for most hot springs in western Canada is not large, and much of what exists is buried in technical reports and scientific journals. The publications given here are a starting point if you are interested in learning more about hot springs in this region.

The first list contains mainly non-technical guidebooks and reference material of broad interest. These books are available in many libraries. The second group consists of technical publications. Many of these reports are hard to find but contain a great deal of useful information. The bibliographies in these reports list much of the remaining technical and older literature. There is a large volume of technical literature on Meager Creek Hot Springs, mostly related to geothermal exploration; the Fairbank and Faulkner map points to some of this material.

WIDELY AVAILABLE NON-TECHNICAL PUBLICATIONS

Gadd, Ben. *Handbook of the Canadian Rockies*. Revised edition. Jasper, Alberta: Corax Press, 1995.

> This is not a trail guide, but an excellent description of the natural history of the Rocky Mountains of Canada. Includes geology, flora and fauna, climate, and a short section on hot springs. Non-technical but very detailed. Contains extensive references to other publications. Essential reading for visitors to the Rockies and East Kootenays.

Croutier, Alev Lytle. *Taking the Waters: Spirit, Art, Sensuality*. New York: Abbeville Press, 1992.

> Sumptuously produced history of hot springs around the world from earliest times to the present. Includes chapters on the mythological and religious history of water and water motifs in art.

Gersh-Young, Marjorie. *Hot Springs and Hot Pools of the Northwest*. Revised edition. Santa Cruz, California: Aqua Thermal Press, 1995.

> This perennial publication was originally written by Jayson Loam. Briefly covers hundreds of springs in the northwestern United States, especially

commercially operated pools and springs that are easy to reach. Includes notes on 20 hot springs in southwestern Canada.

Jowett, Peter. *Nahanni: the River Guide.* Calgary, Alberta: Rocky Mountain Books, 1993.
Although primarily a guide to Nahanni National Park, this book contains excellent information on the natural history of the western Northwest Territories. Essential for anyone planning a visit to any of the springs in the Northwest Territories.

Kaysing, Bill and Ruth. *Great Hot Springs of the West.* Fourth edition. Santa Barbara, California: Capra Press, 1993.
Gives short notes on hundreds of hot springs in the western United States. Nearly half the book consists of maps and listings of all known hot and warm springs in the region.

Kroeger, Paul. "Meager Creek Hotsprings." *Cordillera* (Vancouver: Federation of British Columbia Naturalists), Summer, 1995, pp. 3–6.
Describes some of the special flora at Meager Creek hot springs and emphasizes the fragile nature of hot spring ecosystems. An example of what can be done by dedicated amateur naturalists.

Litton, Evie. *The Hiker's Guide to Hot Springs in the Pacific Northwest.* Revised edition. Helena, Montana: Falcon Press, 1993.
Provides descriptions of 100 hot springs in the northwestern United States, including 13 in southern British Columbia. No commercial springs here; emphasis is on back country hot springs. For most springs, the book also suggests some nearby hikes.

van Everingen, R.O. *Thermal and Mineral Springs in the Southern Rocky Mountains of Canada.* Ottawa, Ontario: Environment Canada, 1972.
Semi-technical, but contains the best detailed descriptions and historical information on springs in the Rocky Mountains of southern British Columbia and Alberta. Out of print, but many libraries have copies.

TECHNICAL PUBLICATIONS WITH LIMITED DISTRIBUTION

Christie, R.A. *Bibliography and Index of Geothermal Resources and Development in Washington State, with Selected General Works.* Olympia: Washington Division of Geology and Earth Resources, Open File Report 94-1, 1994.

> Most publications on hot springs in Washington are listed in this bibliography. Available in large Canadian libraries.

Crandall, J.T., and T.L. Sadlier-Brown. *Data on Geothermal Areas, Cordilleran Yukon, Northwest Territories, and Adjacent British Columbia, Canada.* Ottawa: Geological Survey of Canada, Open File 427, 1977.

> This is hard to find, but it is the most important source for those interested in springs in northern Canada. Includes references to older publications. Copies are available in libraries of the Geological Survey of Canada and the University of British Columbia.

Fairbank, B.D., and R.L. Faulkner. *Geothermal Resources of British Columbia.* Ottawa: Geological Survey of Canada, Open File 2526, 1992.

> This map shows the locations of hot, warm, and cool springs in British Columbia, with temperature and other technical data. Recommended for those interested in tracking down obscure springs and looking for new ones. Available from Geological Survey of Canada offices.

Ghomshei, M.M., and T.L. Sadlier Brown. *Direct Use Energy from the Hotsprings and Subsurface Geothermal Resources of British Columbia.* Vancouver, B.C.: Canadian Geothermal Energy Association, 1996.

> Clear description of some possible uses of geothermal energy in B.C., with emphasis on hot springs. Contains a complete list of all thermal springs known in B.C. Not widely distributed, but copies are available in libraries of the Geological Survey of Canada and for purchase from BiTech Publishers Ltd., 173-11860 Hammersmith Way, Richmond, BC V7A 5G1

Motyka, Roman J., Mary A. Moorman, and John W. Reeder. *Assessment of Thermal Springs Sites in Southern Southeastern Alaska –Preliminary Results and Evaluation.* Juneau: Alaska Department of Natural Resources, Open-file Report 127, 1989.

> Contains good descriptions of springs in the southern half of southeastern Alaska.

Motyka, R.J., and M.A. Moorman. *Geothermal Resources of Southeastern Alaska.* Juneau: Alaska Department of Natural Resources, Professional Report 93, 1987.

> This colour map (scale 1:1,000,000) shows locations of hot springs in southeastern Alaska, with temperatures, notes, and references.

Nelson, J. "The tropical fish fauna in Cave and Basin hot springs drainage, Banff National Park, Alberta." *The Canadian Field Naturalist* (Ottawa) 97 (1983): pp. 255–261.

> A fascinating description of the exotic fish at Banff. Semi-technical but worth the effort if you are interested in the biology of hot springs.

Porsild, A.E., and H. Crum. "The vascular flora of Liard Hotsprings, B.C., with notes on some bryophytes." Ottawa: National Museum of Canada, Bulletin 171, pp. 131–196, 1961.

> Contains a thorough description of the flora of Liard Hot Springs. Technical but essential reading for anyone interested in the unique flora of these hot springs.

Waring, G.A. *Thermal Springs of the United States and Other Countries of the World – A Summary.* Washington: United States Geological Survey, Bulletin 492, 1965.

> Contains a listing with maps and extensive references to the hot springs of the world. Now somewhat out of date but still an invaluable starting point for research.

Index